Cody Choi · *Culture Cuts*

Cody Choi · *Culture Cuts*

Editor and Coordinating Curator · John C. Welchman
Curators · Gregor Jansen; Marie de Brugerolle; Thierry Ollat

Verlag der Buchhandlung Walther König

Contents

Foreword

FOR more than two decades, Cody Hyun Choi has been creating memorable and important works of art. His sculptures, photographs, "database" and other paintings, public projects, drawings, and mixed-media works have been seen in exhibitions worldwide. This exhibition, the first international traveling survey of one of the most challenging and original contemporary Korean artists, reacquaints us with highlights from Choi's diverse oeuvre and traces the developments in his career to date. Working closely with the artist, coordinating curator, John C. Welchman has selected a series of key works, including Choi's path-breaking "Thinkers" series made in the mid-nineties and first seen in New York. Choi has been in sustained dialogue with many artists and issues, including Conceptual Art and the discourse of "appropriation"; the work of Western masters such as Michelangelo, Auguste Rodin, Marcel Duchamp, and Gerhard Richter; histories of modern and contemporary Korean art; and the development of postcolonial theory.

Choi brings these and other sources together in works that are sharply focused and culturally provocative, but also witty and heartfelt. High art collides with commonplace materials and lowbrow allusions; icons of Western art are detoured through Asian ideas about corporeal energy; cultural identities are spun in a centrifuge of illusions and dissent; while the artist's diffident masculinity is probed, tested—and perhaps even redefined.

We would like to acknowledge our gratitude to John C. Welchman, the coordinating curator and editor of this publication for helping to realize a project that has been in discussion for many years.

Thierry Ollat extends special thanks to Gregor Jansen who has done "double duty" as curator of the exhibition in Düsseldorf and co-author of the catalogue. *Cody Choi. Culture Cuts* exhibition is part of the program of the Korea-France Year 2015–2016. It has received the support of the Korea Arts Management Service, The Secretariat of the organizing Comitee of the Korea-France Year 2015–2016, Seoul, Korea.

We are also deeply grateful to the colleagues and staff in our respective institutions, especially the curator in Marseille, Marie de Brugerolle.

The authors of this publication—de Brugerolle, Jansen, Korean art historian, Sumi Kang, artist Mike Kelley, and Welchman—have provided eloquent and informed elucidations on Choi's work. While the makers of the book—in particular Boris Dworschak (design) and Irina Raskin (editorial assistant)—combined hard work, patience, and creativity to produce a fittingly elegant catalogue.

The exhibition and catalogue was not made possible without the generous financial support of the Seoul Metropolitan Government, Seoul Foundation for Arts and Culture, and last, but not least, PKM Gallery Seoul and its director Kyung-mee Park.

First and foremost, of course, we thank Cody Choi, an inimitable spirit whose capacity to lift us up and illuminate our lives makes a profound contribution to the crucial, but frankly mysterious, place where art, personhood, and cultural difference come together.

—Gregor Jansen · *Kunsthalle Düsseldorf*
—Thierry Ollat · *Musée d'Art Contemporain de Marseille*

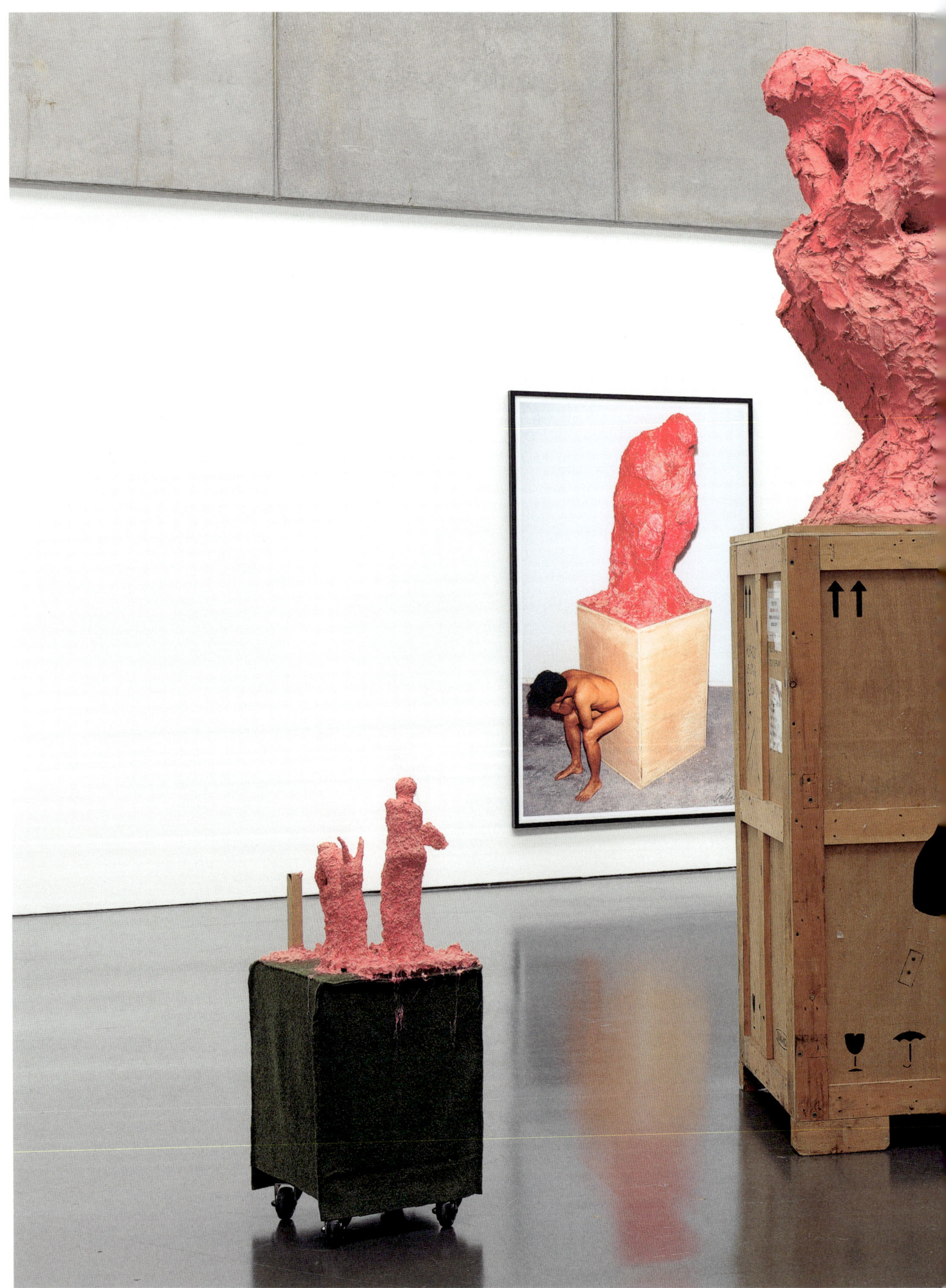

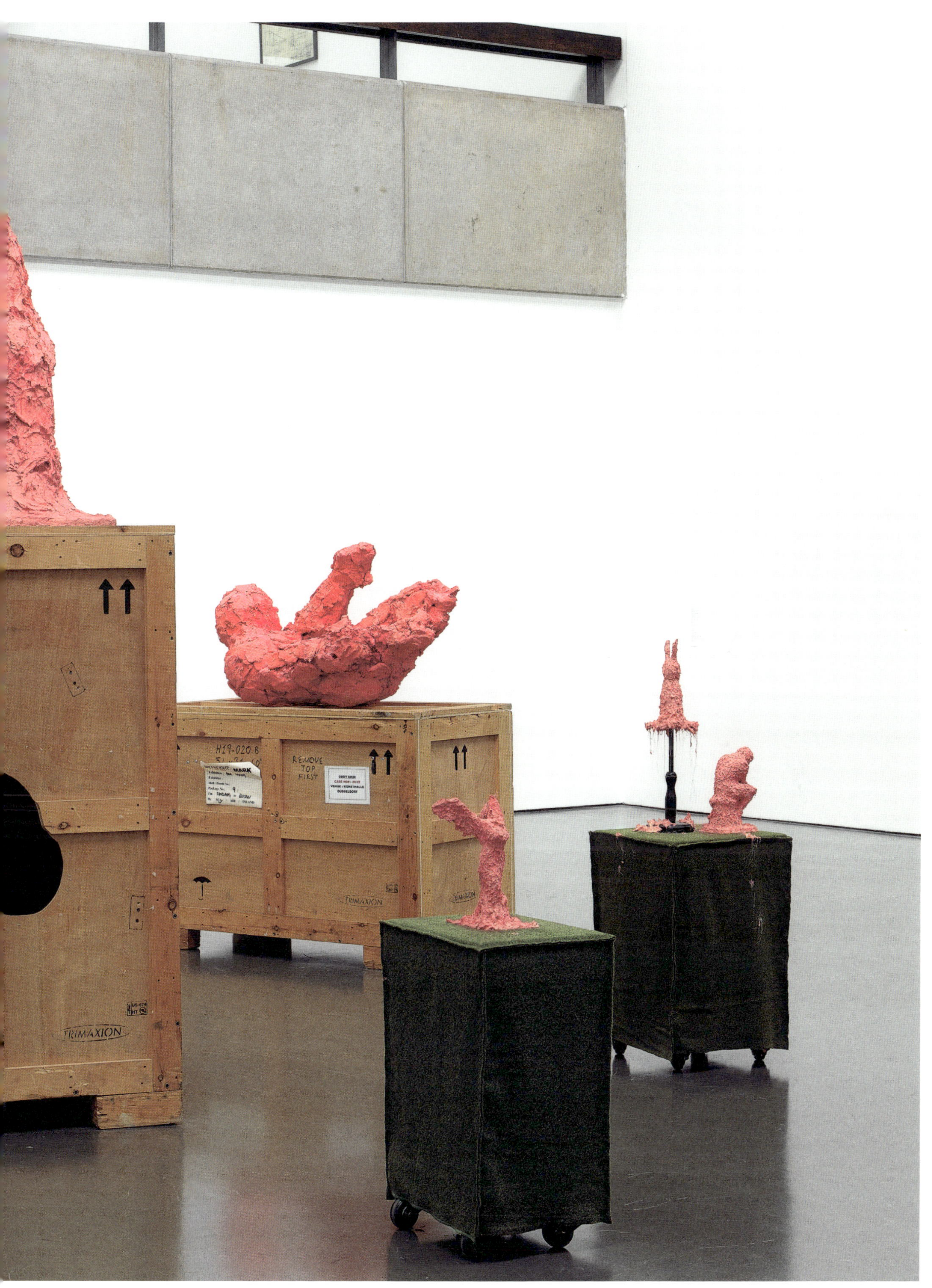

Installation view at Kunsthalle Düsseldorf (2015) showing (f.l.t.r.):

Esquisse 1 · 1995/2014 · Toilet paper, Pepto-Bismol, wood, glue

The Thinker · 1996 · C-print

The Thinker, December #3 · 1996 · Toilet paper, Pepto-Bismol, wood, glue

Untitled · 1996 · Toilet paper, Pepto-Bismol, wood, glue

Esquisse 2–3 · 1996 · Toilet paper, Pepto-Bismol, wood, glue

Artist's Acknowledgments

Research for the exhibition and the catalogue was supported by the generous grants and loans from
Seoul Metropolitan Government; Seoul Foundation for Arts and Culture; Chargée de mission
Arts Visuels Le Secrétariat de l'Année Corée-France 2015–16; Korea Arts Management Service;
CAN Foundation; Kim Yang Hee; Shin Hye Jin; Whang Bong Won; Yoo Sang Duk; Chun Philip;
Peak Jin Young; Jung Sun Mee; Jung Eun Mee.

Thanks to the creators of the exhibition
Gregor Jansen; John C. Welchman; Marie de Brugerolle; Thierry Ollat; Kang Sumi.

Thanks to the studio
Kim Seo Woo; Gigi Sue; Kim Dong Hyun; Lee Jeong Hyung; Jang Joon Ho; Kim Hye Yeon; Na
Eun Min; Jeon Soo Man; Choi Soo Ji; Hong Sung Yeon; Jung Gil Chae; Lee Junwoo; Na Myung
Kyu; Jin Yong Pil; Andrew Hunt.

Special thanks to
Paradise Culture Foundation; Song Eun Art Foundation; Total Museum; PKM Gallery; Lauren-
cina Farrant; Lee Ung Yull; Kim Hyung Soon; Saul Ostrow; Mischa Kuball; Franklin Sirman;
Gary Simmons; Jeffery Deitch; Janine Antoni; Peter Halley; Mike Kelley; Ashley Bikerton; Choi
Hyo Joon; Lee Jun; Kang Yeo Wool; Jung Sook Young; Kim Sung Hee; Kim Te Yeon; Sa Whan
Kyu; Lee Jin Myung; Seo Jin Seok; Lee Gun Soo; Lee Sung Whan; Lee Hye Kyung; Kim Bo
Kyung; Lee Jang Wook; Kim Kab Soo; Kim Ok Chul; Yoo Myng Boon; Yoo Seung Ho; Choi Sun;
Ji Han Kyung; Han Won Seok; Kim Chang Hyun; Huh Ji Young; Hwang Jun Ho; Jinny Huh; Ahn
Sangsoo; Anh Graphics; Holly Choi; Jay Choi; Culturegraphy Press; Lusitania Press; Martim
Avillez; Carole Ashhley; Boris Dworschak; Haung Du; Detmar Westhoff; Laurence W. Rickels;
Nancy Barton; Michael Cohen.

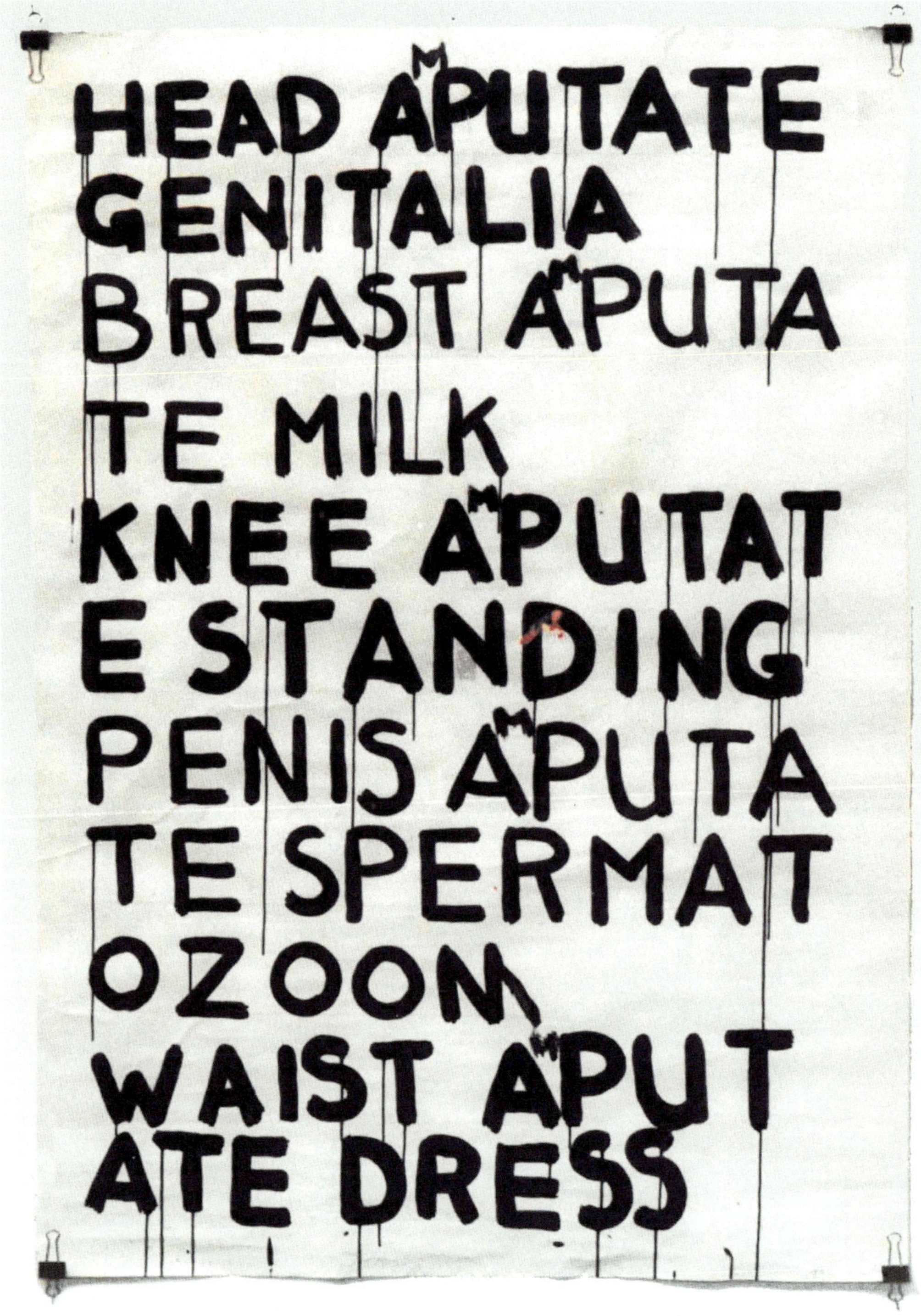

Bad Drawing (Post-Conceptual Poem Based on Western Body Theory) · 1992–93 · Ink on paper

John C. Welchman
Culture Cuts

The "culture cuts" to which Cody Hyun Choi and his work have been subject—and which they have also produced—are of several distinct but overlapping kinds. Their most conspicuous manifestation was engendered by the artist's forced emigration from Korea and subsequent arrival on the West Coast of the United States in the nineteen-eighties. This remove precipitated a thoroughgoing psychological crisis as the young Choi was cut-off from this homeland, his language, a good part of his family, and even his sense of self. But, almost from its beginning, Choi's "family romance" had been formed in a crucible of severance and loss, these deficits including the death of his two sisters and his consequent estrangement from a mother who never managed to come to terms with her tragic bereavement. Some while later his family was subject to another round of losses as its wealth and social prestige were suddenly threatened by one of the abrupt shifts in patronage and obligation that have long characterized Korean politics, finance, and government.[1] These events precipitated the family's emigration to the US and ushered in the next round of dislocations.

It is hardly surprising, then, that having elected to study art Choi almost immediately took up with the "cut" as both a leading subject and a formal language in his early work—a move that included the clipped declensions of writing itself. Begun in 1992 and finished the following year, *Bad Drawing* is a gory, ink-on-paper chorus of bodily severances, whose crude lettering is spiked with thin vertical trails of excess run-off, and interrupted by repetitively amended spelling mistakes in the shock-word, "AMPUTATE," which slices between listed body parts, fluids, and accoutrements, and is itself literally split as it runs on from line to line.

> HEAD AMPUTATE
> GENITALIA
> BREAST AMPUTA
> TE MILK
> KNEE AMPUTAT
> E STANDING
> PENIS AMPUTA
> TE SPERMAT
> OZOON
> WAIST AMPUT
> ATE DRESS

Streaking this strangely fixated post-conceptual poem with the appalling triple logic of decapitation, emasculation, and mutilation, Choi poses sexual pessimism at the extremity of his

---

1.

On questions of governmentality and change in Korea, see Adrian Buzo, *The Making of Modern Korea* (Oxford: Taylor & Francis, 2007) and Christoph Bluth, Korea (Cambridge: Polity, 2008).

Scamps, Scram #1 (Self-Portrait in Energy Level) · 1994 · Wood, banding straps

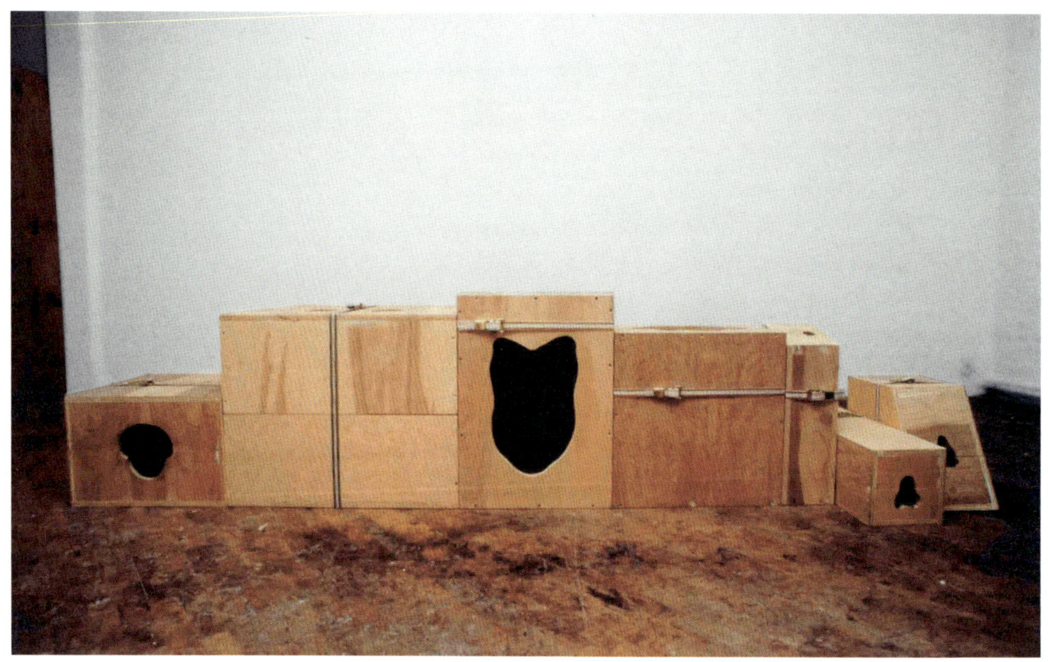

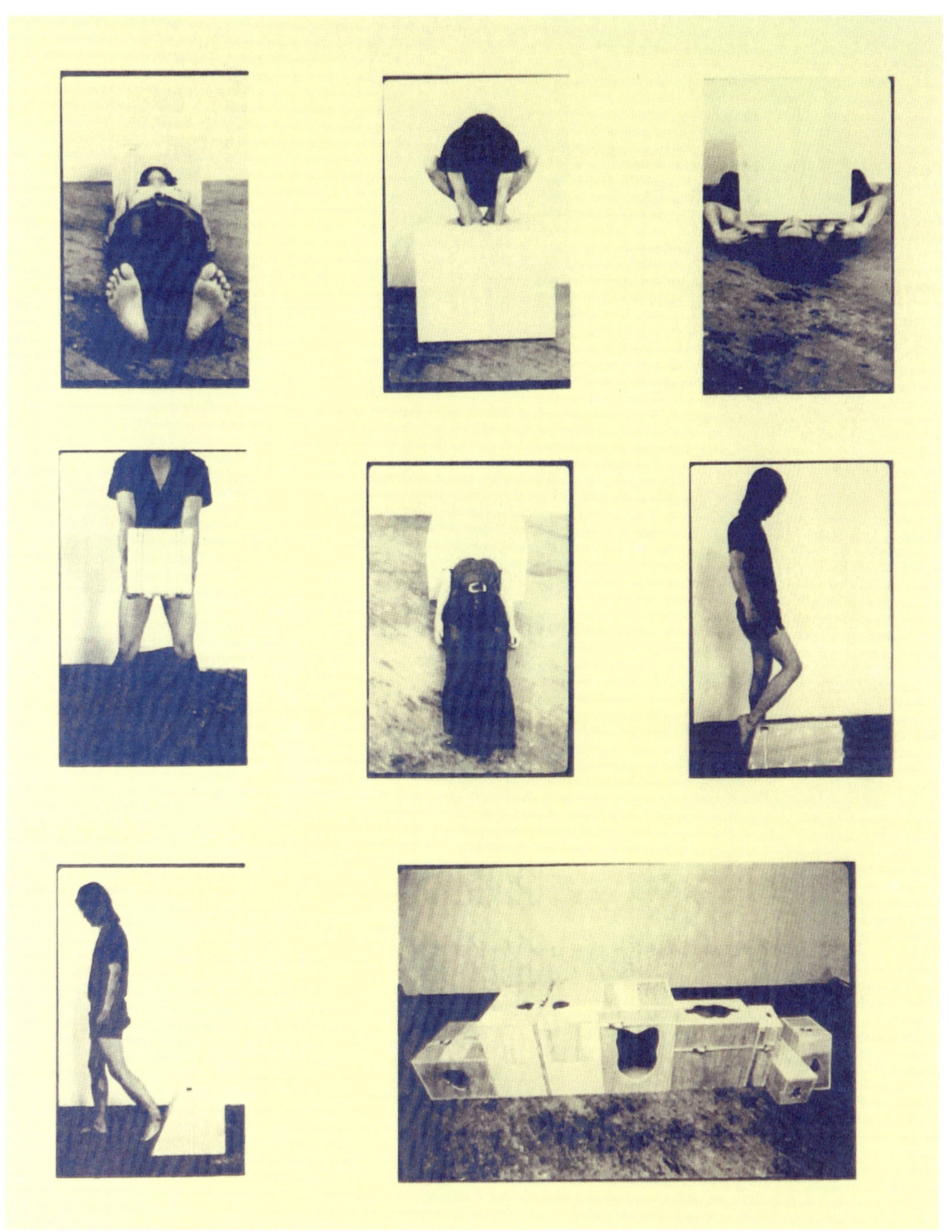

Modeling for Scamps, Scram (Self-Portrait in Energy Level) · 1993 (Blueprint) · C-print

violent foreboding. But such violence is the difficult, perhaps confounding, preface, not the tragic conclusion, of Choi's bodily expedition. For his subsequent work plays out another side of these gruesome castrative fantasies, bringing its repertoire of cuts up against a subtly blunted carnival of appropriations, memorials, excremental stand-ins, and intercultural personae.

The amputative process so starkly poeticized in *Bad Drawing* is reorganized in *Scamps, Scram #1* and *#2* (1994), a doubled installation of differently sized, body-perforated, aluminum and wooden boxes, stacked horizontally on the floor. Building a kind of "self-portrait in energy levels," Choi began by cutting out the shape of his head from a designated "head-box," then placing his head inside for three hours, in both conscious and dormitory states. The process was repeated with a palm-box (into which Choi set his hands for thirty minutes while seated "like a frog"); an abdomen-box (in which he stored forty minutes of energy generated by flipping over onto his stomach); a penis-box (energized with a twenty-minute insertion analogous to an episode of sexual intercourse); a big-toe-box (replete with direction-oriented movement energy); and, finally, a heel-box (forming a model of the transfer-point that conducts energy from the walking body to the traversed environment). Set within Choi's boxed energy field is a breast-box, taken from fellow-artist Janine Antoni, who occupied her box for twenty minutes (to lend lactative energy—and transgendered incorporation—to the male-dominant portrait).[2]

In "Scamps, Scram" a series of pre-emptive cuts staunch the flows and connectedness of the organic body, relocating its energies in isolation boxes emblazoned with the negative likenesses of particular energy-bearing (and energy-producing) body parts. Choi is clearly looking back—to the machine-denominated portraits of Francis Picabia and the mechanical eroticism of Marcel Duchamp—and forward—to the "desiring machines" and organless bodies described by Gilles Deleuze and Félix Guattari. From the Dadaists, he has absorbed the parody-effects of mechanistic subversion, from Deleuze and Guattari, something of the rhizomous, refracting logic, and anti-Oedipal drive of "schizoanalysis." But Choi has in no way reduced these points of contact to diagrams or illustrations. He resists, for example, the anarchic, dysfunctional deconstruction of mechanomorphic rationality proffered by the Dadaists, while deliberately holding on to his own precipitated subjectivity in the form of borderline energies willfully deposited in his holding tanks.

Choi's dialogue with the body-without-organs and the desiring machine is more complex. What he shares with the thought of Deleuze—apart from superficially similar strategies of the cut (the schizoanalysis of the philosopher and the cut-out body parts and larger deracination of the artist)—is a perception of the artwork as a kind of symptom. Symptomatic appearance is not, however, reducible to the legible traces of a particular unhealthy body, nor is it simply the sum or system of traces left by a particular disease. Instead, as Deleuze has argued throughout his writings, the artwork may be staged as a configuration of affective devices that together constitute a new symptomological field, a new way of seeing or thinking the experiences of life.[3] "Nonorganic vitality," Deleuze noted, flows through bodies that are "organically defective" and

2.
Choi described the material constitution of *Scamps, Scram* and some of the issues it raises in a letter to the author, June 2, 1998.

3.
Other works from the nineteen-nineties, including Damien Hirst's *Pharmacy*, are also convened around this symptomological design; and, though seldom Deleuzian in reach or sophistication, the critical practice of a cultural symptomology is now well-established; see, Marjorie Garber, *Symptoms of Culture* (New York: Routledge, 1998).

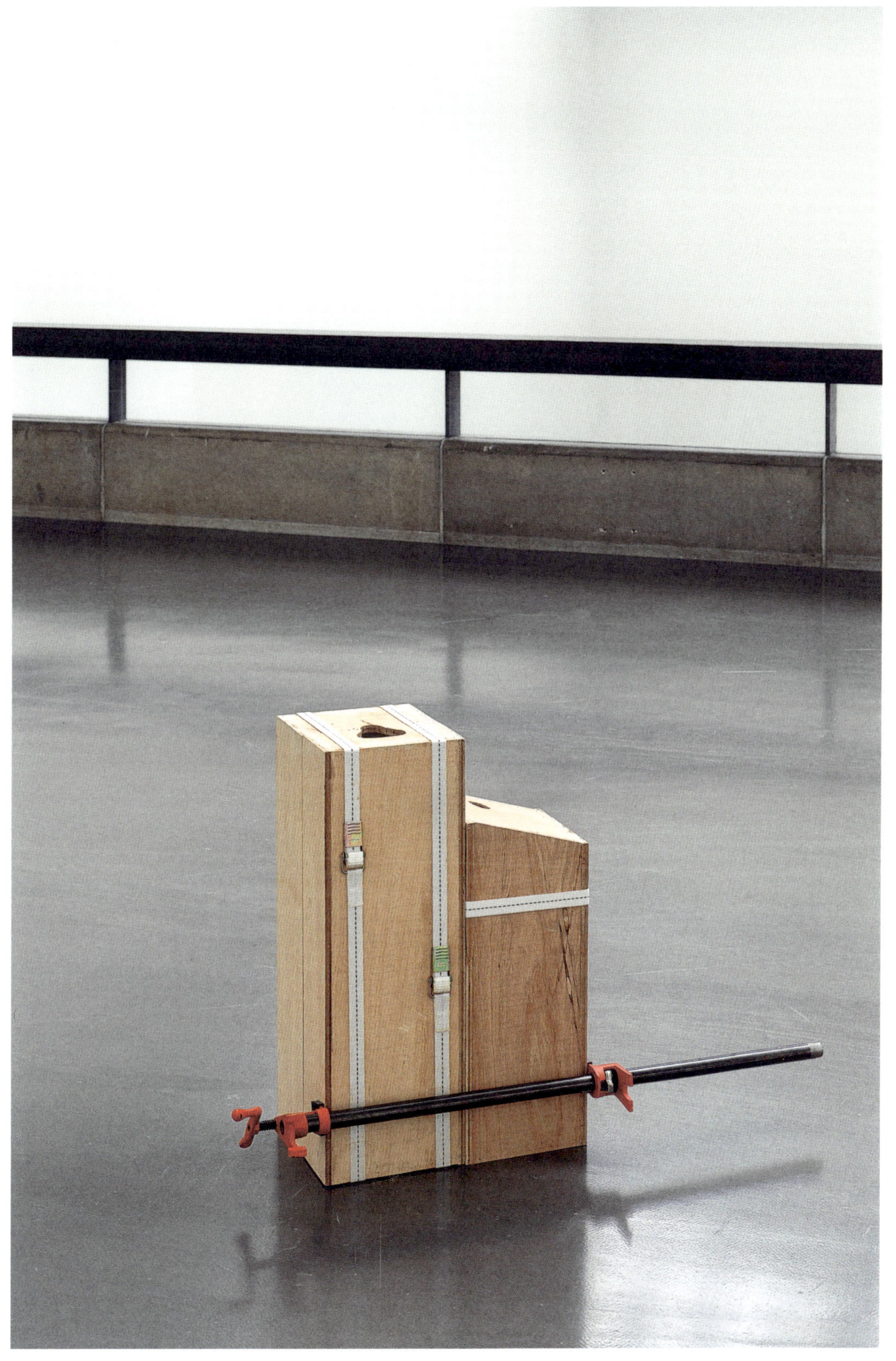

Box Animal Face · 1994 · Aluminum, wood, banding strap
Installation view at Kunsthalle Düsseldorf (2015)

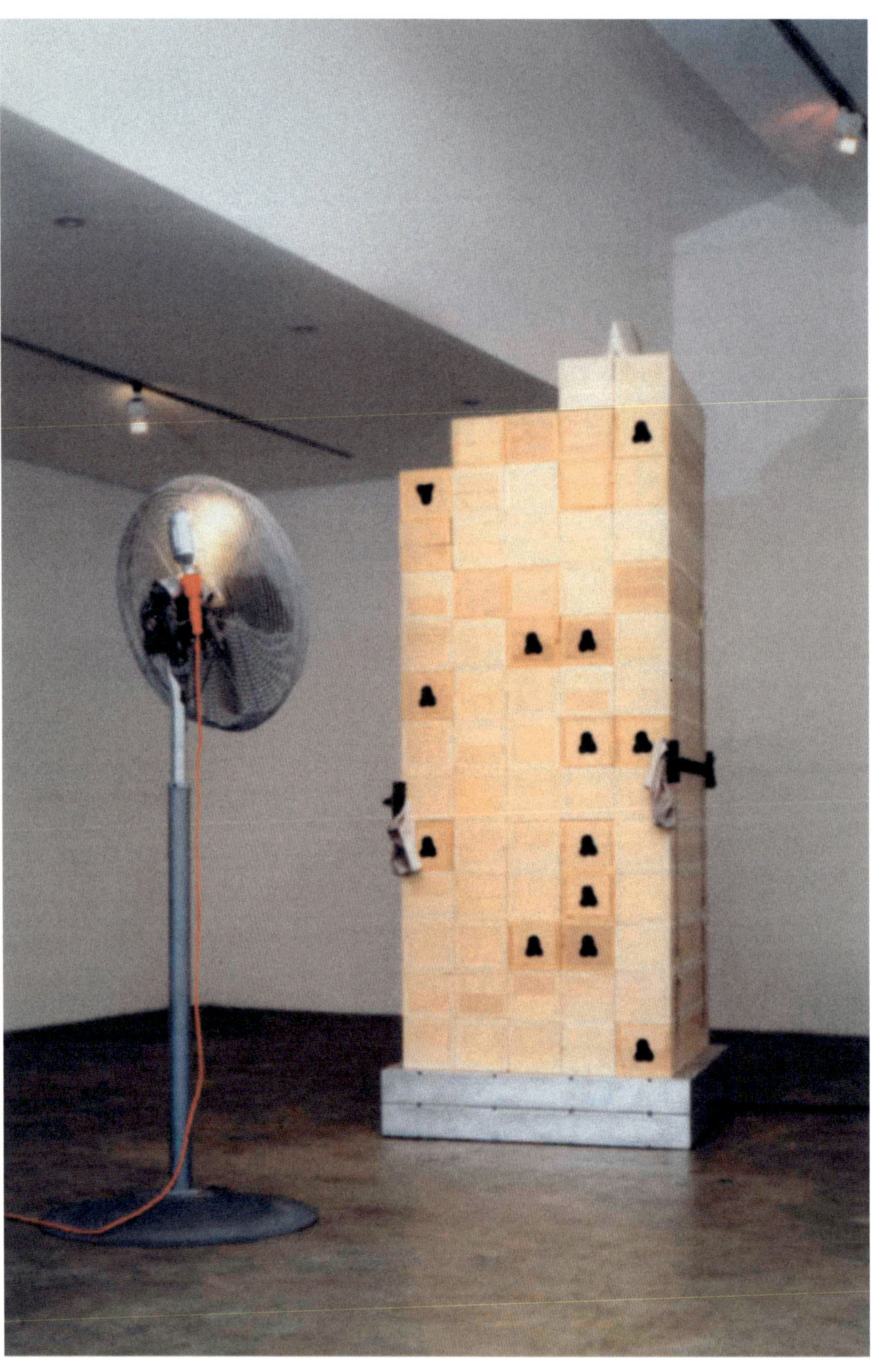

Cody's Ego Shop (Study of Male Energy) · 1994 · Wood, aluminum, plastic, cotton socks, steel, banding straps, cassette player, industrial fan

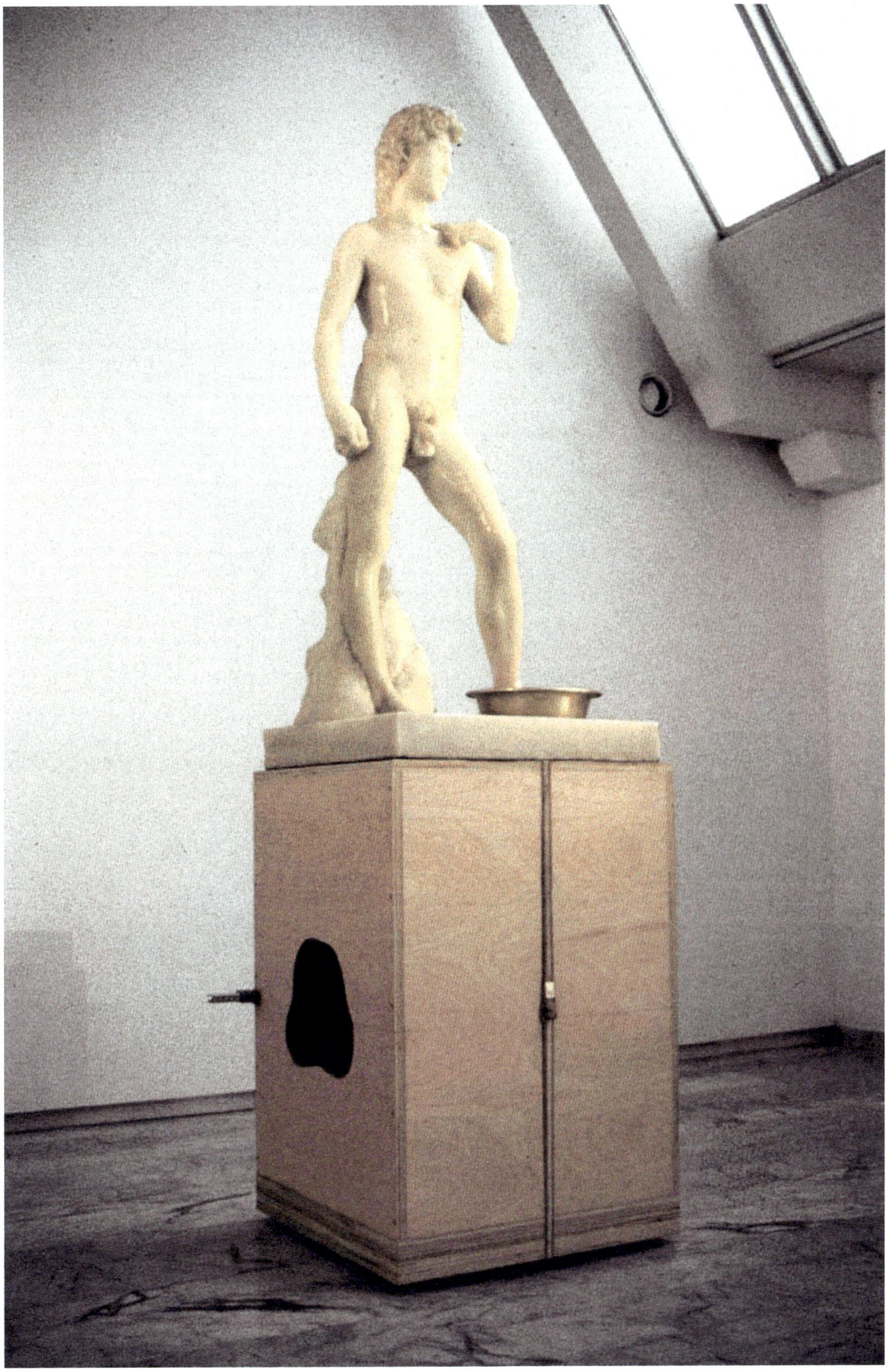

Cody's Legend vs. Freud's Shit Box · 1994–95 · Wax, Pepto-Bismol, banding straps, yellow tin, aluminum, wood, steel
Installation view at Musée d'Art Contemporain, Marseille · Courtesy of Musée d'Art Contemporain, Marseille

the body-without-organs emerges as "an affective, intensive, anarchist body that consists solely of poles, zones, thresholds, and gradients."[4] When Choi states, then, that the "disruption in the flow of desire" engendered by his amputated boxes "leads to the border of the physical order"[5] he appears to inscribe his own regime of cuts within that system of intensive thresholds and gradients appealed to by Deleuze.

The closest approach to such disembodiment, "disorder," and "visceral unconscious-ness"[6] arrives in "Box Animal Face" (1993–94), a series of works assembled from another round of cuttings-out from plywood boxes, to which Choi affixed various clamps and binding straps. Supplying the works with random subtitles ("face," "crazy," "stinky," et cetera), Choi's alliance of these evacuations with the counter-human conditions of a "becoming-animal" allows us to locate an important genealogy for the virtual body in the tradition of corporal surrogates mapped out in the Western and international art worlds from Hans Bellmer to Cindy Sherman and Yasumasa Morimura. But Choi's work seems precisely caught between two fundamental artistic tendencies in—or symptoms of—counter-organic life attended to by Deleuze: those, like the meatish images of Francis Bacon or D. H. Lawrence's "defectives," which pulverize and dissect the organic body; and others, such as the pictographic bodies of Paul Klee or preactive characters of Samuel Beckett, whose abstract virtuality is explored to the point of exhaustion, a limit-term that allows that which is nonorganic to offer itself up as a series of thresholds. For Choi, however, there is an energy, or potential, within his (or any) constituent organs, that may be decanted from them and unironically stored. This power is more literal than the forces or processes alluded to by Deleuze. It is also irreducibly predicated on a non-Western concep-tion of body-energy that cannot, perhaps, even be cut into—or out of—Deleuze's particular system of cuts.[7]

Clearly, Choi's move from the pent-up sexual energies of "Cody's Ego Shop" (1994) through the "shit boxes" of *Cody's Legend vs. Freud's Shit Box* and *Cody's Legend vs. Genghis Khan's Shit Box* (both 1994–95) to the congregation of seven, coarsely textured, hunched-over thinkers, their bodies patched together with layers of toilet tissue drenched in Pepto Bismol first seen in *Cody Choi: The Thinker* at Deitch Projects in New York (1996–97),[8] provided a means for the artist to challenge—and gradually to dismantle—the inexorable logic of the cut. The cuts ad-ministered in these works become first terms and preliminary actions that engender a series of reparational moves whose effects are, by turns, restorative and therapeutic.

Dubbed "The Macho Tower" by the artist, the mini-skyscraper of sixty-six tied boxes bored into with the negative outlines of the artist's genitalia that constitutes "Cody's Ego Shop" is topped by a replica of Albrecht Dürer's *Praying Hands* (ca. 1508)—wrapped in a transparent

---

4.

Gilles Deleuze, "To Have Done with Judgment," in *Essays Critical and Clinical*, trans. Daniel W. Smith and Michael A. Greco (Min-neapolis: University of Minnesota Press, 1997), 131. This summary of the body without organs arises in the context of a discussion of the "defective" bodies of D. H. Lawrence. Smith's introduction offers a useful outline of the relationship between Deleuze's writ-ings and the idea of a critical "symptomology"; see ibid., xvi–xvii, xxi, li, 177 nn 25, 26.

5.

Choi, letter to the author, June 2, 1998.

6.

These are Choi's terms, noted in ibid.

7.

In several statements, Choi noted the influence on his thinking of readings in the Tao beginning around 1996.

8.

"Cody Choi: The Thinker," Deitch Projects, New York, December 7, 1996 to January 4, 1997.

plastic bag)—hung with Choi's discarded cotton socks, accompanied by a hidden tape loop of lascivious male laughter, and wafted by drafts from an industrial fan. The commerce of smells, hot sexuality, and cooling breeze mixes with peals of lewd, disembodied laughter, and the liberatory sublimation of the praying hands to form a "desiring machine."[9] The sensate flows that fuel the machine are typically redolent signs of male sexual surplus, which Choi turns on and off against their point of origin in his chamber of precipitated libido.

These flows merge with a set of historical references, important for Choi's work as a whole, to the conceptualization of the "cut" and the production of cultural stereotypes with which it may be associated. Choi's earlier projects engaged aspects of the Western conceptualization of severance, imagined in the social and cultural spheres in a conjugation of technical procedures, including dissection and photographic cropping, with cultivation of the language of appropriation (in a lineage that reaches from Cubist collage to the "cut-ups" of William Burroughs[10] and beyond), and in psychoanalysis as a process decisive in the very scene of the "birth of subjectivity"—as Jacques Lacan put it, "the subject begins with the 'cut.'"[11] It is important, however, that the sensual elements of unadulterated machismo that pervade the *Ego Shop* also carry with them intimations of two key moments in Korean national memory, which are grafted onto the already provisional template of Choi's encounter with Western art and thinking. The relevance of the first, the so-called "Butcher's Ethic"[12]—denominated by a coarse, ribald masculinism associated with the rural and working classes during the premodern Chosŏn (or Joseon) dynasty—is immediately obvious. The second, layered onto this, but subject to the intercultural displacements of postcolonial experience, refers the reattribution of such behaviors to US popular culture in the nineteen-sixties. Choi's work reaches across these shifting categories, trespassing along the phantasmal divide between residual dynastic machismo, its transference onto Western culture (and back again) and the real-time conflicted desires of male sexuality.

The two Legend pieces refract the intensities of the *Ego Shop* in an exchange system of father figures and proper names relayed through an abstruse symbolism organized by medicines, receptacles, and conceptual sanitation.[13] For the Freud piece, Choi had himself life cast from head to toe in candle wax, striking the pose of Michelangelo's *David* (1501–04), a work originally intended as one of a series of statues of prophets to be positioned along the roofline of the east end of Florence Cathedral. The culturally recoded figure has his left foot planted in a tin Korean washbasin filled with Pepto-Bismol, while a contoured circumference

---

9.
This description and the installation details of "Cody's Ego Shop," derive from an undated text by the artist.

10.
The efficacy and implications of Western fetishizations of the "cut" continue to be asserted—and challenged. Manuel Luis Martínez, for example, notes that "the logic of … [Burrough's] cut-up is imperialistic: strategically offensive in a martial sense, and authoritarian in its politics"; see, Manuel Luis Martínez, *Countering the Counterculture: Rereading Postwar American Dissent from Jack Kerouac to Tomás Rivera* (Madison, WI: University of Wisconsin Press, 2003), 54.

11.
Tom Eyers, *Lacan and the Concept of the "Real"* (New York: Palgrave Macmillan, 2012), 135.

12.
The origin of the "Butcher's Ethic" can be traced to the outlaw folk hero, Im Kkeokjeong (?–1562), a butcher by trade, who was the "unclean" leader of a group of bandits that included slaves, peasants and fallen *yangban* (scholar-officials).

13.
In a text describing this piece, Choi insists that the Pepto-Bismol stands for "heterosexual love."

proportional to Choi's upper inside thighs and lower back has been excised from the strapped-up wooden pedestal (the "Shit Box" of the title),[14] allowing the artist to bend into the voided space as if seated on a Western-style toilet. Like the stretchers of a canvas—and the toilet bowl itself—the pedestal is for Choi an "oppression structure,"[15] which he works with and against in a schizoanalytical exchange of physical and psychic energies. As in his later works, the shit box/pedestal is severed in two, infiltrated with a cut-out body part, then forced together using straps and clamps whose bonding agency symbolizes Choi's struggle to repatriate the split. The bands and vices are "gears" that conjoin the boxes as contradictions while Choi "activates" the cut-outs performatively by depositing his body energy into the boxes and saving it there as a metaphorical residue.

In the Ghengis Khan version, Choi assumes the unassisted squatting position of a non-Western lavatory-user within the hollow shit box/pedestal, in which position his head protrudes through a differently shaped orifice. Binary oppositions between East and West are parodied here in a pantomime of bathroom etiquette, bodily switches, and decontextualized rituals of medicine and hygiene. Yet, Choi seems to suggest, any redemptive reversal, any hard-won escape route from the hothouse of ethnic and cultural stereotypes, is—for now at least—more likely to remain desired, even delusional, than to issue in some kind of social amelioration. For the shit boxes form a pair with the legendary Choi, relaying inverse presentations of the artist as subordinate and hero, dizzying us in a spin of homage, debasement, and substitution.

If "Cody's Ego Shop" and the shit-box works turn on insinuations of sexuality and excretion, *The Thinker* installation extrapolates the referential anxieties of the latter in a scene of manic repetition and material dissimulation and crosses the fraught implications of both with a powerful allegorization of the stakes of the *remedial*. Here, Choi offers a brazen and arresting reassessment of visual modernity's privileged conjugation of the Western mind and body bound up in a new post-appropriative logic that grants us access to some of the wider issues raised (and flouted) by the artist around the interacculturated body and the philosophy of digestion. As I have argued elsewhere, Choi's intervention is locked in compulsive dialogue with both the material and conceptual attributes as well as the social and historical coordinates of Auguste Rodin's signature *The Thinker* (1880–1904)—a Michelangelesque refrain of scorched bronze and simmering clay answered by the declamatory outrage of Choi's puce-pink, Pepto-Bismol papier-mâché.[16]

Looking to Rodin's contemporarsy, Friedrich Nietzsche, will help us to tease out some of the complex layers of material, historical, philosophical, and intercultural reference that converge in *The Thinker* and to examine the alternative posed by the artist to the violence of the cut, the expenditures of sexuality and the voiding of excretion. Nietzsche understood interpretation itself through a privileged gastroenterological metaphor according to which the body ceaselessly assimilates, absorbs, reduces, and incorporates that which is foreign to it. This actice consumption is staged in the face of the philosopher's fear of its (now literal) processes

14.

Choi, letter to the author, June 2, 1998.

15.

Ibid.

16.

John C. Welchman, "Culture/Cuts: Post-appropriation in the Work of Cody Choi," in *Art After Appropriation: Essays on Art in the 1990s* (Amsterdam: G+B Arts International, 2001), 245–61. My discussion here draws on this earlier essay.

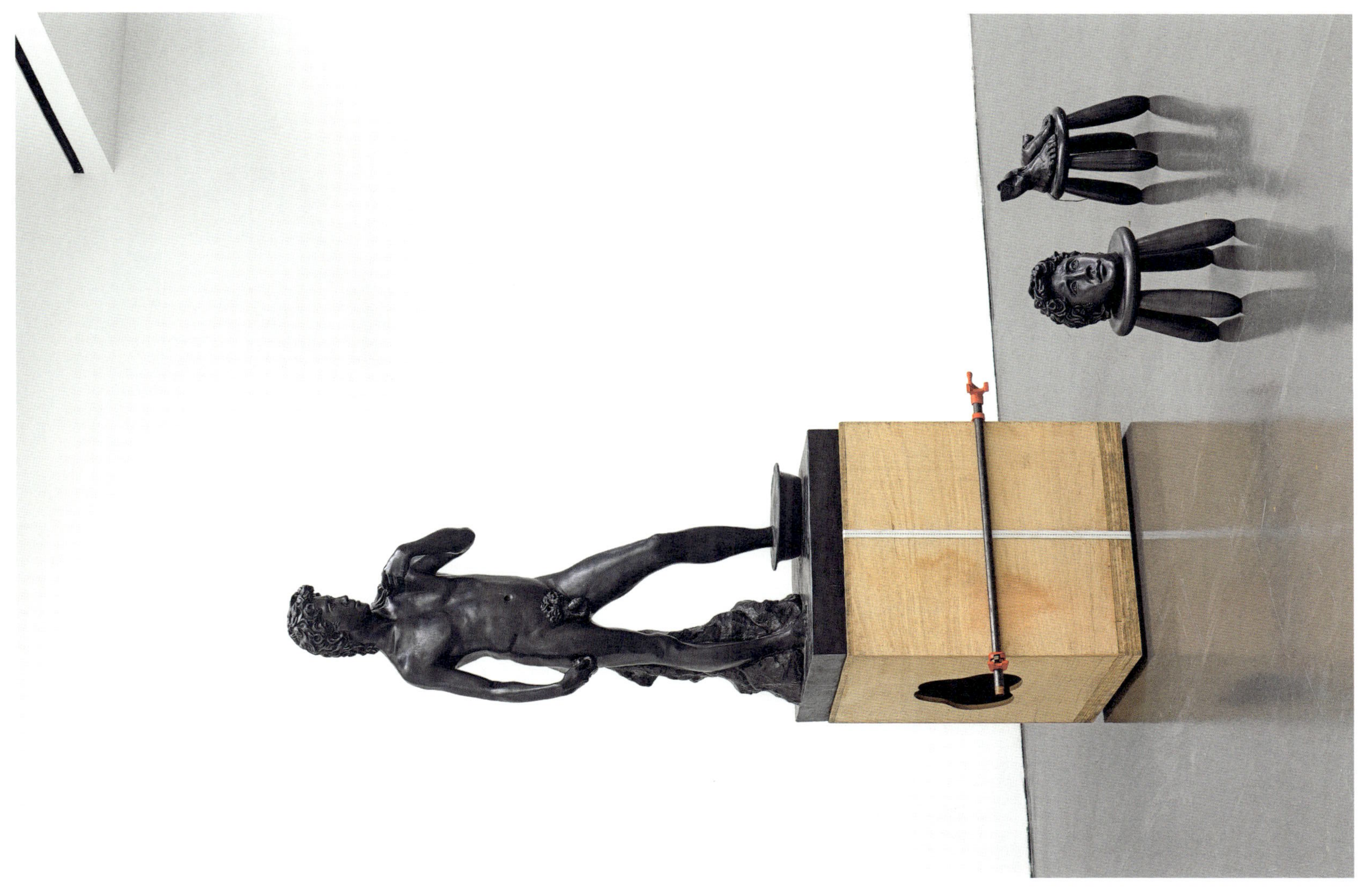

Cody's Legend vs. Freud's Shit Box · 1994–95 · Bronze, wood, steel
Installation view at Kunsthalle Düsseldorf (2015)

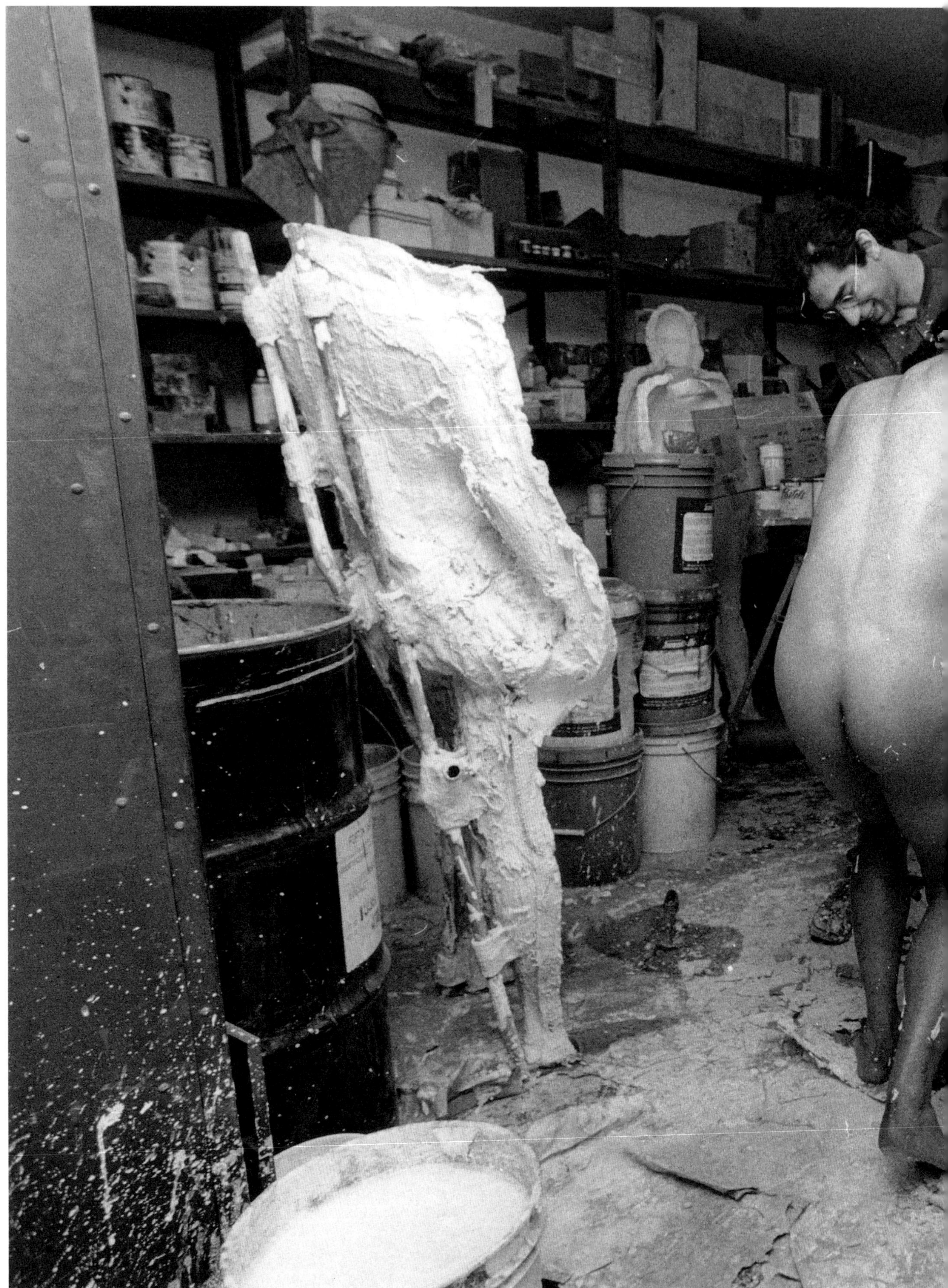

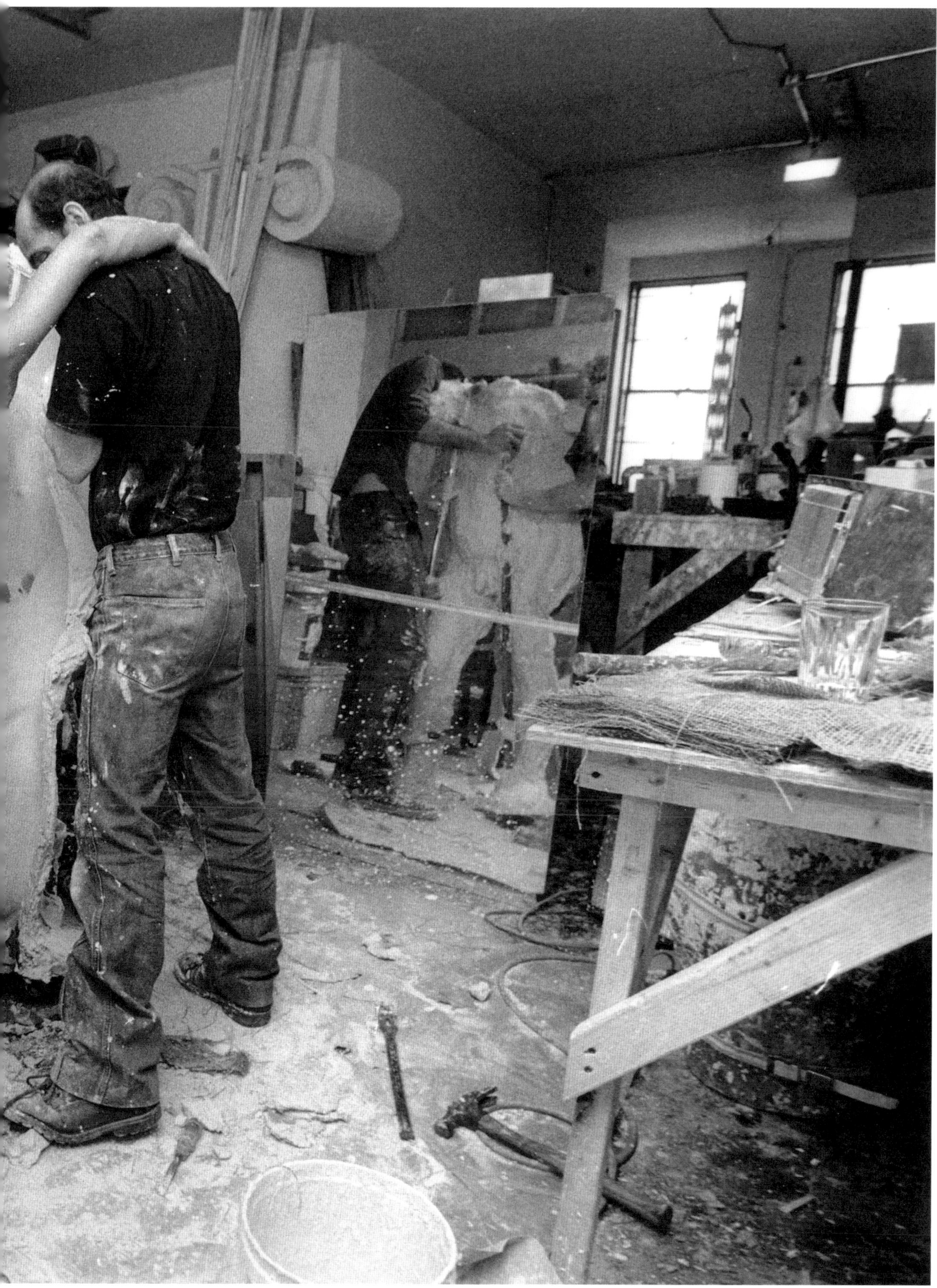

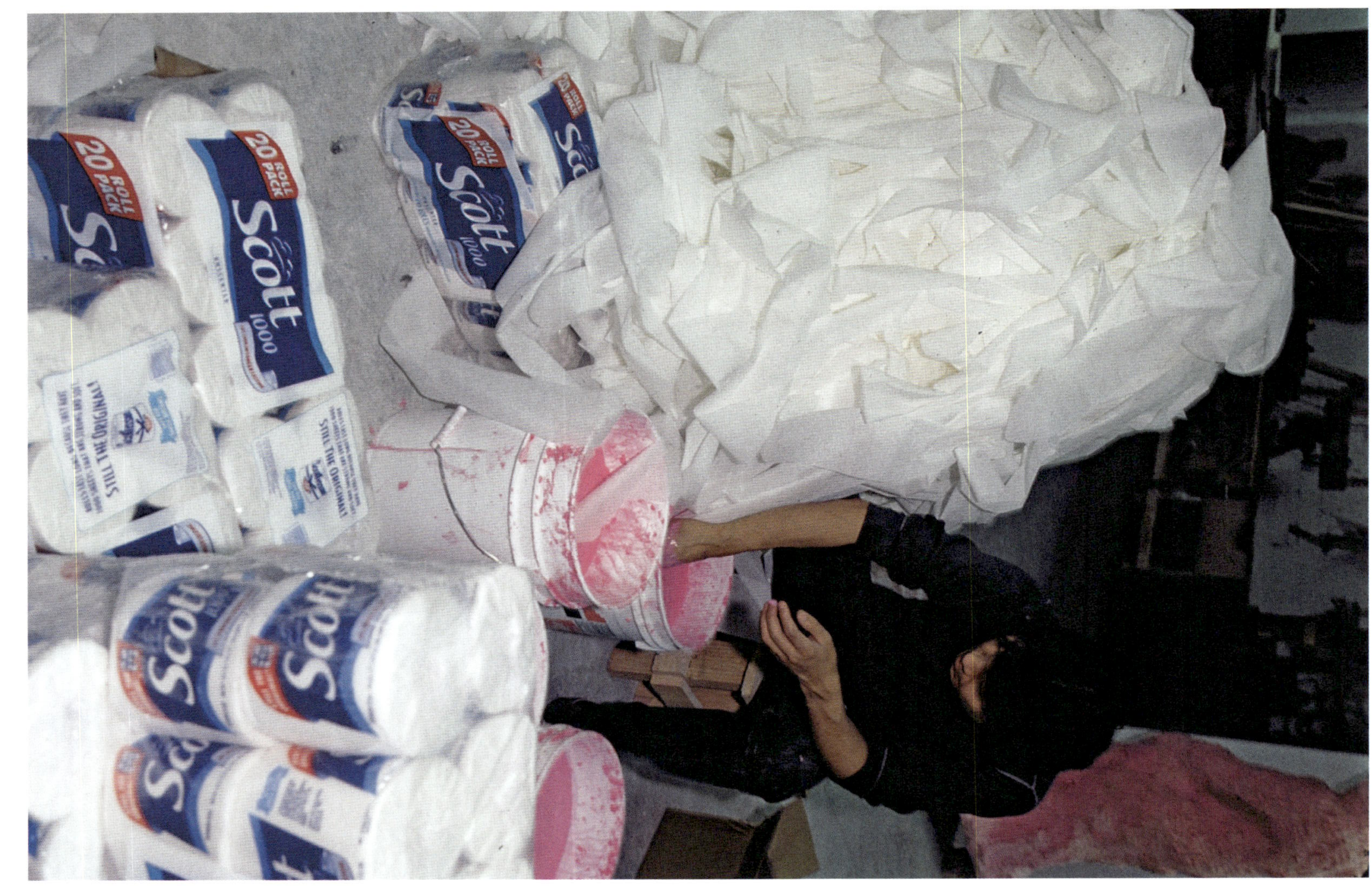

pp. 24–25 · Production process of *Cody's Legend vs. Freud's Shit Box* in Choi's New York studio (1994)

Cody Choi in his studio, New York

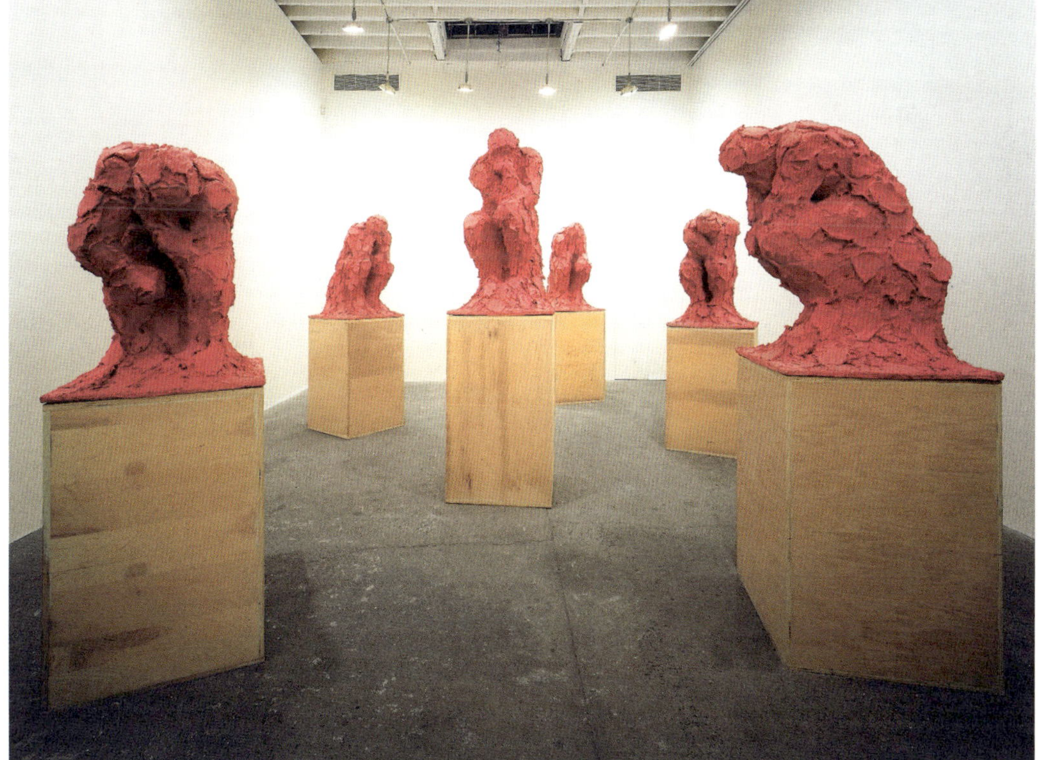

Empty Pepto-Bismol bottles, Cody Choi's studio, New York
The Thinker · 1996 · Toilet paper, Pepto-Bismol, wood
Installation view at Deitch Projects, New York City · Courtesy of Deitch Projects, New York City

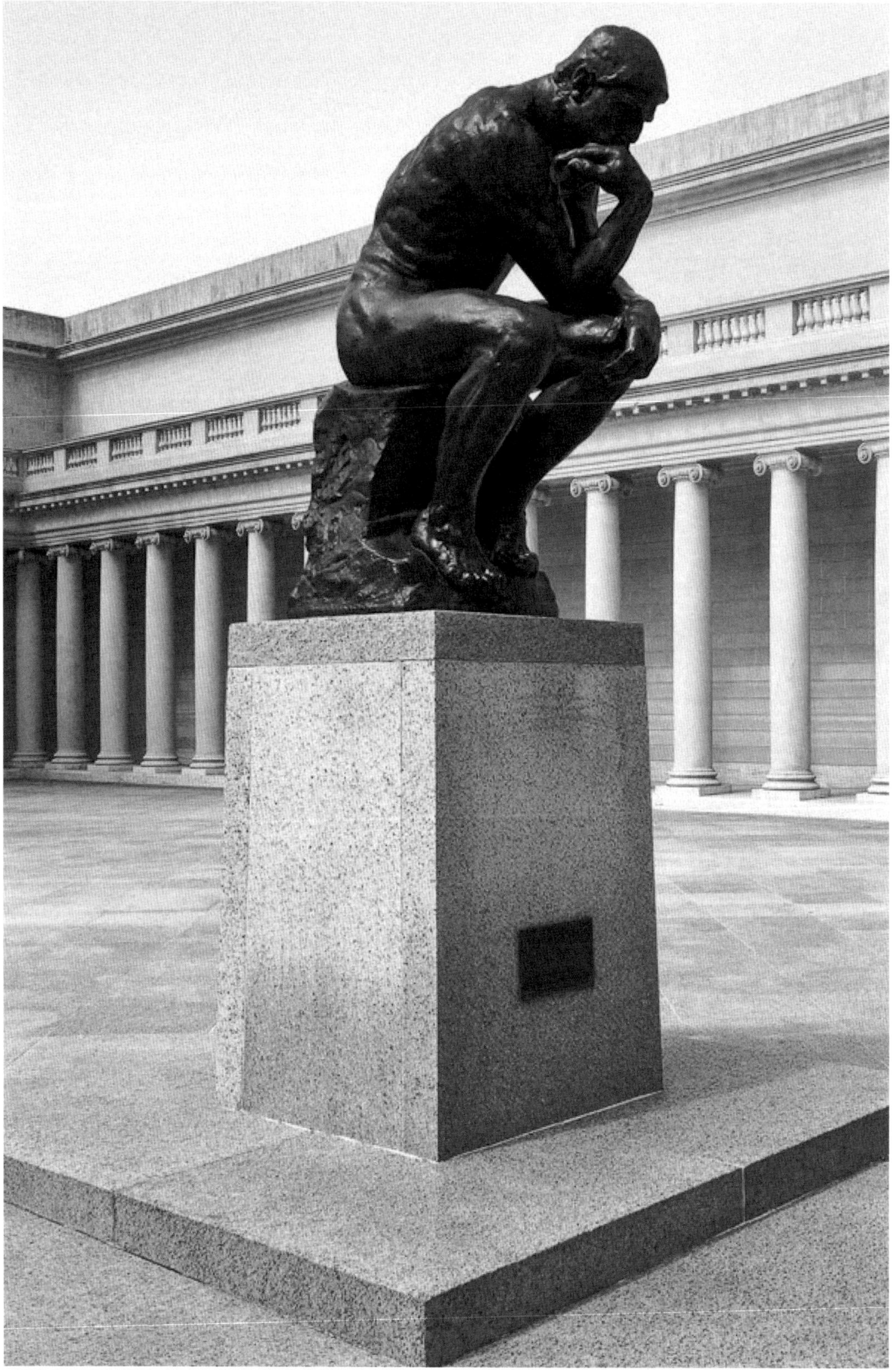

Auguste Rodin (1840–1917) · *The Thinker* · 1904 · Cast bronze
Legion of Honor Fine Arts Museums of San Francisco. Gift of Alma de Bretteville Spreckels

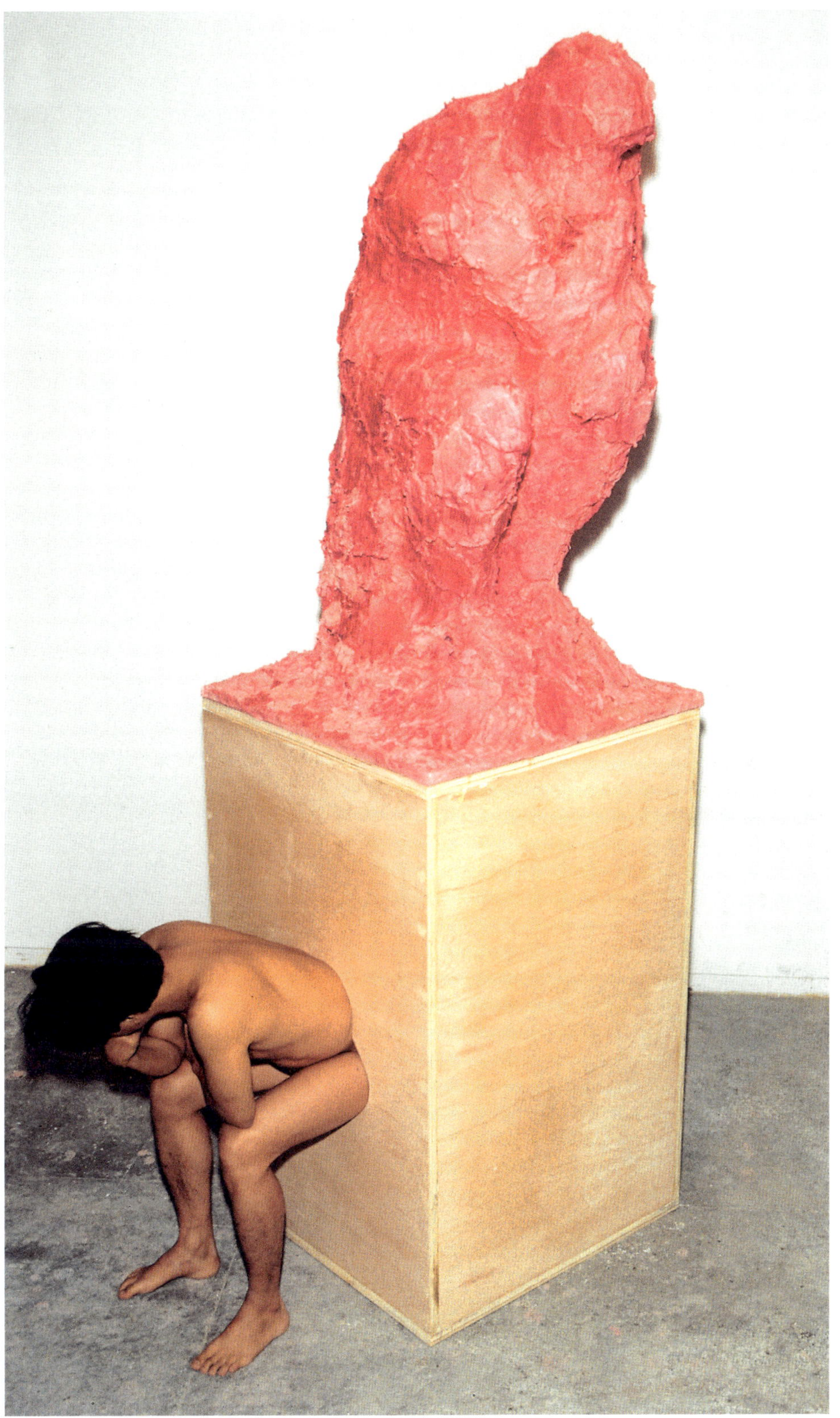

The Thinker, December #3 · 1996 · Toilet paper, Pepto-Bismol, wood "beneath the skin: bloody masses, full intestines, viscera, all those sucking, pumping monsters—formless or ugly or grotesque, and unpleasant to smell on top of that!"[17] Nietzsche's consternation about the "aesthetic" of "the human being under the skin" is not just reversed by Choi in some celebration of bodily internality—as might be argued for the paintings of Francis Bacon. Instead, Choi remetaphorizes Nietzsche's tropes, building "formless," "ugly," and "grotesque" "monsters" that are, simultaneously, paragons of high culture and covert images of the artist's body; insisting on the active energies of "sucking and pumping" (and siphoning-off); flaunting body-smells, and intimating bodily fluids that for Nietzsche only "awaken shame"; and finally packaging the result in a pink-hued parody of Nietzsche's fearful "bloody masses."

Nietzsche also correlates digestive assimilation with nationalities and their differences, leveling some of his most disparaging remarks at a "German nation" that was fundamentally "dyspeptic," incapable of exercising proper dietary regulation, and hobbled by a debilitating gastronomic democracy "which finds everything tasty." Choi, of course, works from the other side of this divide, playing the part of a foreign body who is putatively accorded "equal rights" and then supposedly broken down by the enzymes of acculturation. The interlocutor in one of Nietzsche's *Assorted Opinions and Maxims* might represent the point of view at stake in Choi's position: "Society's stomach is stronger than mine, it can digest me."[18] In a sense, the artist's objects are products of his own cross-cultural digestion that refuse to be repatriated—to go quietly—back to their bodily point of origin. The repertoire of cuts set out in and around a forest of genital- and shit-boxes can now be seen as a defense against the terrible choices of Choi's art: that it be relentlessly fed back into the originating body, layered into it like arty tissue; or that it be voided excrementally and forever lost or abandoned.

For the last two decades Choi has fought back against the uncompromising virulence and passive aggression of his own self-representation. Complicated—and in part fostered—by his return to Seoul a decade and a half ago, much that he has achieved since the mid-nineteen-nineties can be seen as a kind of rapprochement with the better implications of contexts and circumstances that had once appeared only alienating or hopeless. In turn these revisions have been crossed with, and often trumped by, the artist's attention to new or different situations that drew strength—as opposed to being drained by forfeits and disillusionment—from various social and subjective conjunctions including fatherhood, technology, community, public outreach. and economies of giving and distribution (rather than taking and storing). Choi took up, then, with a reparative fortitude that confronted the cuts and fragmentation of the box-pedestal works with something like the "partitive cohension" or "knotted interdependence" examined by Alain Badiou in his *Theory of the Subject*.[19]

17.
Friedrich Nietzsche, *The Will to Power*, trans. W. Kaufmann (New York: Vintage Books, 1967), section 906. See also, chapter 9, "The Body and Metaphors" in Eric Blondel, *Nietzsche: The Body and Culture*, trans. Seán Hand (Stanford: Stanford University Press, 1991), 201–38.
18.
Friedrich Nietzsche, "Assorted Opinions and Maxims," in *Human,*

All Too Human, trans. R. J. Hollingdale (Cambridge: Cambridge University Press, 1986), section 152; cited in Blondel, *Nietzsche: The Body and Culture*, 229.
19.
Badiou's "topolgical principle of partitive cohension, of knotted interdependence" is outlined in Alain Badiou, *Theory of the Subject* [1982], trans. Bruno Bosteels (London: Bloomsbury Academic, 2009), 227ff.

It would be a mistake, however, to imagine that the reparative turn in Choi's work was easy, consistent or even successful. We can discern a transitional phase in the later nineteen-nineties and early in the first decade of the twenty-first century, when the artist was still resident in New York. The shift he negotiated from the twentieth to the twenty-first centuries ran in parallel with the dispensations of the new millennium.[20] Questions of identity, corporeality, and the cultural dialectic between Asia and America were replaced by a synthetic regime of technological co-productions. Repudiating what he termed the "philistinism, snobbery, and sensualism" endemic in postmodernism's critical self-reflexivity and its nineteen-nineties redactions (including aspects of his own work), and refusing, in particular, its "putrefaction of the code,"[21] Choi participated in the invention of another era. His new materials were software and the desktop computer; his new symbology organized as a succession of fantastic animal-landscapes; while a new conceptuality emerged from the Oedipal relation staged between the artist Father, the keyboard Son, and the shifting software that programmed among them. Governing these forms and thematics was the artist's abiding concern to use basic elements of the new technology as machines for the recovery of "inspiration," armatures to secure creative work against the ravages of cultural "exhaustion" and "mental cruelty."[22]

As if to compensate for the succession of family splits that had underwritten his upbringing, immigration, and alienation, Choi began to work with his son, Joy, on the child's no-frills Packard Bell home computer. The animal-landscape configurations they produced using a "Crayola Magic 3-D Coloring Book" program were subject to various transfers and modifications and then printed on material "mesh" with the VUTEk system, backed with stretched and framed canvas. The weave of collaborations and revisions thus engendered were leashed to the technical apertures opened and closed by a prefabricated palate, the exigencies of printing and its supports, and the fixed but quasi-infinite regimen of morphological permutations preset in the system. Manipulating the logic of the default, Choi maneuvered the pixelated palate back to a premodernist regime of limitations—associated with the demands of commission, sanctioned narrative usages, the dictates of patronage, and the urgencies of location—suggesting at the same time that the software parameters, whose image-repertoire is coextensive with its template, may be antithetical to the standard stoppages of the nineteen-eighties, when the default was set to a message level that embraced the entire "critical" orientation of cosmopolitan postmodernism.

What resulted was a gaudy, virtual bestiary whose organization and effects are quite different from the post-Romantic animal allusion developed by visual modernism. For while they often stand for various forms of volitional abandon, his animals are not caught up in that singular allegiance to the pathetic fallacy, routed from primary coloristic identities to fatalist menace in the cows, horses, and forest-dwelling fauna of Franz Marc. Nor are they configured as startling, interruptive agents of Surrealist dreamwork. Formed in compounds, layers and folds, their garish hybridity emerges in a mode almost antithetical to the visceral dissection and pickled display so prominent in Damien Hirst's sectioned mortuary vitrines. Instead,

---

20.

My remarks on Choi's later work were first formulated in an essay for *Monthly Art* (Seoul, Korea, 2000), published in Korean.

21.

Cody Choi, e-mail to the author, March 8, 2000.

22.

Ibid.

Database Painting, Tiger#01 · 1999 · VUTEk ink on mesh, mounted on canvas
Datebase Painting, Whale #00 · 1999 · VUTEk ink on mesh, mounted on canvas

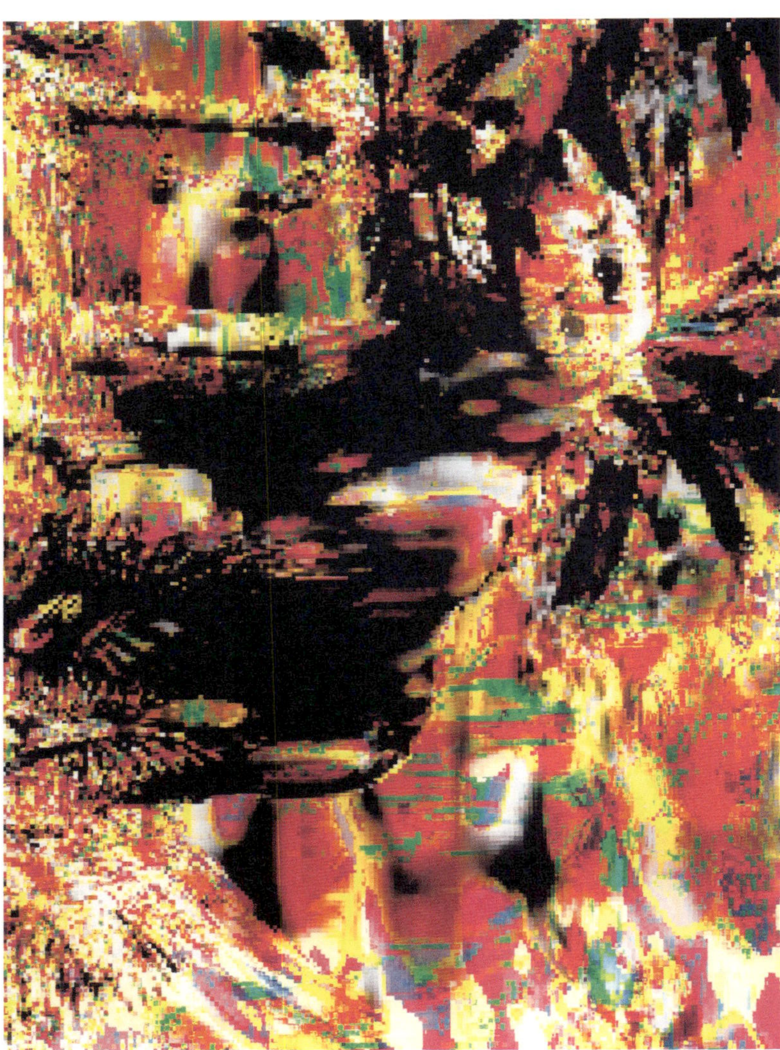

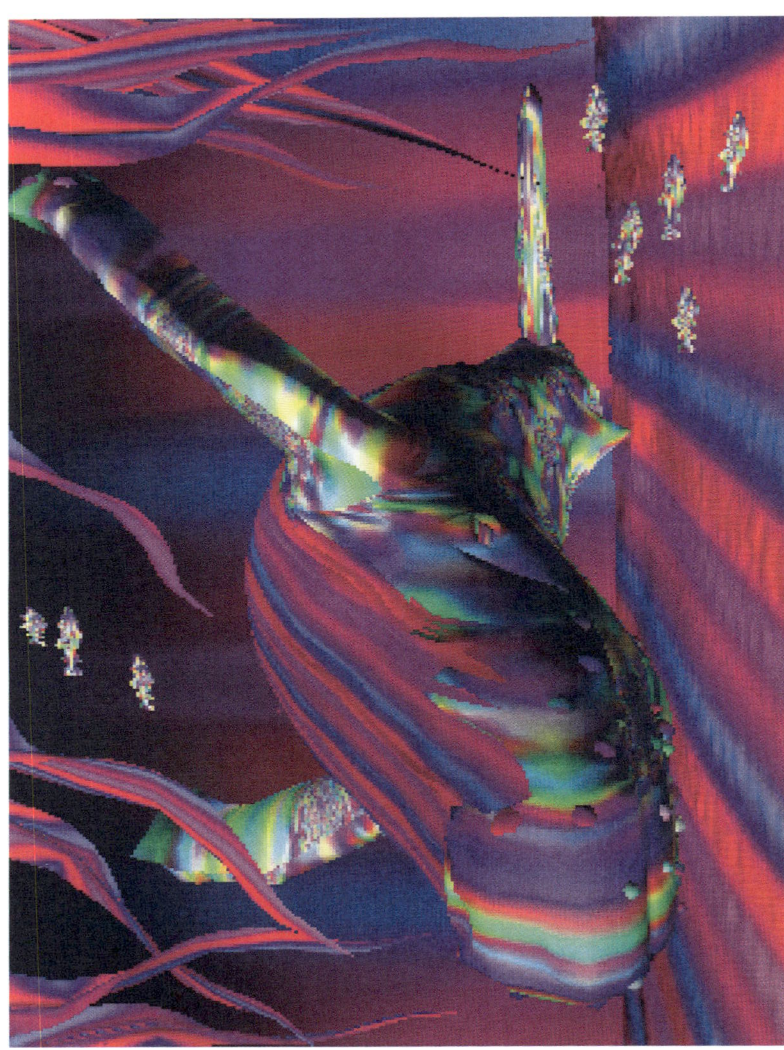

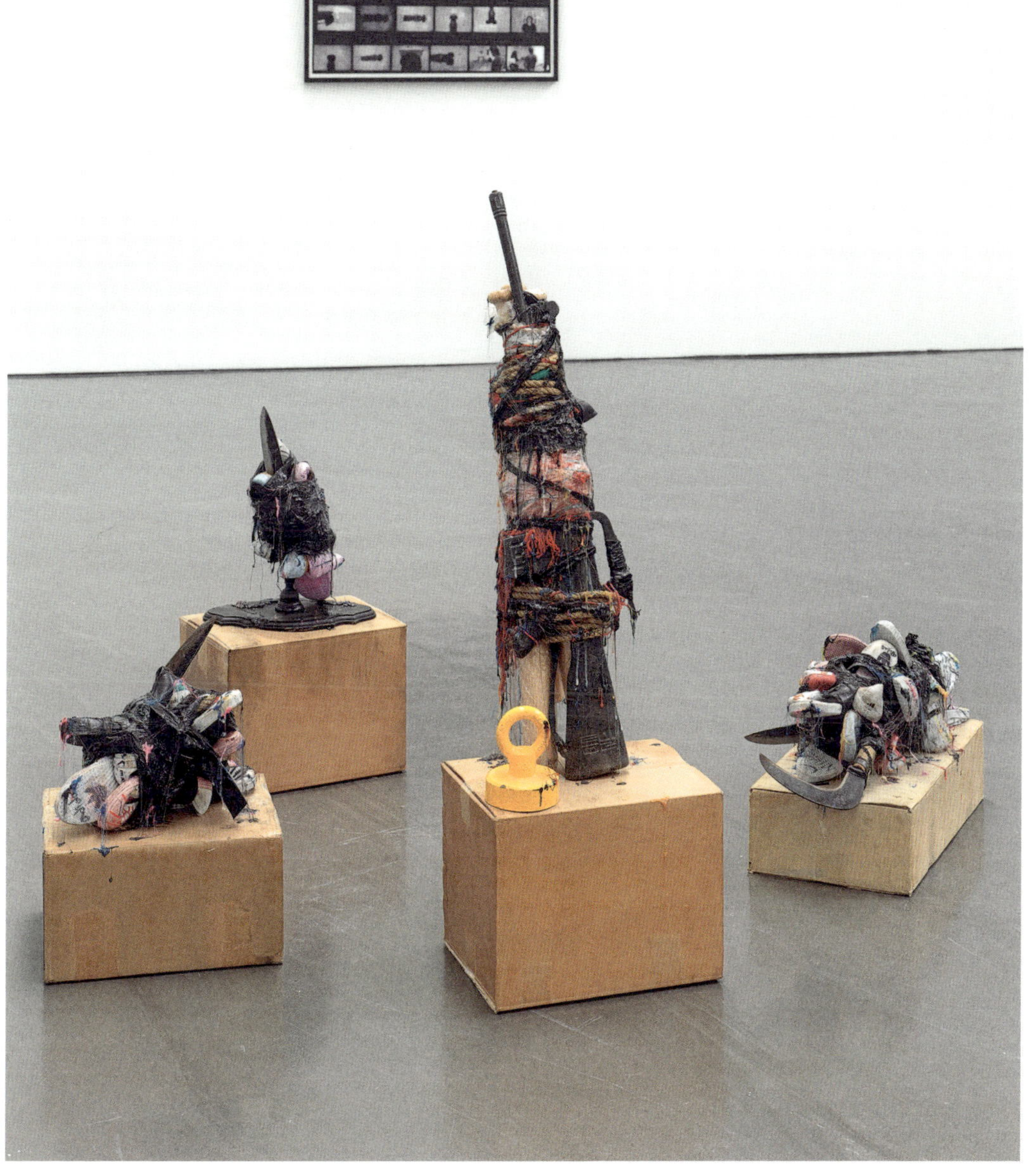

The Gift Exchange 1–4 · 2009 · Rubber tire (made in USA), Korean cast iron, children's shoes, marker pen, wood, paper
Installation view at Kunsthalle Düsseldorf (2015)

the attributes of Choi's zoomorphic imagination are governed by a double principle of pleasure and appropriation. Infused with a sense of postmodern marvel, what sets Choi's beasts apart is an invigorating lightness that looks over to the benign creatures of the fairytale, while passing by the sinister beasts of the nursery rhyme, and peering back to the mythological hybrids of medieval and ancient imaginations. Sharing something of the compounded nature of Deleuze's "contrapuntal conception of Nature,"[23] Choi's hazy, pixelated fauna, done in impossible reds and greens, dissolve the framing structures of their origin with a measure of that "paradisiacal" world "full of color in a state of identity, innocence, and harmony" that Walter Benjamin correlated with the absence of shame in his early essay, "A Child's View of Color."[24]

Traversing a line of genealogical filiations set out between father and son, Choi's new work also precipitates a refurbished family romance whose narrower and rebarbative dimensions were first glimpsed in the "Cody's Legend" pieces of 1994. Choi's stake in the elementary software program is an act of renunciation locked in a gesture of exchange, as complete in its way as the flight of an American football in a local park, or a one-on-one under the basketball hoop. Only the orientation of the participants' skills and capacities is reversed. Choi Sr. is not the master of the game, the giant athlete, the regulator who administers the structure of the adult-child encounter or secures it in a bond of tutelage. Instead, at the beginning at least, he is relegated to a confounding form of millennial infancy, made to feel younger, less competent and thus more vulnerable than his son, who is able at the age of five effortlessly to manipulate the program. Choi's is a backwards journey that commences in a preinfantile incompetence quite at odds with either his parental seniority or his art world "mastery." The work succeeds when Choi's intervention in the creative theater staged by Joy results only in the redemption and accentuation of childhood fantasy. The result is an allegory for a thousand paintbrushes— the energy that supplies a new spectrum for creativity—drawing out a virtual rainbow that, as Benjamin put it, "refers not to a chaste abstraction but to a life in art."[25]

When he returned to Seoul from the US in 2004, Choi immediately encountered another, defiantly inverted, round of the almost hallucinatory bombardment of (now) binational images and materials which had confounded him two decades earlier. The edginess and potential violence of this reencounter is palpable in works from "The Gift Exchange" series (2009) which featured fake Nike children's shoes inscribed with markers, impaled by traditional Korean iron knives and bonded with American tire rubber. It took a more oneiric and phantasmal form in the associated paintings, where blurs, streaks, and flares of long, blond hair—redolent of his impossible West Coast dreaming—stream across the canvas leaving the face that governs them as a remote island of physiognomic form at the edge of the image.

These interests were focused through an exhibition titled *The Gift* (2009)[26] where the bifurcations of Choi's everyday and artistic lives over the last quarter century were crosshatched

---

23.
Gilles Deleuze and Félix Guattari, *What Is Philosophy?* trans. Graham Burchell and Hugh Tomlinson (New York: Verso, 1994), 184-85.

24.
Walter Benjamin, "A Child's View of Color" (1914-15), in *Walter Benjamin: Selected Writings, Vol. I: 1913-1926,* ed. Marcus Bullock and Michael W. Jennings, trans. Rodney Livingstone (Cambridge, MA: Harvard University Press / Belknap Press, 1996), 51.

25.
Ibid.

26.
The Gift, Lucas Schoormans Gallery, New York, September 24 to October 23, 2009.

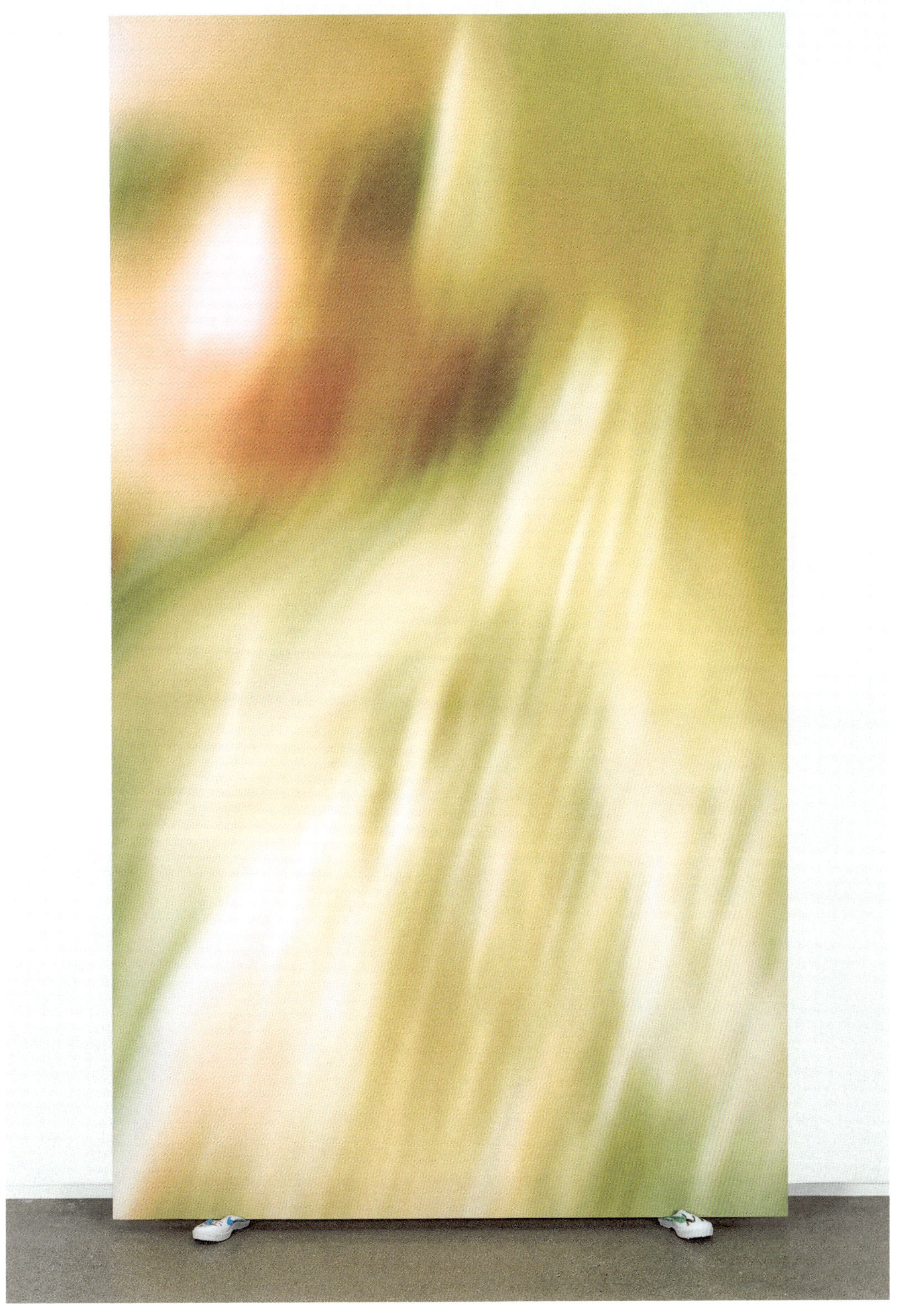

The Gift 4 · 2006–09 · VUTEk ink on canvas, children's shoes, marker pen

with deflation and delirium. The hair paintings such as *The Gift 4* (2006–09), for example, braid his early erotic dream life, in which, as for many Koreans in this era, the desire for "California girl" golden hair spawned a whole subculture of bleaching parlors and hairdressing salons. In the nineteen-nineties the craze switched from girls to boys, and ten years later had become as common and anodyne as urban Gothic or ankle tattoos in globalized youth culture. The exhibition addressed once more the give-and-take between cultures; but while reversing his early accentuation of "taking" it didn't shrink from the artist's angry growl about what he describes as the bastard love children of "American pseudoculture." Gifted or consumed, cut or reparatively regenerated, Choi and his work have always lived on the edge.

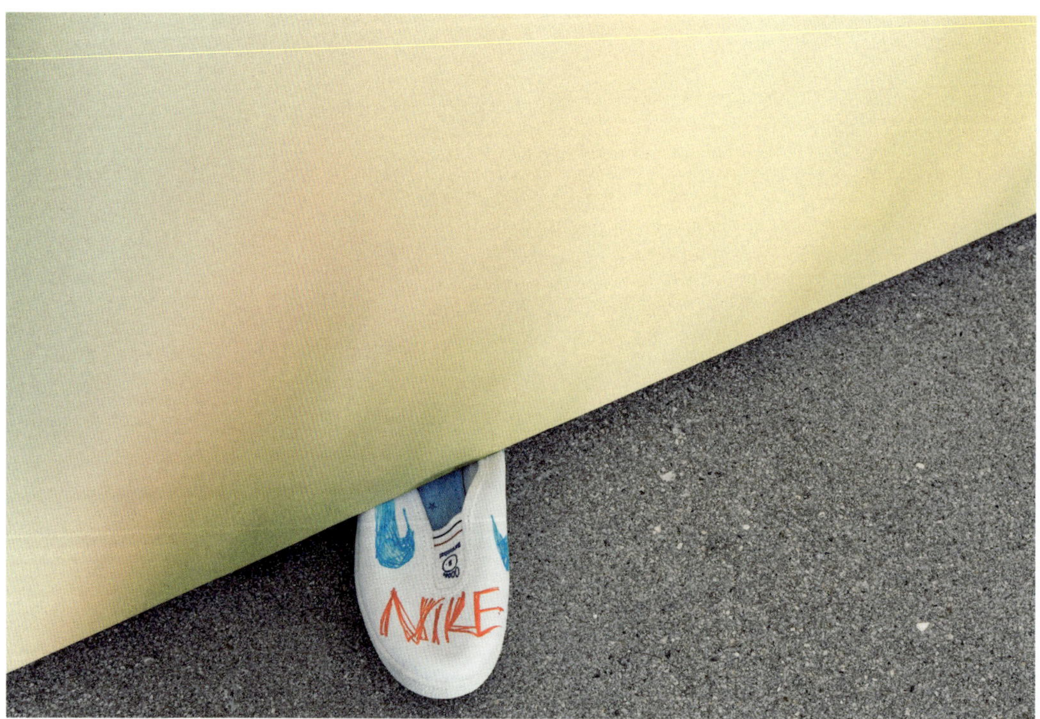

The Gift 4 (Detail) · 2006–09 · VUTEk ink on canvas, children's shoes, marker pen

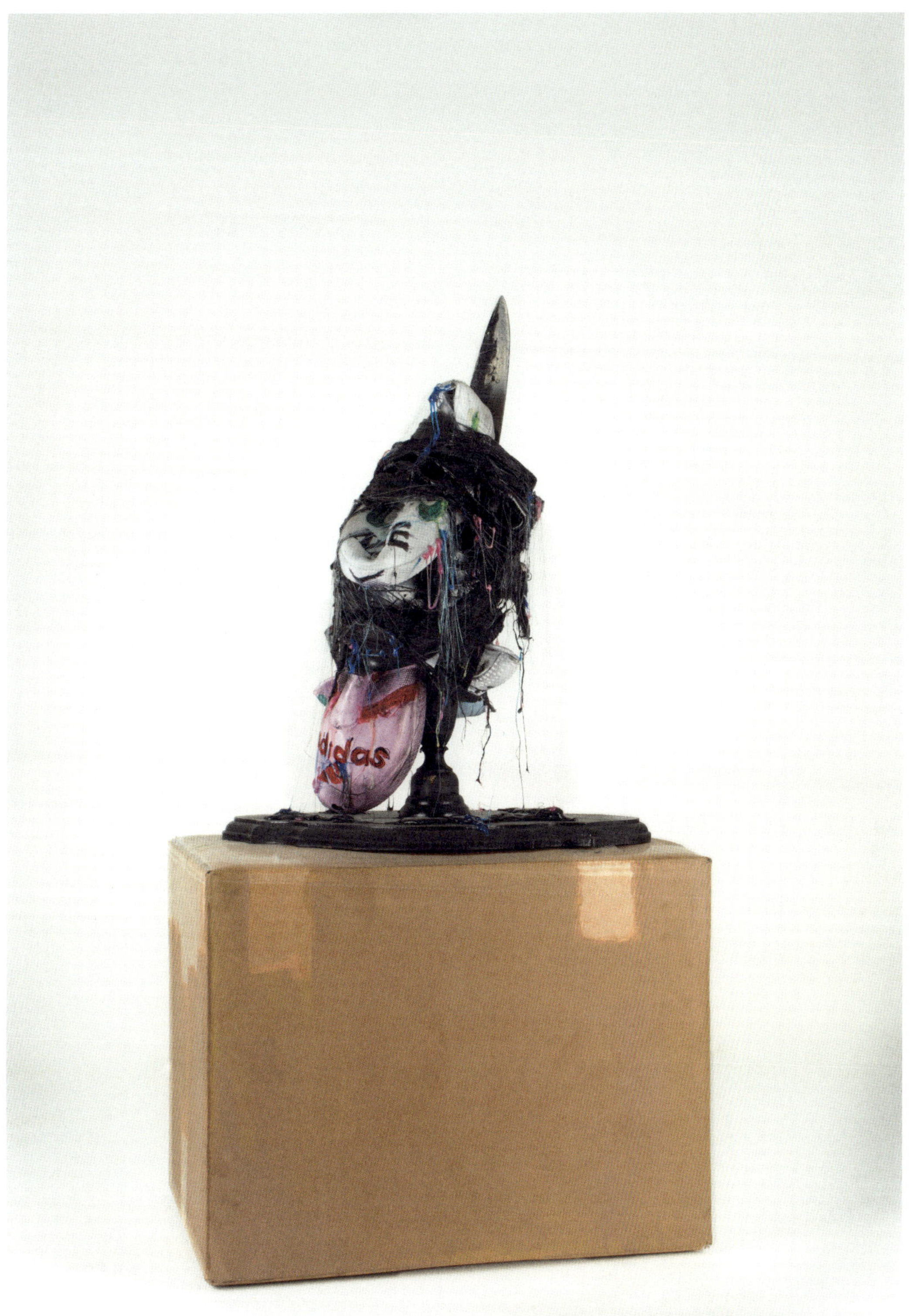

The Gift Exchange 2 · 2009 · Rubber tire (made in USA), Korean cast iron, children's shoes, marker pen, wood, paper

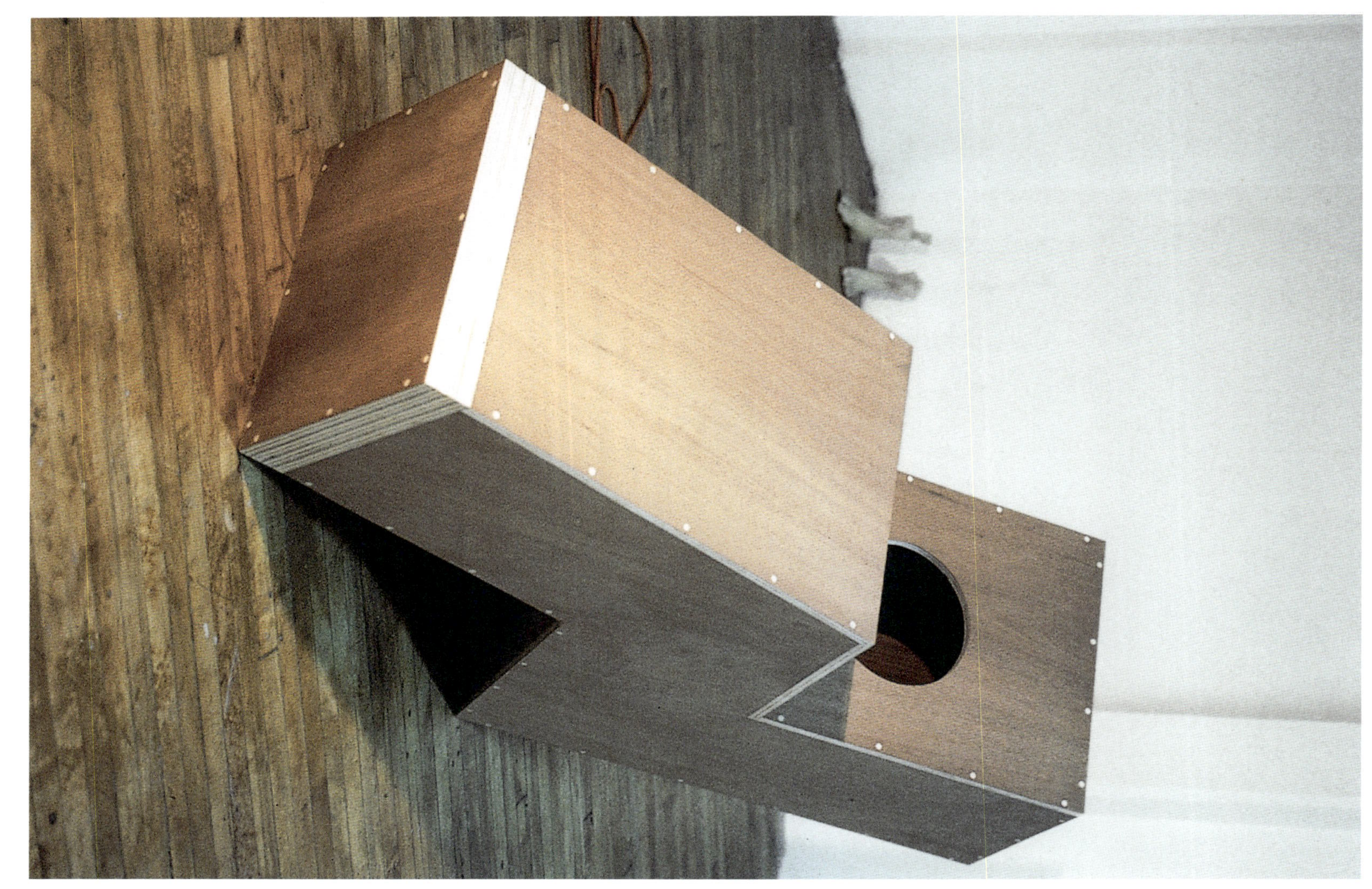

The Last Gasp (Sitting Coffin, Energy Container) · 1994 · Wood, CD player
Courtesy of Musée d'Art Contemporain

Marie de Brugerolle
Cody Hyun Choi: Canons/Cannons

Marie de Brugerolle

First meeting, first steps (mid-nineteen-nineties)

I MET Cody Choi in 1995 in his studio on Greenwich Street in New York, having been invited there by Dennis Elliot who was the director of ISP program in New York. After *Hors Limites: l'art et la vie* opened in November 1994 at the Centre Pompidou in Paris, an exhibition addressing the origins of happenings, "events" or performance art for which I was adjunct curator, I went to the Museum of Modern Art in New York to work on a Bruce Nauman retrospective. It seemed to me that there were connections between Choi and Nauman, notably in their shared interests in constrained bodies, the use of language as a tool, and the redeployment of objects and materials from American consumer society—sublimated by philosophical inquiry.

A number of important pieces were installed in Cody's studio. They were significant not only in terms of the artist's own work and development, but also in relation to their historical context. It was here that I discovered the "Bad Drawing" series (1992–93) and the wooden boxes of *Cody's Legend vs. Freud's Shit Box* (1994–95) as well as those that made up "Cody's Ego Shop" (1994). Cody was also finishing a series of "Edge Paintings" (1995). Three pieces in particular caught my attention: *The Last Gasp (Sitting Coffin, Energy Container)* (1994); the "David" from *Cody's Legend vs. Freud's Shit Box*; and *High Heel Neurosis (Study of a Female Energy Balance Against Gravity)* (1994–95).

A post-appropriation digest

T HE *Last Gasp (Sitting Coffin/Energy Container)* (1994) is a sound sculpture that functions as both a reappropriation and a unique investigation—with nod to René Magritte and Mike Kelley. It might be termed a "digested appropriation," a gesture that no longer refuses to make something new from something old, offering a shameless ricochet of an artistic form that is constitutive of modernity itself. For the "life-sized" wooden coffin of *The Last Gasp* is indebted to a series of paintings by Magritte featuring coffins in which the Belgian Surrealist offered a new perspective on several key images associated with the origins of modern art in France: *Perspective II, Manet's Balcony* (1950), *Perspective I: Madame Récamier by David* (1951), and the related *Perspective: Madame Récamier by David* (1951). Magritte also created a bronze sculpture based on the latter, *Madame Récamier by David* (1967), that is almost the same size as a real piece of furniture, and a little larger than the original painted by Jacques-Louis David in 1800. The decision to reproduce Magritte, who himself remade—or hijacked—works

---

1.

The earliest version of *Perspective II: Manet's Balcony* appears to be
a red chalk drawing made ca. 1948–49.

by his predecessors, is anything but haphazard. For each of the three French painters from whom Magritte "borrowed" salient forms—François Gérard (1770–1837), David (1748–1825), and Édouard Manet (1832–83)—are associated with the rupture that marks the passage from the ancien régime or a "classical" order to the onset of the modern. Building on this turn, Choi was attuned to both the irreverent "pastiche" of dominant models of Western visual culture and to metahistorical and metaphysical considerations related to his "applied" philosophy.

I remember our conversations about the writings of Gilles Deleuze and especially Jacques Lacan when I returned to New York in 1997, when Cody was beginning to think about a return to Korea. He said that he felt he had "absorbed everything" that modern Western philosophy could teach him. Once, when we were walking in the gardens of the Nogushi Museum in Queens after an afternoon spent with friends, Cody told me about his new research. He was studying traditional Chinese philosophy with a "master," and at the same time starting to hang out with a group of young "hackers" who were teaching—and debating with—him about digital culture. I can picture Cody commenting on the calm beauty of the museum's rock gardens, recalling how Mike Kelley had told him how much he admired Isamu Noguchi, while at the same time beginning to walk with a heavy, applied step. At that moment I noticed the beauty of his shoes, made from the best materials by one of the trendiest Korean designers. To my mind, until that time Cody had worn old shoes that clashed with his American biker's jacket. In response to my questions Cody answered that his philosophical work was beginning to have an impact on his body and his way of walking, and that he was beginning a period of transition.

It was then that I remembered Magritte's shoes (*The Red Model*, 1934) and the *High Heel Neurosis* piece that Cody had been working on when we first met. On Cody's feet, as it were, Magritte's shoes had literally become plastic forms—a pastiche of the Belgian painter who knew how to ridicule his own work, especially in his so-called *Période vache* in the later nineteen-forties. Magritte's self-parody targeted the hegemony of the Parisian artistic scene, and is not insignificant that all this transpired in 1948, during the Cold War, when the world was split into two on either side of the Iron Curtain.

The impact of a dominant aesthetic canon refers to restrictions (of the body, of taste, of making) mandated by convention. The very title *High Heel Neurosis (Study of a Female Energy Balance Against Gravity)* (1994–95) could be sounded out as "High Hell," alluding to the fact that in both Western and Asian traditions, women's feet were often subjected to aesthetically-occasioned "torture." We are familiar with the foot binding originating in the courtly etiquette of tenth century imperial China and not eradicated until the early nineteen hundreds that prevented women from walking could inflict lifelong damage. Accompanied by an explanatory diagram that seems to account for why "office girl's legs are beautiful," Choi's wooden sculpture has something in it of another Chinese ritual, "Death by a thousand cuts"—a photograph of which came into Bataille's possession in the mid-nineteen-twenties.[2] Cody explained to me how lifting the sole of the foot unsettles the posture and also blocks the correct irrigation of the brain, due

---

2.

Lingchi or "Death by a thousand cuts" is a Chinese torture that consists of cutting away the flesh of a living person piece-by-piece, opium being administered to prolong the suffering. Georges Bataille writes of the practice in *Les Larmes d'Eros* (The Tears of Eros, 1959), noting that the photo he reprinted was published for the first time in George Dumas's *Le Traité de Psychologie* (Treatise on psychology, 1923–24) and that Adrien Borel, one of the founders of the Société psychanalytique de Paris, gave it to him in 1925.

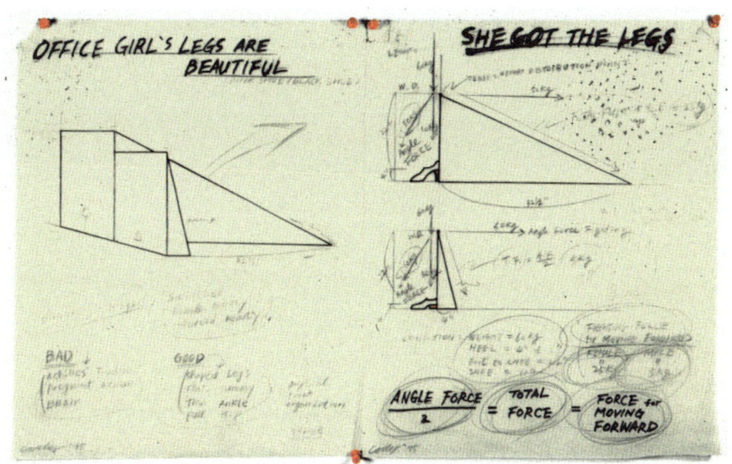

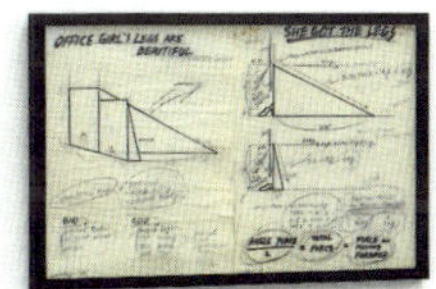

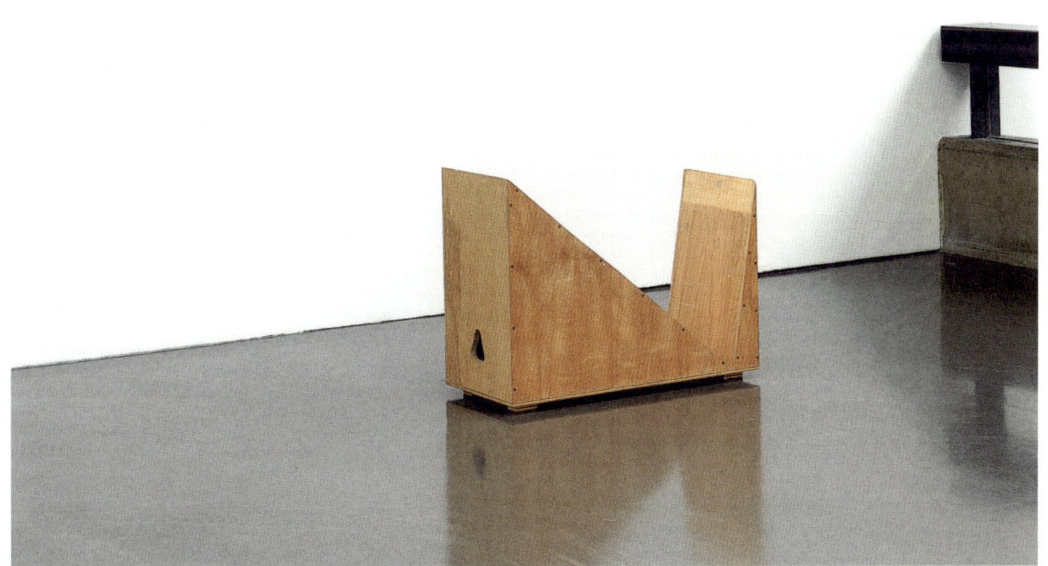

High Heel Neurosis Drawing (Study of Female Energy Balance Against Gravity) · 1994–95 · Ink, pencil on paper
High Heel Neurosis (Study of Female Energy Balance Against Gravity) · 1994–95 · Wood
Installation view at Kunsthalle Düsseldorf (2015)

to the anchoring and circulation of corporeal energies. We can see how archaic and modern myths combine endlessly to recreate "canons" that are little more than "straightjackets."

In everyday French parlance, *canon* is used to designate a beautiful girl or a handsome boy, as well as a weapon of war ("cannon" in English) that propels balls, or the barrel of a gun. Like the English "canon" it also denotes a code of laws (as in the canon law of the Catholic church), a more general established principle, or a group of exemplary literary or other works—rule-governed, often dogmatic, systems established by convention. Choi's work is anchored in a unique metahistorical reading of the processes according to which art was canonized at the turn of the twentieth century. As we will see, the question of rules and of the canonization of contemporary practices corresponds to the criticism of a type of colonization. It is in dialogue with artists belonging to moments of rupture such as Michelangelo, and refers to an ability to constantly reactivate the question of modernity as an unfinished project. It is about an aesthetic that goes beyond the will to imitate, reminding us of the ultimate value of art.

This raises the question of artists who work outside the studio, such as Robert Smithson, who wrote explicitly about the "fall" of the studio since the time of Michelangelo.[3] This reconfiguration achieved a kind of critical mass a few years later when John Baldessari commenced his "post-studio" course at the California Institute of the Arts, Valencia, California, making his class into a place of translation and transmission. Today, Baldessari often receives small groups of artists in his studio to continue the discussion.

I remember my first visit with Cody to Louise Bourgeois, at her Chelsea home, one spring Sunday. Louise welcomed us as usual, having asked her perennial question: "Do you have a cold? And your friend, is he ill?" Her fear of germs didn't limit her curiosity about young artists, and "living room" conversations quickly became fraught with staged irony. The pink color of the Pepto-Bismol used by Choi fascinated her. So Louise began to imagine badly stitched figures in fabric, puffy figures that sometimes turned pink.[4]

Choi's "David" disturbs canonical rules in two respects: in relation to neoclassical values and in relation to kitsch. It is anti-canonical by virtue of its challenge to classicism as much as for its annexation of mass-produced materials. Its "form" is not simply the opposite of that posited by convention, it is "beyond recovery" and unclassifiable. For starters, it is not called "David" but *Cody's Legend vs. Freud's Shit Box*. It is an iconic statue in the antique sense of the term—that is to say, a portrait of an individual—whereas Michelangelo's sculpture is not a "proper" portrait, but rather the representation of an idealized figure. It is also a heroic nude, following a tradition dating back to antiquity that was accentuated under Augustus, the first Roman Emperor (27 BC to 14 AD). It is also the product of an aesthetic, mystic, and political

3.

On this subject, see the exhibition catalogue, *Robert Smithson: Une rétrospective, le paysage entropique 1960–1973*, ed. Maggie Gilchrist and James Lingwood (Marseille: Musées de la ville de Marseille, 1994). In the first head text for his essay "What Really Spoils Michelangelo's Sculpture" (1966–67), Smithson cites Clement Greenberg's discussion of Michelangelo's relation to pictorial illusion (see page 167): "However, what really spoils Michelangelo's sculpture is not so much its naturalism as, on the contrary, its unnaturalistic exaggerations and distortions which place themselves more in the context of pictorial illusion than in that of sculptural self-evidence." Clement Greenberg, "Modernist Sculpture, Its Pictorial Past" (1952), reprinted in *Art and Culture: Critical Essays* (Boston: Beacon Press, 1971), 161.

4.

In 1995, while assisting Robert Storr with the Bruce Nauman retrospective at the Museum of Modern Art, New York, I also worked for Louise Bourgeois. Her series of sculptures in stitched pink fabric represented figures of often exaggerated size, such as *Three Horizontals* (1998).

program: Apollonism. If Michelangelo's *David* (1501–04) symbolizes the Florentine Republic, unseating Donatello's *Judith and Holofernes* (1455–60), one measure of its audacity is attested by the moment chosen for his figure's pose: an almost lascivious contrapposto, the calm before the battle. David represents the oppressed minority that wins thanks to its courage and wit, faced with a giant who is, by all appearances, stronger and better armed. Choi transfers the message of this allegory to postwar relations between Korea and the United States—and to postcolonial experience itself. To attack this monument is literally to appropriate both an academic model and a universalist project by means of a work the scope of which is political because it is aesthetic.

This is where the exemplary force of Choi's work is located: a strong aesthetic in the service of philosophically-inclined political thinking, yet deeply vested in corporeal materiality. Molding his own body in the pose of Michelangelo's figure, the artist is in dialogue with both the Florentine "original" but also with Auguste Rodin who was criticized for having "molded from nature" by way of a life cast.[5] To make a wax mold, instead of carving directly into a block of marble, poses questions about the history of sculpture in a "post-medium" era. The idea of "post-medium" was first suggested by Rosalind Krauss, who stressed the insufficiency of Clement Greenberg's notions of modernist purity and its replacement with practices defined by heterogeneity, interdependence, indeterminacy, and, ultimately, obsolescence.[6] To paraphrase the artist Morgan Fisher (who was, in turn, paraphrasing Walter Benjamin): "It is when something is obsolete that it can become revolutionary." Krauss's point of view is the opposite of what is implied by the postmodern condition, or by Conceptual Art, installation-based practices and relational aesthetics: moving on from the white cube is not inevitable, perhaps not even possible. In effect, the technical extension of media restores the autonomous and specific nature of the work of art, so that the "white cube"—in its role as an ideal space—becomes, like Michelangelo's block of marble, the immanent gangue from which the work is to be released.

So, how does Choi's work question post-medium specificities?

To answer this question we need to understand that the very interaction between ancient and modern practices leads quite directly, in concept and fact, to the persistence of the medium. When Choi named his sculpture and thus created a "portrait," he was no longer working in the heroic mode. For his nudity is fashioned after nature and is not subject to the canon. We see a man of wax with one foot in a basin of Pepto-Bismol—literally, "a giant with feet of clay," who displays his flaws, pain and weakness. Here, the contrapposto is a way of maintaining a precarious balance, one that connects it in a different manner to the sculptural work of Bourgeois, who also speaks of this sensitive, fragile tension in her work.

The rhetoric of the "exemplary" cedes its place to a hybridization of ways of making—and being—and in this Choi uses the "ruse of the *metis*" about which Michel de Certeau

---

5.

When first exhibited at the French Salon in 1877, critics accused Rodin of having cast *L'Âge d'airain (The Age of Bronze)* from a living model. Even if Rodin proved his intentions, a certain level of doubt persists.

6.

See, Rosalind Krauss, *"A Voyage on the North Sea": Art in the Age of the Post-Medium Condition* (London: Thames & Hudson, 1999) and *Under the Blue Cup* (Cambridge, MA: MIT Press, 2011).

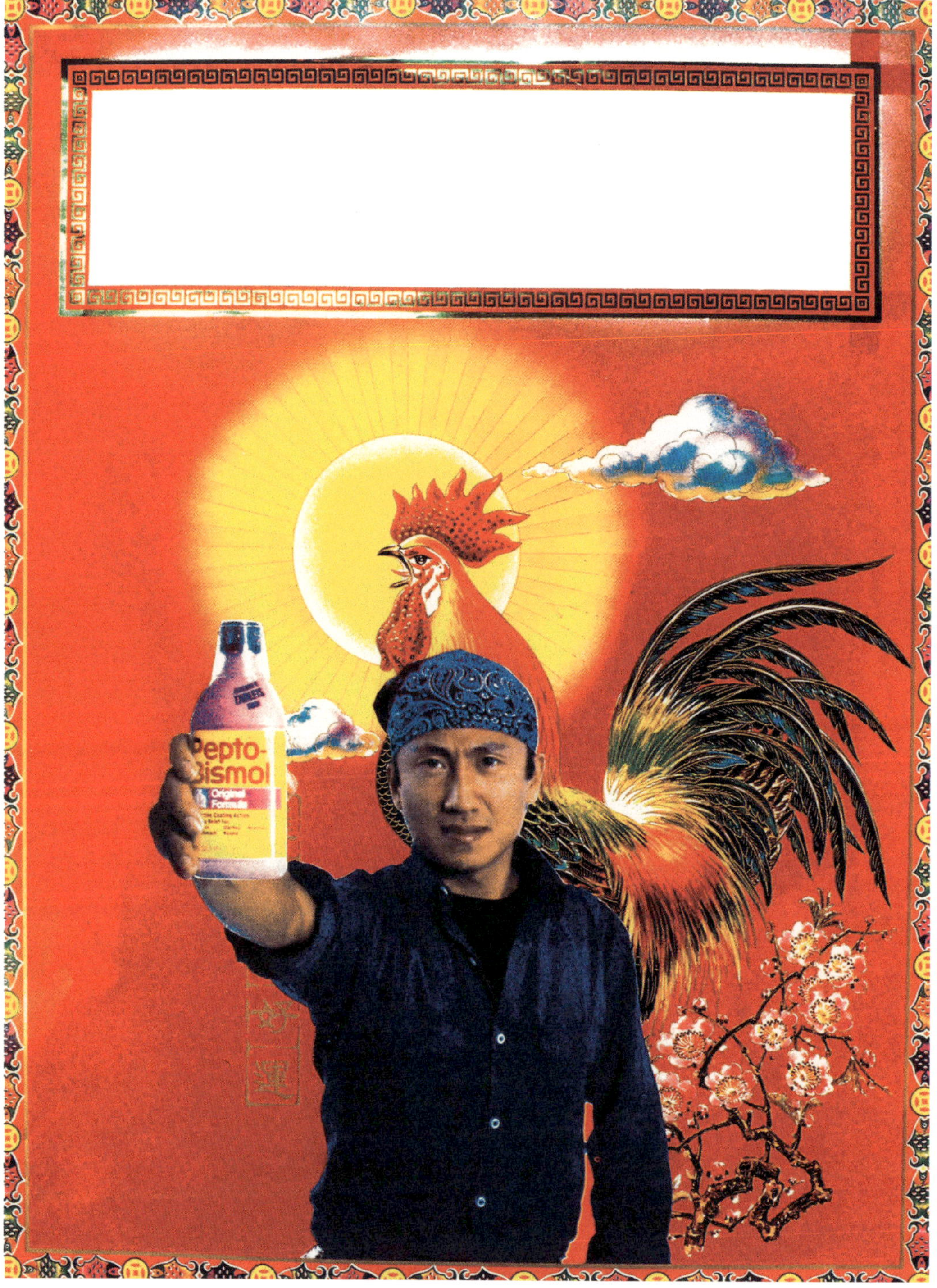

Golden Boy Poster (Heidegger in Bagesvaerd Church) · 1986–91 · C-print

writes—the apparent appropriation of the rites and traditions of an invader so as to be able to ensure the survival of one's own traditions.[7] One could speak here, of syncretism, or even of anthropophagy in a symbolic sense, methods for thinking a world in transformation. In Choi's work, the plinth is replaced by a pierced box, the evacuated form of which corresponds precisely to the hips of the seated artist. It is the measure of a single individual, and any use of the work must adhere to this scale. We are reminded of the first "corridors" of Bruce Nauman, which were also presented with the constraint of adapting themselves to the unique nature of the artist.[8] Choi built his "legend" from these two disparities: an antique model derived from biblical history and a box of excrement. The artist "performed" the two parts of his sculpture by first molding his body and then shaping its outlines in the negative excavation. This emphasis is reinforced by the photographs that accompany various steps in the production process. The gap becomes a trace, marking an absence, the reverse side of the mold, the hole of the cut. Similarly, the constitution of a volume in wax is one stage in the technique of lost wax casting (to create bronze sculptures, for example). But Choi makes the maquette into the final form, and the shipping crate or "waste" into a plinth. In this way he inverts the founding principles of the rules of art, calling into question the established borders between the techniques that frame disciplines. It is by these means that the work opens-up new articulations between codes: the artist becomes the vector for such new perspectives, and momentarily incarnates the stakes.

Golden Boy Poster (Heidegger in Bagesvaerd Church) (1986–91) is based on a similar move. I remember seeing the poster that informs this piece with Cody for the first time in a small gallery in New York, and hearing his comment on "pseudo-heroes." In *Golden Boy Poster*, Choi brandishes a bottle of Pepto-Bismol, the popular stomach medicine, probably first used in art by Ed Ruscha in screen prints such as *Pepto-Caviar Hollywood* (Cirrus Editions, Los Angeles, 1970). Text and image are fused in Ruscha's work as they are in Cody's, and there is a line of force that underpins the work. The repurposing of consumer products—taken up by other artists in the LA scene, notably Paul McCarthy (ketchup, syrup, and sundry foodstuffs) and Mike Kelley (deodorizers)—offers a social critique directed by what John C. Welchman terms "digestive" philosophy, but also a masquerade or disguise.[9] McCarthy, for example, explains that ketchup designates the fake blood used in films, the abundant and outrageous gore that makes the artificial obvious. Printer's ink,

---

7.

See, Michel de Certeau, *L'invention du quotidien, 1 arts de faire*, (Paris: Gallimard, 1970), 63–64. De Certeau notes that, "various theoretical comparisons will allow us to better characterize the tactics, or the polemology, of the 'weak.' The 'figures' and 'turns' analyzed by *rhetoric* are particularly illuminating in this regard. Freud already noticed this fact and used them in his study on wit and on the forms taken by the return of the repressed within the field of an order: verbal economy and condensation, double meanings and misinterpretations, displacements and alliterations, multiple uses of the same material, etc." Michel de de Certeau, *The Practice of Everyday Life*, trans. Steven Rendall (Berkeley: University of California Press, 1984), 39. De Certeau distinguishes between the ruse and the "bricolage" of Lévi-Strauss, which is both a tactic and a strategy.

8.

See, for example, Bruce Nauman, *Performance Corridor* (1969). Here the dimensions of the corridor are based on the proportions of the artist's own body. Two wooden panels are installed twenty inches apart, one extremity being open and the other closed-off by the wall on which they lean. Lacking instructions, the spectator may enter the corridor but does know what is at the end of it. This first corridor arrived just after Nauman's film exercises, notably *Walking with Contrapposto* (1968), in which Nauman's body is posed in a contrapposto stance.

9.

See John C. Welchman, "Culture/Cuts: Post-appropriation in the Work of Cody Choi," in *Art After Appropriation: Essays on Art in the 1990s* (Amsterdam: G+B Arts International, 2001), 245–61; and "Culture Cuts" in the present publication.

and traditional screen print inks, are replaced by foodstuffs, perverting the artisanal process. Reversing the dichotomies between rough notes/work of art, hero/clown, and crate/plinth, Choi uncovers a dimension that is already at work—though not always discussed—in Michelangelo: an intermittently macabre humor, and a penchant for the grotesque.

As Smithson noted:

> If one considers Michelangelo's grotesque sense of humor "pictorial illusion" then one sees art in terms of realistic and natural content. Modernist criticism recoils at the sight or thought of Michelangelo, because the organic is threatened by what Wolfgang Kayser calls "the annihilating idea of humor." Realistic and naturalistic criticism fears the cosmic laughter inherent in the grotesque (grotto-cave)—the abyss.[10]

It is the fall of the studio that modernism fears.

Withdrawn body = hole of spirit (or dead end?)

LIKE Nauman and Kelley among others, Choi takes on the figure of the "trickster," or Divine Rogue.[11] By hijacking conventions he marshals an economy of negativity to produce twisted meaning. The holes in the wooden crates give birth to new figures—outlines of a phallus, an arm, a head, create a new, fragmented body, established by a founding absence. It could represent something that is missing, or a space for play, or for breathing, as with a musical instrument, to allow air to circulate and sound to pass.

The Last Gasp becomes, then, *The Last Gaps*, the mark of a separation between East and West, between different systems for the representation and understanding of the world, between language and the inarticulate. With sardonic corporeal humor, Choi creates a musical coffin the sonorities of which generate an atmosphere made up of all of the "body's airs": belches, flatulence, hiccups, even a "musical vagina." The circle is thus complete—from Madame Récamier to the renovated "perspectives" according to which she is perceived, from David to Magritte by way of Choi, the seat of the Muses has taken on a real form and become a sound sculpture. The performative nature of the piece brings to mind Kelley's *Performance Related Objects* (1977–79), "instruments" that were themselves in dialogue with Luigi Russolo's *The Art of Noise* (1913) and its argument for a future music constituted by everyday noises.[12]

10.
Robert Smithson, "What Really Spoils Michelangelo's Sculpture" in *Unearthed: Drawings, Collages, Writings*, ed. Eugenie Tsai (New York: Columbia University Press, 1991), 73.

11.
Present in all civilizations, the figure of the buffoon or the clown upsets the rules of societies. On the myth of the "trickster" see

Carl Gustav Jung, *Le Fripon Divin: un mythe indien* (Paris: Georg, 1997). See also, Jung, *On the Psychology of the Trickster-Figure*, ed. Herbert Read (London: Routledge and Kegan Paul, 1968).

12.
See, Luigi Russolo et al, *The Art of Noise: Destruction of Music by Futurist Machines*, trans. Robert Filliou (Sun Vision Press, 2012).

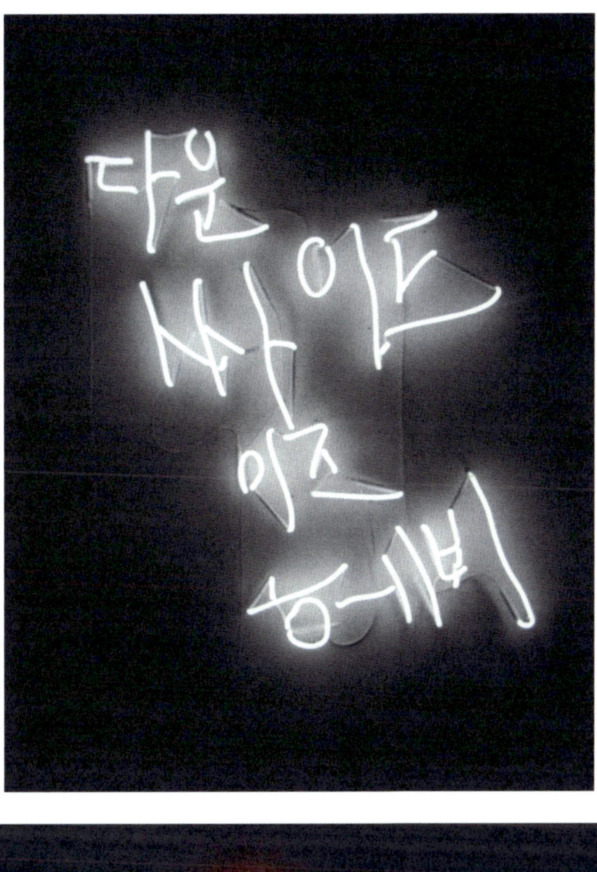
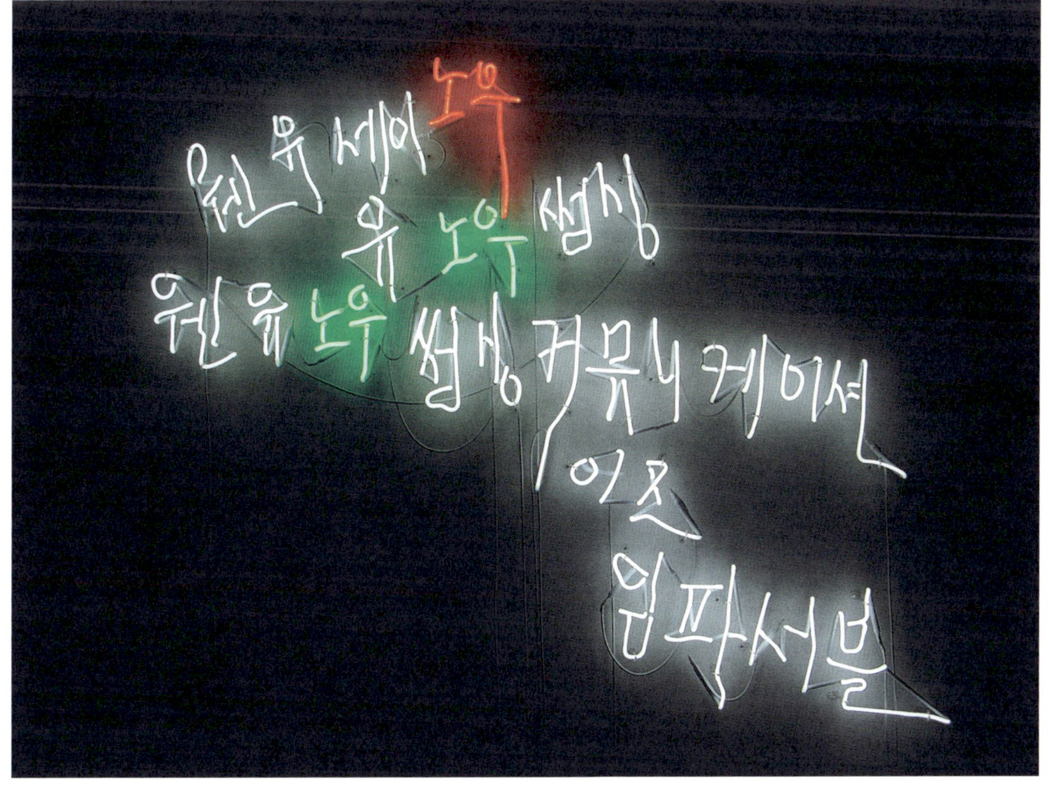

Down Side Is Heavy · 2010–11 · Neon lights

When You Say No, You Know Something, When You Know Something, Communication Is Impossible. · 2010–11 · Neon lights

CHOI is adept at making witty remarks and puns, both written and spoken. He is aware that the alphabetical script of the Korean language, famously invented in the fifteenth century, became a means of resistance under the Japanese occupation in the first half of the twentieth century.[13] Remembering, also, the symbolic nature of illuminated writing (especially in the work of Nauman), Choi's use of these signs to write texts in neon offers to renew the struggle by releasing another round of resistant meanings. *Down Side Is Heavy* (2010-11) and *When You Say No, You Know Something. When You Know Something, Communication Is Impossible* (2009-11) use modernist codes to circulate proverbs invented by the artist that announce the renewal of Eastern philosophy—as it might be applied to a Western system. Fortified by a custom variant of the linguistic "wit" about which Freud wrote in his essay on "Jokes" (1905), Choi uses the dominant language to illustrate its own loss of momentum ... and the gift is returned to the sender.

"I believe in Roman Jakobson's claim that language is a dominant "cultural form." The neon works arose from my first experiences after returning to Seoul from the United States in 2004. There are so many billboards in Korea—in a mix of languages, English, Chinese, and Korean. Some of them are in English but use the Korean alphabet, some of them are Chinese with the Korean alphabet, some are the reverse and some of them are all mixed up. What kind of culture is that? Recently, the English language has become one of the most important issues in Korea. Some rich parents force their children to have tongue surgery so that their English pronunciation will be more natural. They want to be like Americans in speech, while their manner must be humble, in line with Chinese Confucian precepts. This gives rise to a new race of Koreans. I was angry at this development, so I translated a paragraph of Chinese philosophy into English and transferred it to the Korean alphabet on a neon billboard. What results is not a binary opposition, but a multiple overlapping."[14]

Recent paintings such as *No Ego No Suffer* (2001-13), mounted on a swatch of ancient fabric from a mourning garment, testify to a form of melancholic nostalgia for the historical Korea—epitomized by the Choson dynasty, an era noted for a renaissance in the arts that underwrote Korean cultural identity and which Choi wants to help reinvent. The impertinent humor Choi shares with Baldessari recurs in the "Double Bill" series (2012)—also in dialogue with the history of art—and in his recent "Episteme Sabotage" series (2014). Here, Choi remakes some of the key paintings of modernity: Edvard Munch's *The Scream* (1893) in *Episteme Sabotage-Shit,* (2014); Manet's *Olympia* (1863) in *Episteme Sabotage-Flower from East* (2014); and—fast-forward a century—Ruscha's *Hollywood Boulevard* (1973) which is transformed into *Episteme Sabotage-Stone* (2014). Under each reproduced painting a piece of white fabric—the artist's discarded underwear or T-shirts—is marked with a painted message.

13.
From the sixth to the fifteenth centuries, the Korean language was based on a system of ideograms, close to Chinese *kanji*, comprising over ten thousand signs. In the fifteenth century, Sejong the Great imposed the *Hangul*, an alphabetical system, in order to spread literacy as widely as possible. Scorned at first by the educated classes, in the twentieth century this vernacular writing became a form of resistance under the Japanese occupation.

14.
Cody Choi, conversation with the author, winter 2015.

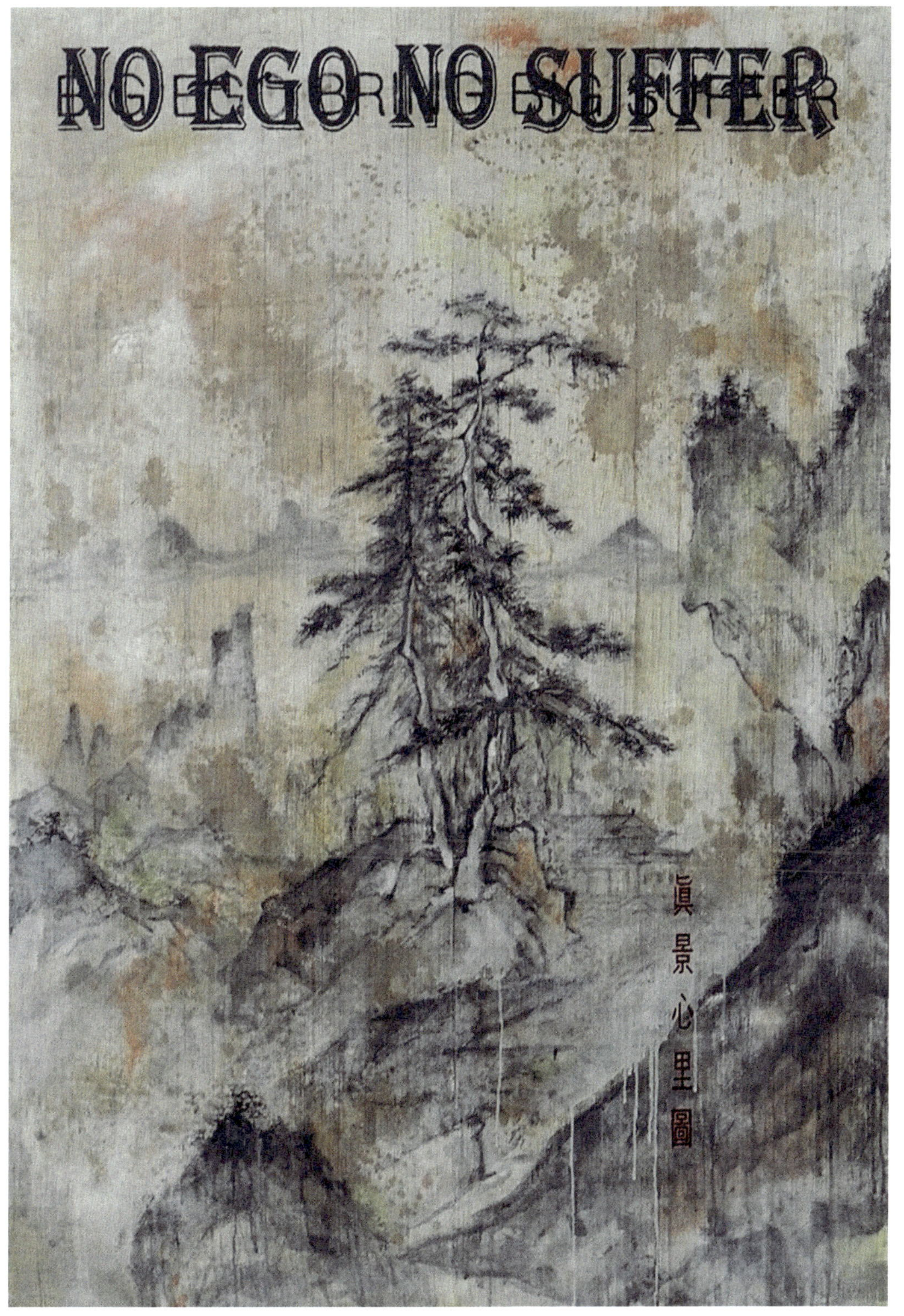

No Ego No Suffer · 2011–13 · Chinese ink stick, cashew paint, shell powder, bone glue, hemp cloth

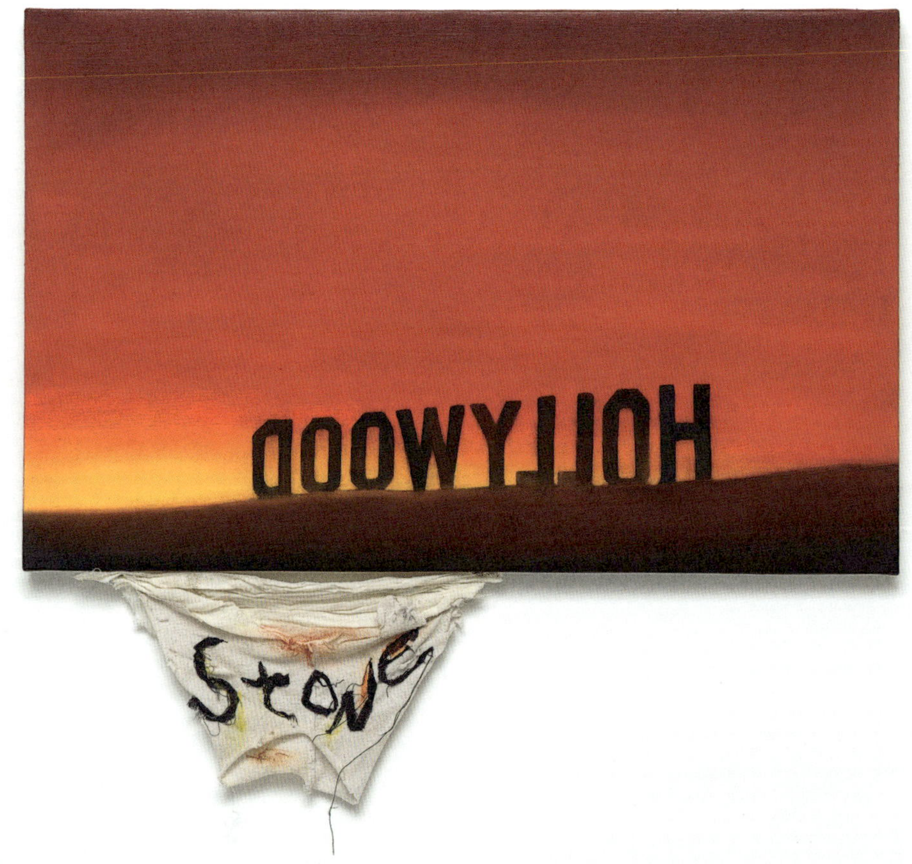

Episteme Sabotage–Stone · 2014 · Oil on canvas

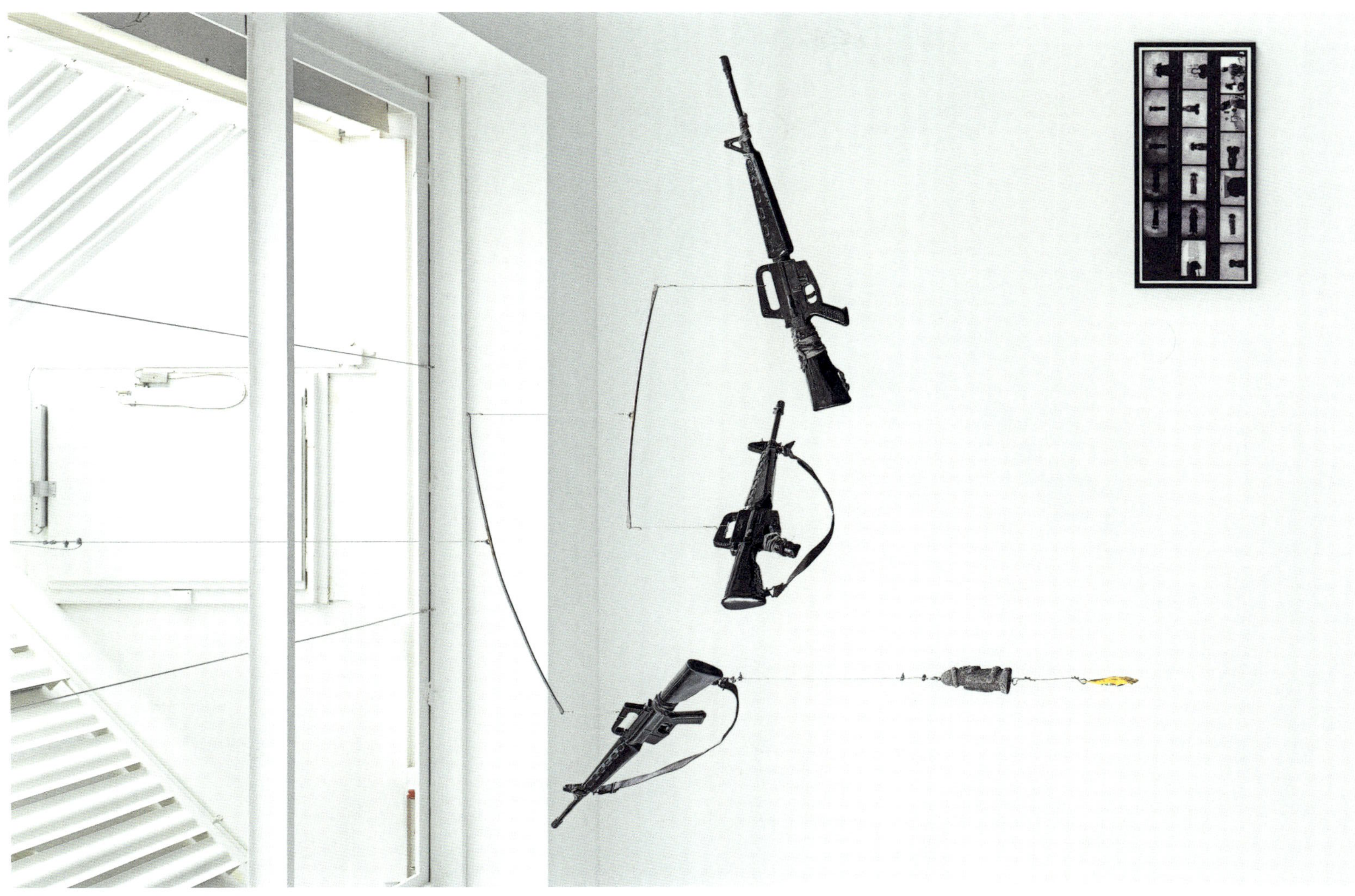

Border Bounder, mắm · 2011–12 · Steel, plastic, cloth, stone, cashew paint
Installation view at Kunsthalle Düsseldorf (2015)

The cuts and amputations Choi inflicts on these (and other) pieces relate to aspects of colonial and postcolonial history that are often ignored in the sanctioned narratives of modern and contemporary Korean art. The "Episteme Sabotage" works, such as *Made in USA* (1986–2002), *Bonder Bounder, mĕ́m* (2011–12) and *Gift Exchange 2* (2009), are boomerangs originating in some sense from a potlatch.[15] We know that when certain gifts are received they confer a debt; I want to suggest that these works can be understood through the principle of "counter-gifting" or giving back. The small, fetish-like totem of *Bonder Bounder, mĕ́m*, (2011–12) a sort of plastic phallus, for example, invokes the monumental stones symbolizing fertility that can be found all over Korea. The life-sized plastic weapons suspended on either side of it in this mobile are a nod to the phallocentrism propagated by Hollywood films and Western cultural marketing. The debt-laden counter-gift becomes a treacherous, even poisoned, offering. On the tiny plinth of *Gift Exchange 2* (2009) fake pink and green plastic "Nikes" are wrapped in rubber. This strange "wrapped gift" also contains a knife blade pointing upwards: it is a contemporary totem that, through the metonymic effects of its parts simultaneously standing-in for—and contending against—a global commodity system, represents a backlash, a kind of postcolonial effect. Choi told me about the American army blankets he used for his painting series "Pepto-Bismol Hit and Overlay, Rambo" (1989–90), but also recalled the smooth tires sent from the US to Korea with which he and other Korean kids would play. These old, retreaded tires, donated scraps that doubled as an efficient mode of Western dumping, were repurposed in Korea to produce fake Nikes—part of a whole ghost product line of commodity objects simulated after brand name "originals" sold in the West. A fair backlash?

Looking beyond their real life and real world locations, Choi's use of these scraps and fragments relates to a conceptual counteraesthetic that brings his work alongside that of certain feminist artists such as Mary Kelly. The base materiality informing *Post Partum Document* (1973–79), for example, is evoked in Choi's *Night Soiler No. 90-2* (1990–92), a painting made with stained layers of his daughter's excreta that he had first buried and then dug up. For the artist it was a case of delivering an offset to a monocentric, enunciative apparatus, opening it up to new perspectives, suffusing it with humor, and bearing witness to history by pointing outside of its margins. Here, beauty is revealed as a weapon.

15.

Potlach is the act of giving, and receiving in return, during ceremonies in which objects are exchanged but no money changes hands. Practiced widely in the Pacific region and by American Indians, the main purpose of potlatch was to avoid war. However, gifts create a debt that must be honored, with the consequence that villages might be utterly destroyed in cases where the exchange is based on a superior counter-gift. See, Marcel Mauss, *The Gift: Forms and Functions of Exchange in Archaic Societies*, trans. Ian Gunnison (London: Cohen & West, 1966); originally published as "Essai sur le don: forme et raison de l'échange dans les sociétés archaïques" in *L'Année Sociologique* in 1925; and Georges Bataille, *The Accursed Share, Volume 1: Consumption* (New York: Zone Books, 1991).

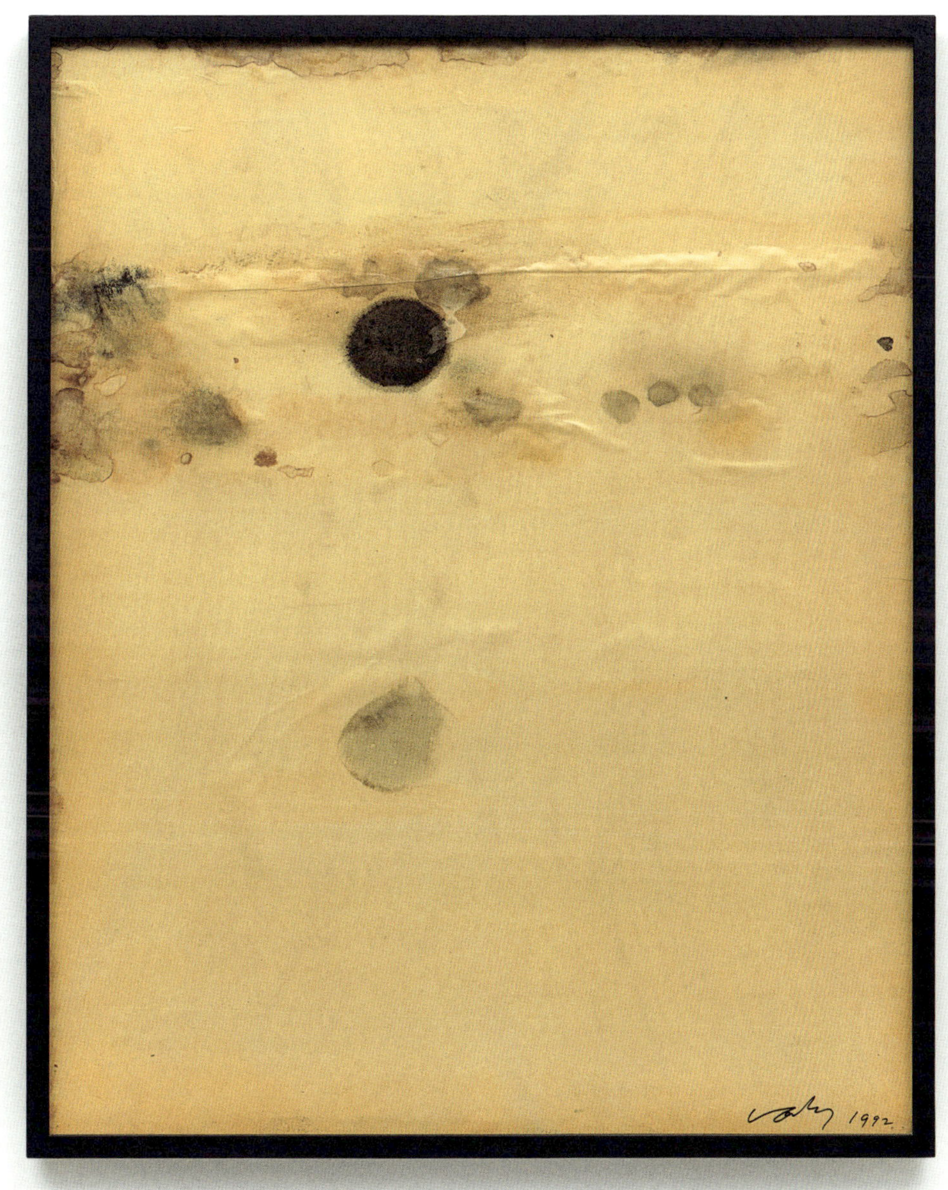

Night Soiler No. 90-2 • 1990–92 • Meconium (from Cody Choi's daughter) on Korean paper floor, buried under the ground for two years and stretched on canvas

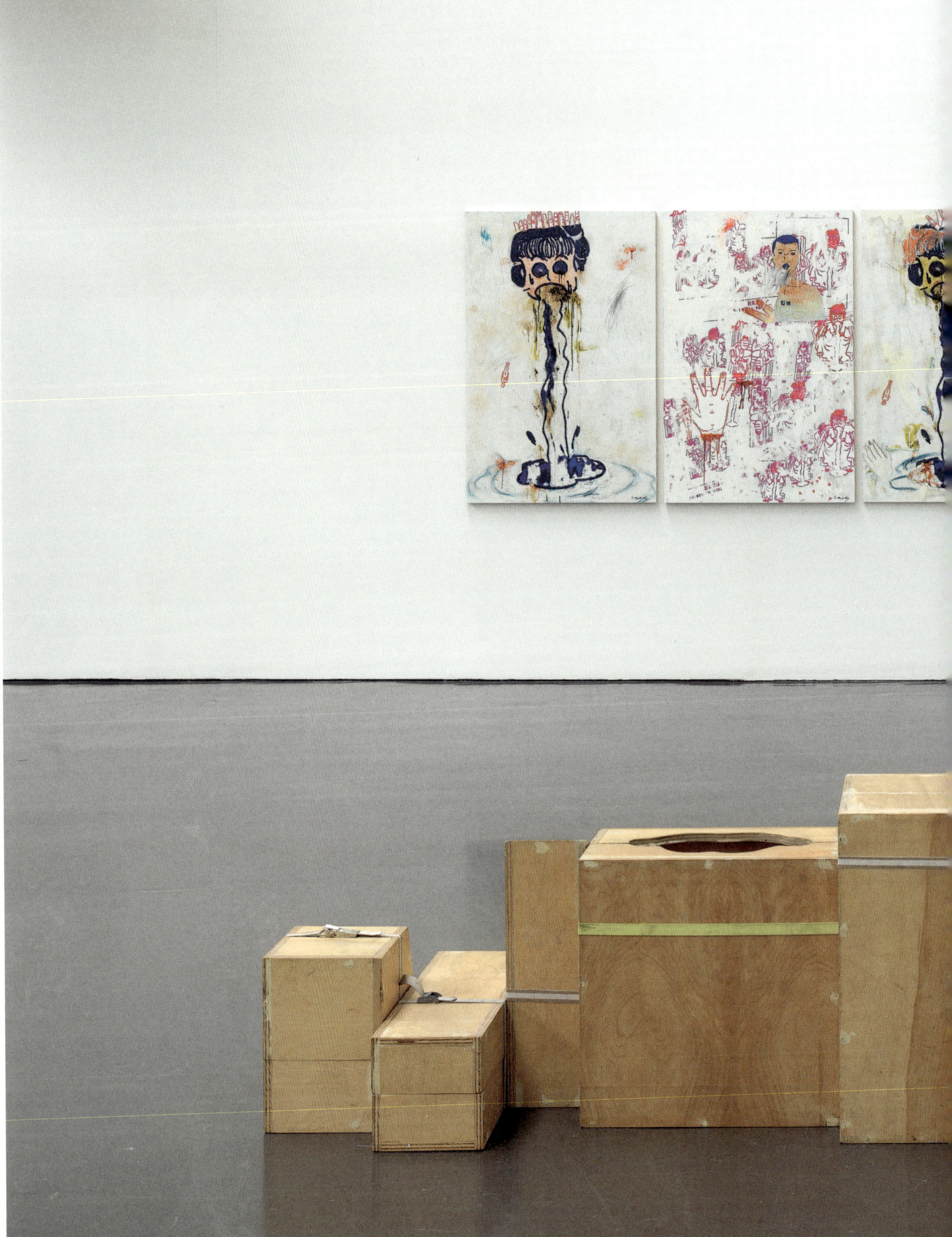

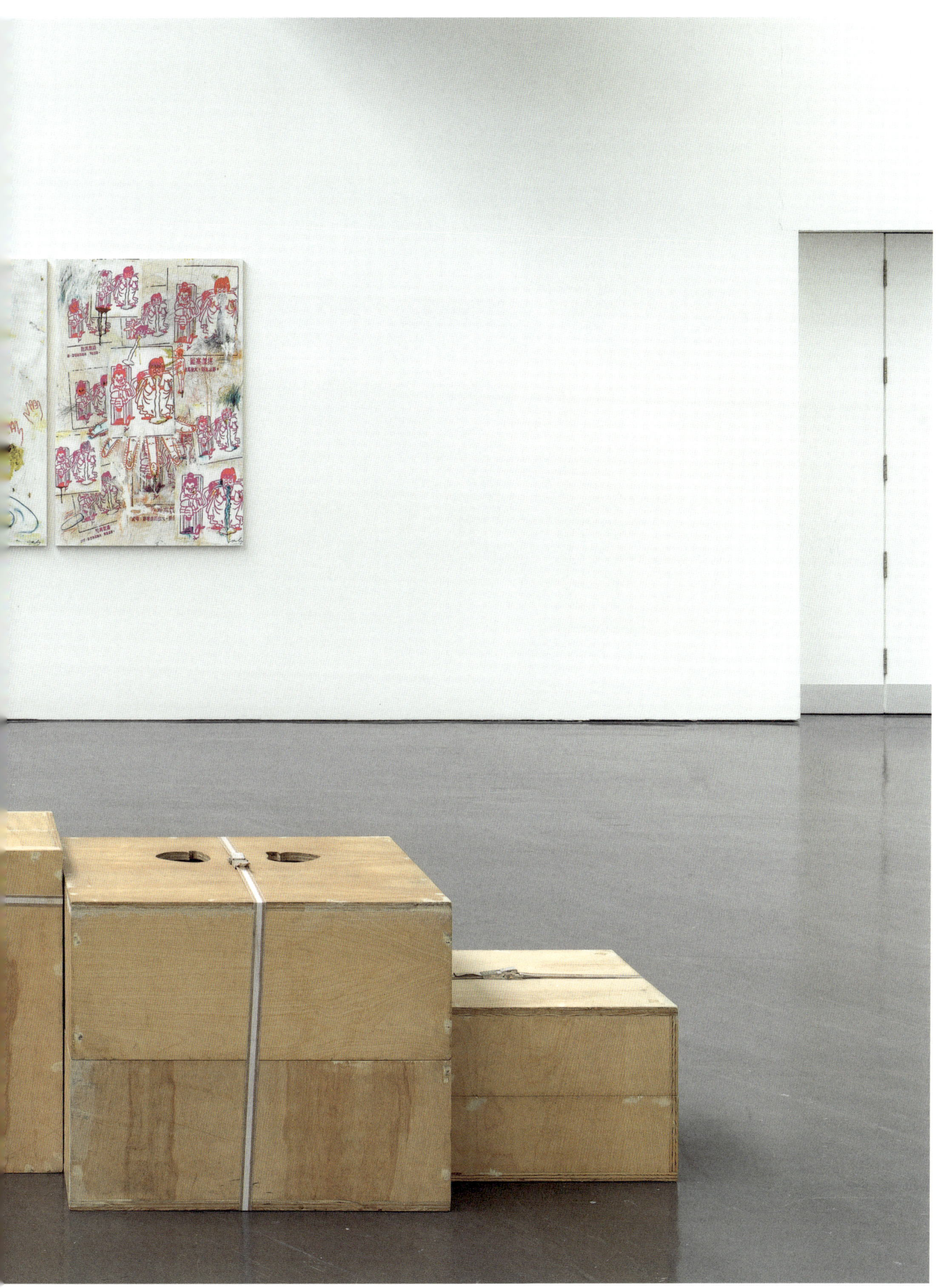

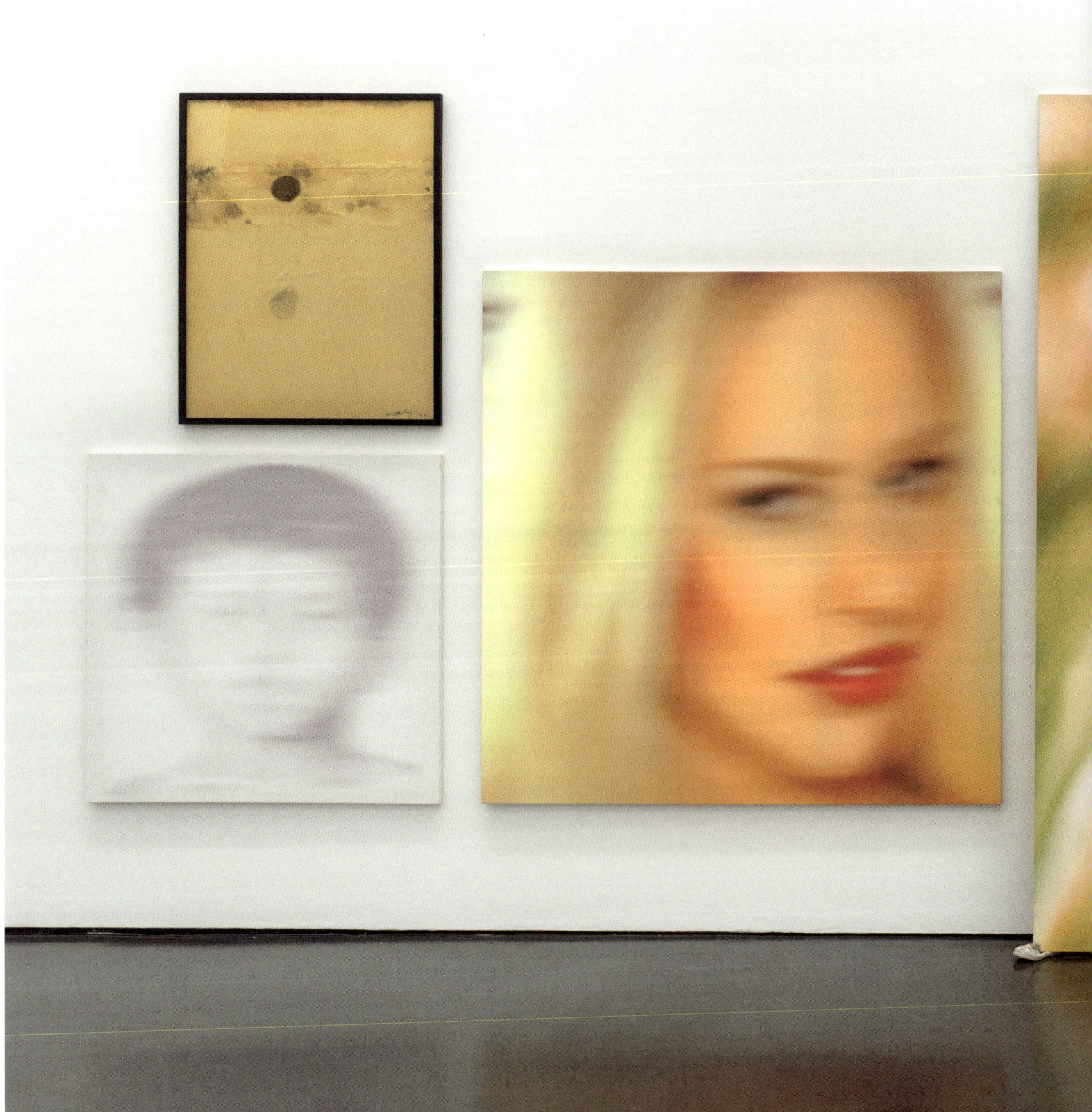

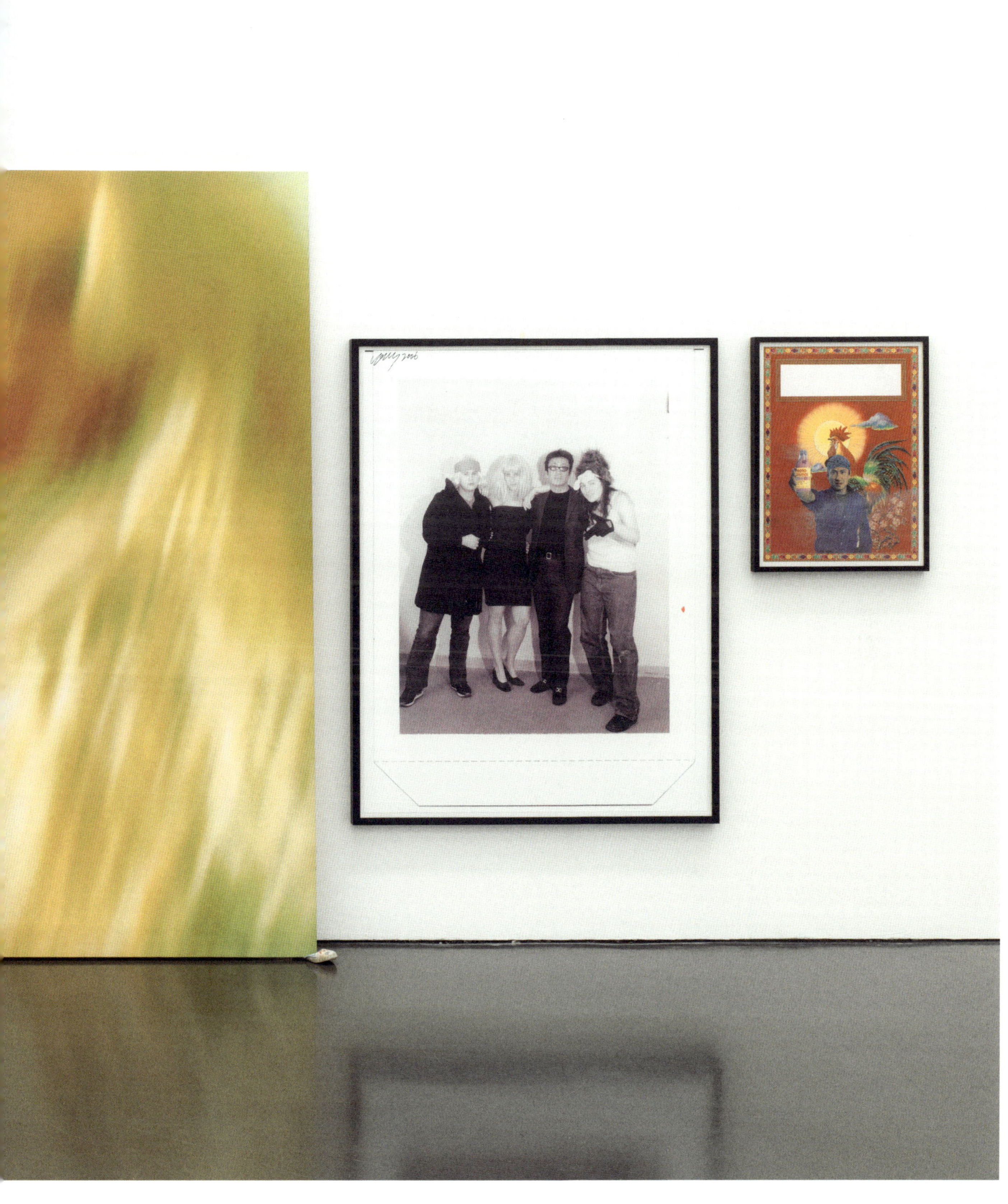

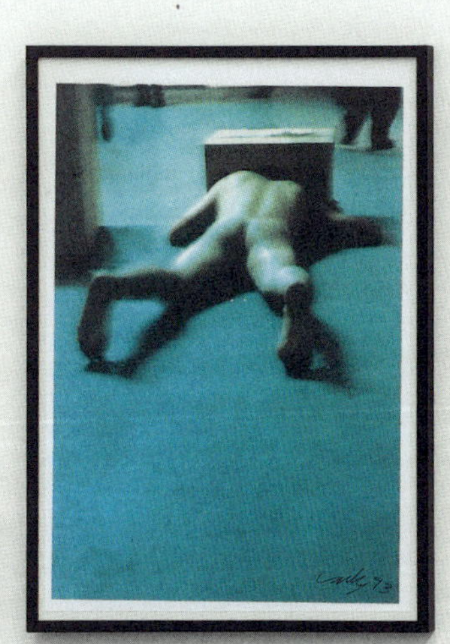

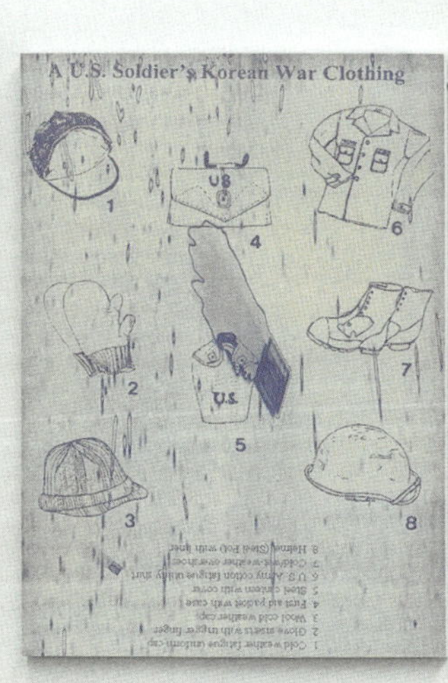

A U.S. Soldier's Korean War Clothing
US
US
1
2
3
4
5
6
7
8
1 Cold weather fatigue uniform cap
2 Glove inserts with trigger finger
3 Wool cold weather cap
4 First aid packet with case
5 Steel canteen with cover
6 U.S. Army cotton fatigue utility shirt
7 Cold-weather overshoes
8 Helmet (Steel Pot) with liner

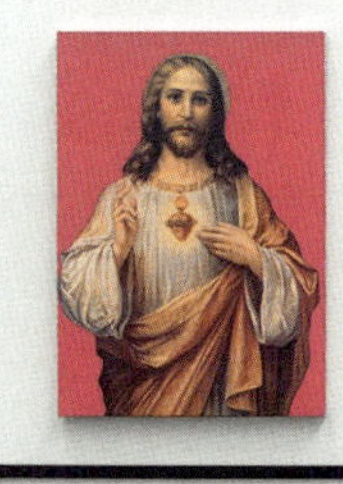

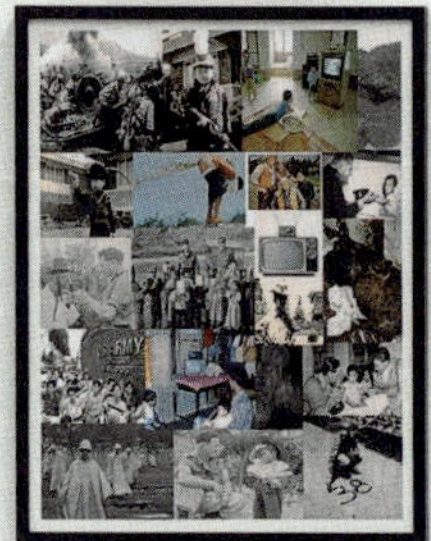

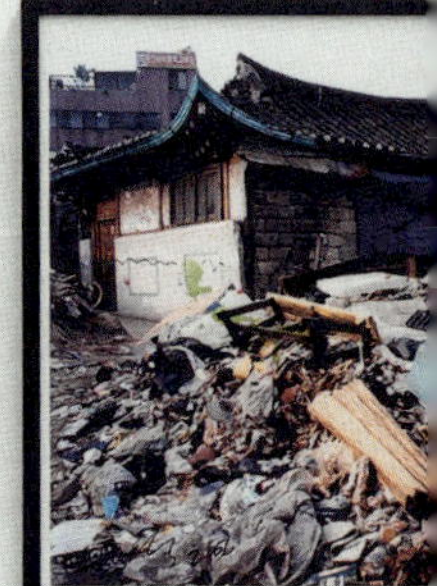

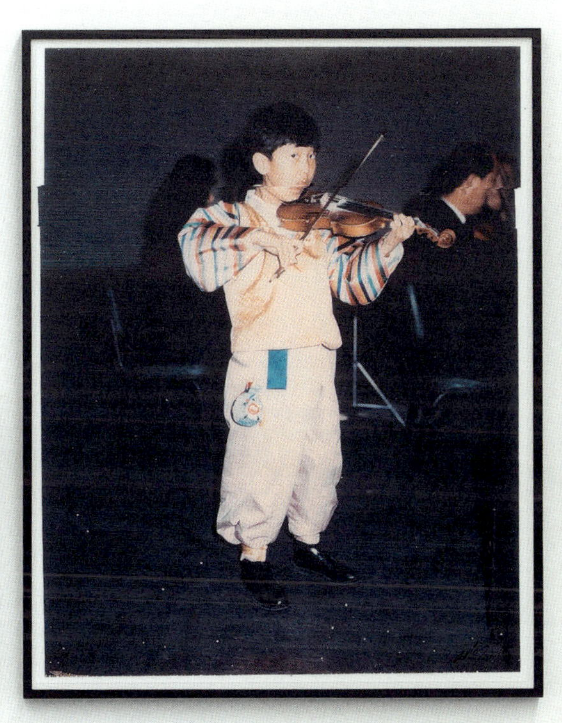
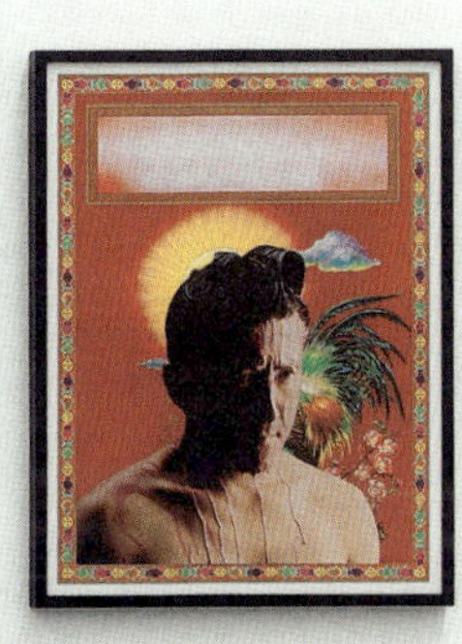
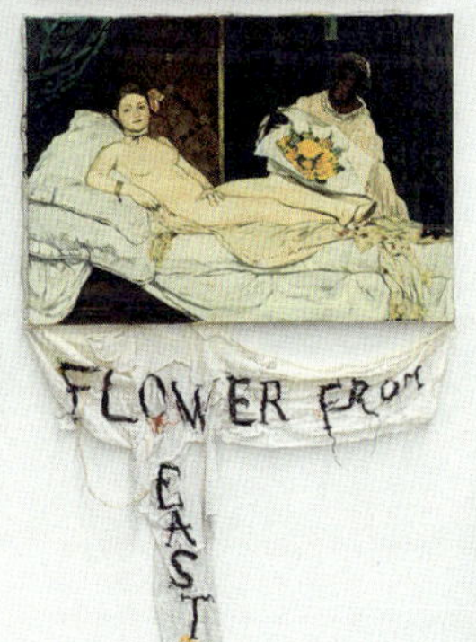

FLOWER FROM
EAST

JUNE 19.1967

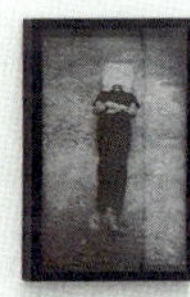

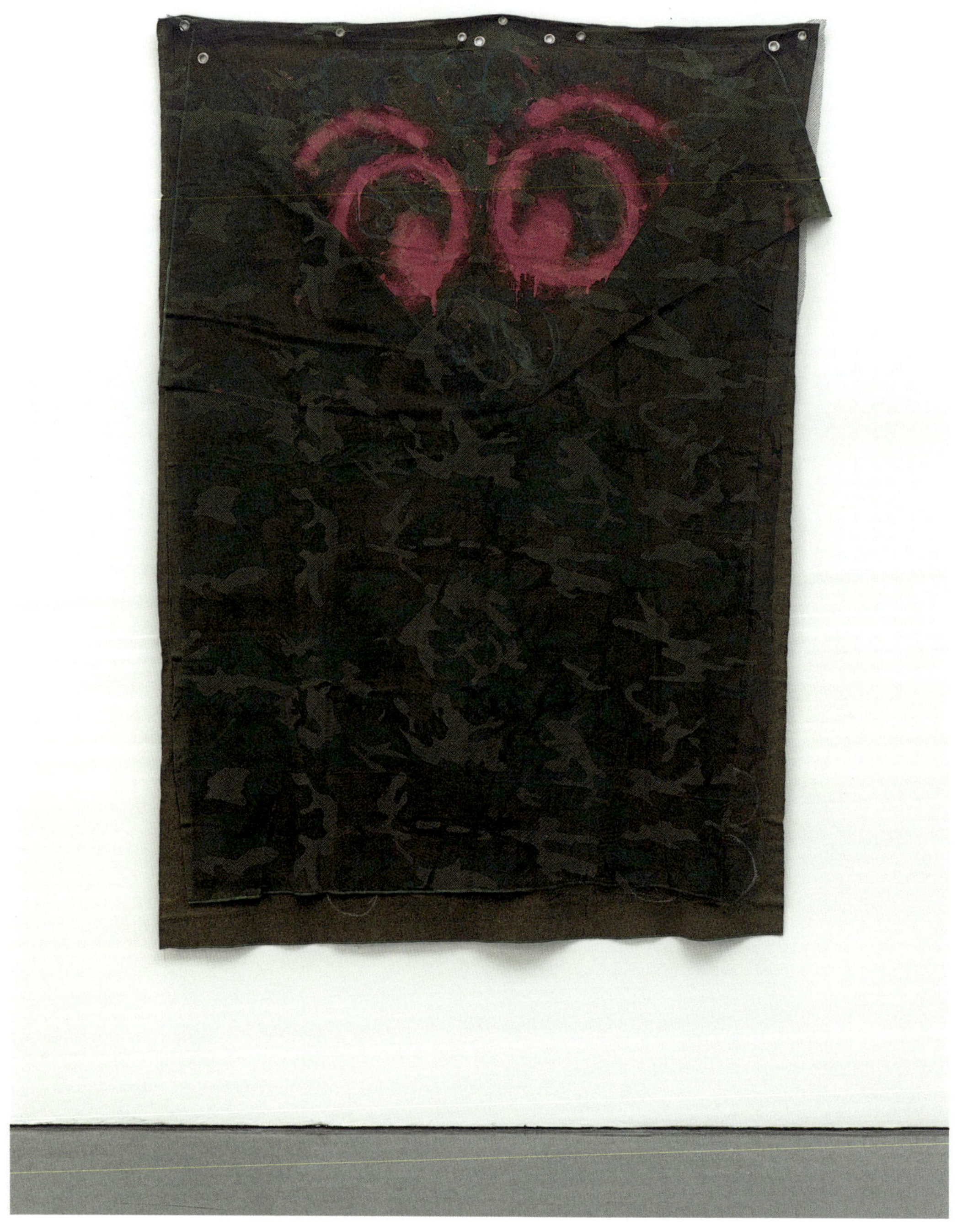

PP. 54–59 · Installation views at Kunsthalle Düsseldorf (2015)
Pepto-Bismol Hit and Overlay, Rambo 2 · 1989–90/2013 · Pepto-Bismol, acrylic, mosquito net on US Army blanket

Mike Kelley

Dyspeptic Universe: Cody Hyun Choi's Pepto-Bismol Paintings

Kelley wrote this brief essay on the Korean-American artist Cody Choi shortly after he completed his degree in fine arts at Art Center College of Design, Pasadena. It was first published in *Cody, Dip The Pink* (Seoul, Korea: Ya-Jung, 1992), and reprinted in *Cody Choi: XX Century* (New York: Deitch Projects, 1999) and Mike Kelley, *Foul Perfection: Essays and Criticism*, ed. John C. Welchman (Cambridge, MA: MIT Press, 2003). A couple of years after its appearance, Choi redirected his interest in Pepto-Bismol from painting to sculpture in a striking series of pedestal-mounted statues modeled on *The Thinker* of Auguste Rodin, made with toilet-tissue papier-mâché drenched in the pink medium. This version of the text is from *Foul Perfection* with notes by Kelley and myself.

—John C. Welchman

IN the United States there is a medicine for stomach cramps and diarrhea called Pepto-Bismol.[1] The medicine is a bright pink liquid familiar to everyone—so familiar, in fact, that an American traveling to another country is shocked to find no equivalent for it there. It is sufficiently ubiquitous in the United States that we've come to mistake it for a "natural" product: there must be some, interior, reason for its color. The pinkness itself *must* have some soothing quality; its pinkness must be a by-product of an element integral to its curative powers. Nonpink medicines are lacking this special something. Standing in some foreign airport examining the row of stomach medicines—all of them pinkless—is a revelatory experience: you have your first conscious thought that Pepto-Bismol might be pink because it has been dyed with food coloring. That's when art comes to mind. "Art," because you've been duped. The façade of the pink remedy was so seductive it made you believe that something merely decorative was actually essential.

Cody Choi is a cultural emissary to America, seeing things as exotic that Americans take for granted. Arriving from a Korea, where pink has different connotations, he is in America to reveal our cultural biases, to make us see the normal and familiar as strange and discomforting. His paintings are overtly decorative, but only to point out the fact that decoration is physically

---

[1.]

Bismuth subsalicylate, the active ingredient in Pepto-Bismol, relieves such symptoms as upset stomach, indigestion, nausea, vomiting, heartburn, and diarrhea. The original variant of Pepto-Bismol was introduced in 1900, and distributed nationally in 1918 under the name Bismosal by the Norwich Eaton Company. A year later the product was rebaptized as Pepto-Bismol, and the formula remained relatively stable for the next eighty years. Following the brand's acquisition by Procter & Gamble in 1982, Pepto-Bismol tablets and caplets were launched. Even the P & G archivist was unable to explain why Pepto-Bismol was made pink.

effective. Would Pepto-Bismol work as well as it does if it were not pink? No, it wouldn't. It couldn't. I can think of only one other artwork that actually incorporates Pepto-Bismol: Charles Ray's *Marble Box Filled with Pepto-Bismol* (1988). A large open-top, white marble cube filled to the brim with Pepto-Bismol, Ray's piece takes as given the medicinal associations of its featured liquid. The box seems to conflate minimalist sculpture and the vomitoriums of ancient Roman arenas. To those versed in Western art history the mix is an unsettling one, producing a feeling of stability gone sour. Pepto-Bismol aside, it's even hard to recall many artworks that are colored pink. For some reason pink has been deemed an unsuitable color for art. Perhaps it's art's "noble" stature that occasions this relegation. For, when pink is used, it is generally seen as perverse, as something purposefully wrong. John McCracken's plank sculptures from the nineteen-sixties are a case in point.[2] Done at the same time as the minimalist work of Donald Judd and Carl Andre, these hot-colored versions of minimalism could not be understood as anything other than contradictory. They seemed to be caricatures of minimalism because their color was so unserious, so inappropriate to the sculpture's simplicity of form. Generally, pink is used in fine art as a weapon, deployed deliberately because of its inappropriateness. It is a color too loaded with cultural associations from outside the art context to sit comfortably within it. What, then, are these associations?

Well, the primary cultural reference of the color pink is its association with young girls. Pink is the color of little girl's rooms, dresses, and playthings. Measured against this scene of identification, its "inappropriateness" to art unmasks the masculine orientation of the art world. In the art context, pink things come off as effeminate. Pink is also thought of as a "decorative" color, and decoration bears similar gendered connotations. It is frilly and useless: it dwells in the home and not in culture; it's about façade, not truth. A government building would never be heavily decorated, or pink—either of which would make it seem untrustworthy. But perhaps it is this feminine aura that has made Pepto-Bismol such a popular product. When one is sick, one wants to be mothered. One wants to adopt a submissive "feminine" role and be cared for. Pepto-Bismol appears as an image of soothing mother's milk to the adult infant suffering from colic. Symbolically, that is everyone.

All of these images—with their associations of sickness and organic, perhaps pathological, decoration—are summoned up when we look at Cody Choi's Pepto-Bismol paintings. My biggest question is: How will these paintings understood in Korea? Are their associations too American to translate? Will the paintings be viewed, simply, in the lineage of abstract expressionism—and thus exude a kind of cultural exoticism to their Korean viewers? The problem of intercultural translation is addressed in the paintings themselves, however, by the fact that some of them are painted on American army blankets. As a child, Choi was profoundly influenced growing up surrounded by the cast-offs of the Korean war. The intrusion of American culture was ever present, and perhaps unwelcome. If the pink shapes are the figures in his paintings, the army blankets act as the grounds.

2.

Kelley discusses McCracken's plank pieces and some of the associated qualities of pink in his essay on Paul Thek, "Death and Transfiguration," in *Foul Perfection*, pp. 138–49. ress, 2012).

Many abstract expressionist paintings adopted from surrealism the notion that visual space is analogous to bodily space. The amorphous space occupied by the abstract shapes and painterly gestures is the inner space of the human body: the dark space of the body cavity or the more mysterious space of the unconscious mind. With the demise of abstract expressionism and the rise of less psychologically oriented (and more concrete) painting, such as color field, this idea of painted space slowly waned, and then itself become concretized. Gerome Kamrowski, a painting teacher of mine and an automatist of the Pollock generation, once described this as a shift from "inner space" to "science fiction space."[3] The black void is now not the domain of the psyche, but of "outer space." This conception of space is territorial and not symbolic. When I look at Choi's paintings, I see the dark space of the army blanket as a territory in dispute, as the site of a war of cultures in which various socially specific poetic systems battle it out. Can we assume, then, that this is what viewers on both sides of the Pacific Ocean might discern: that these paintings are glimpses of an unstable world—a dyspeptic universe?

3.

Gerome Kamrowski, in *Gerome Kamrowski*, Evan M. Maurer and Jennifer L. Bayles, eds., exh. cat. (University of Michigan Museum of Art, Ann Arbor, August 30 to October 16, 1983), 2. For a summary of Kamrowski's career, see Paul Schimmel, *The Interpretative Link: Abstract Surrealism into Abstract Expressionism, Works on Paper 1938–1946*, exh. cat. (Newport Harbor Art Museum, Newport Beach, July 16 to September 14, 1986), 100.

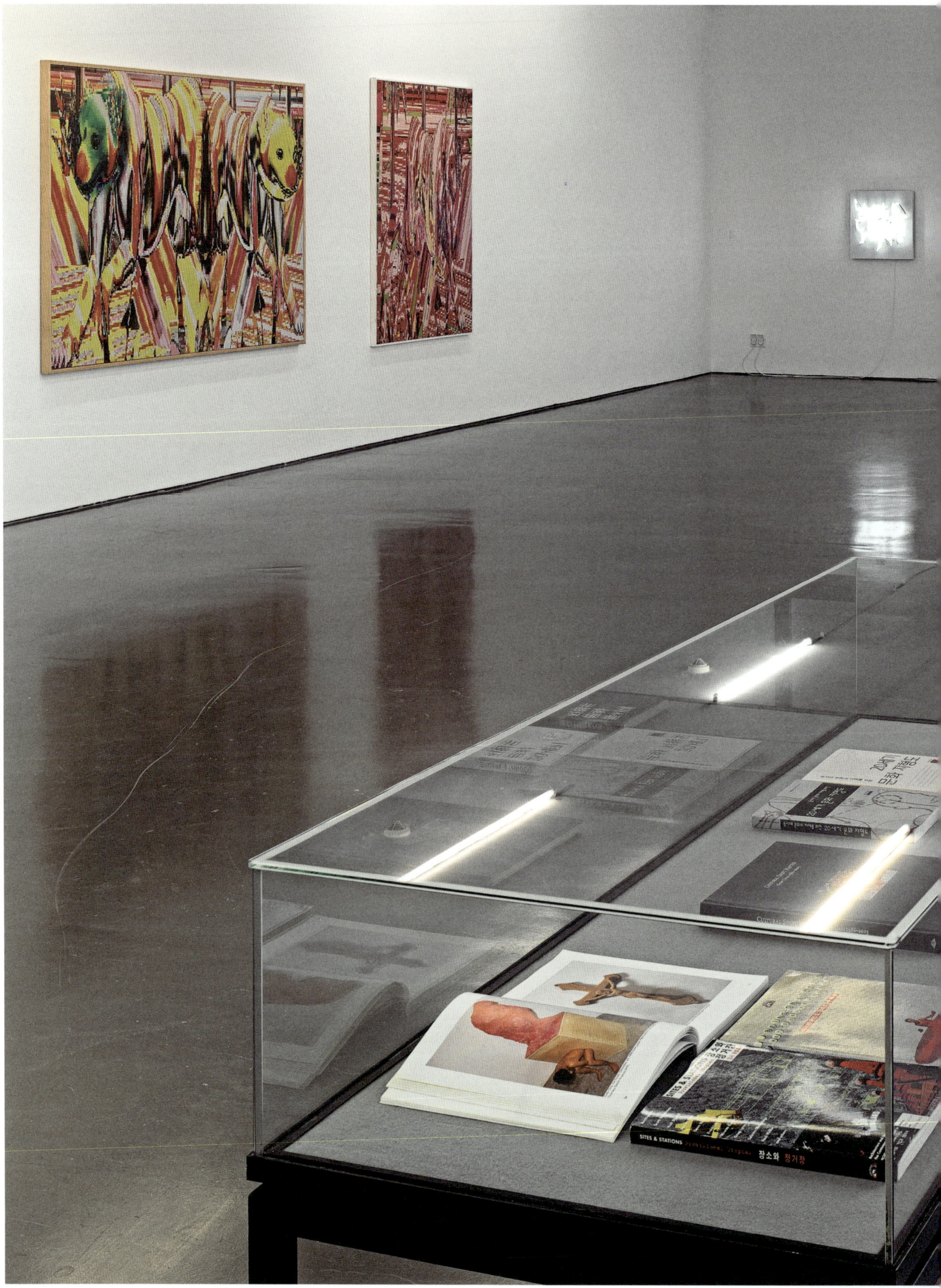

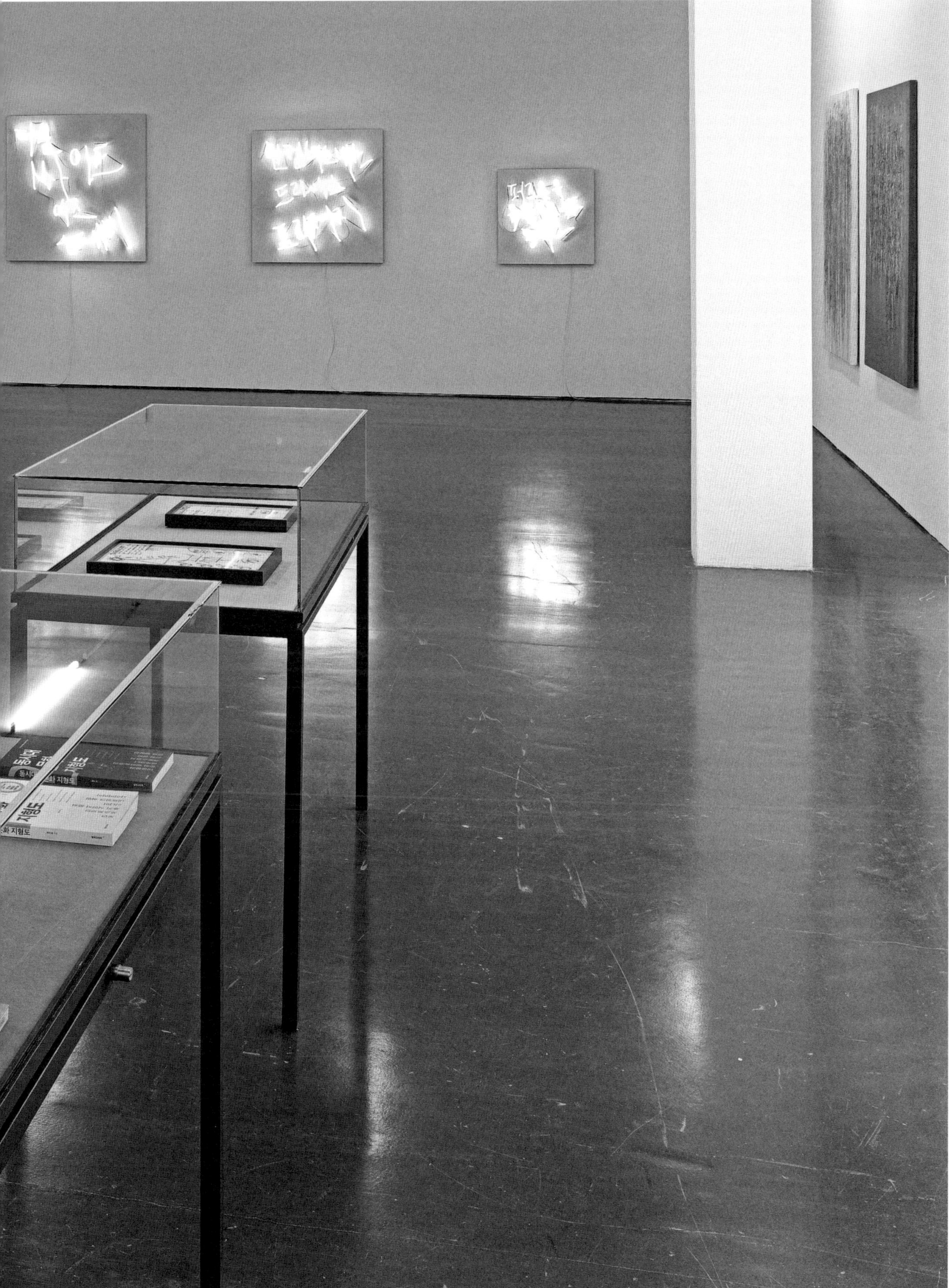

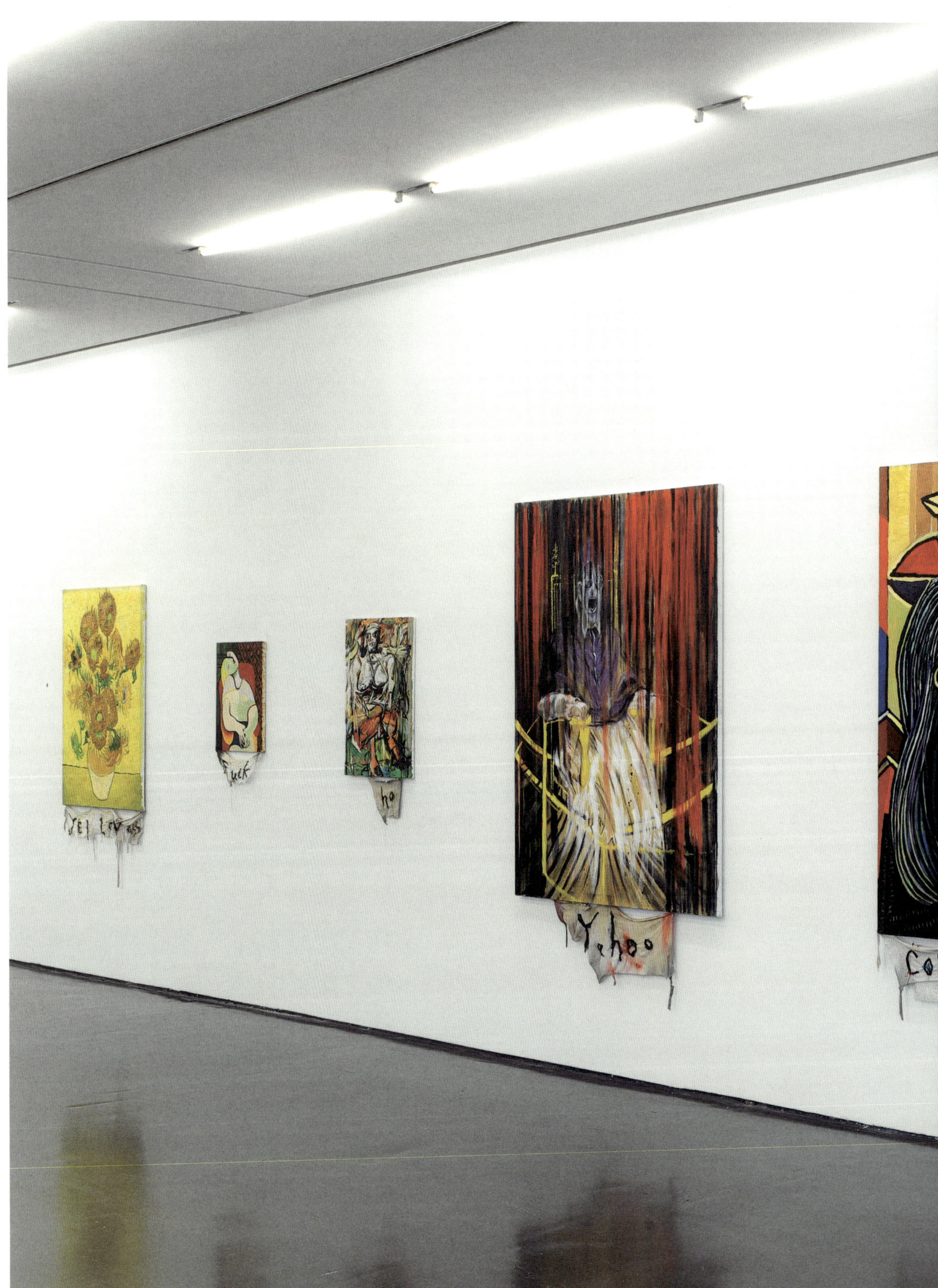

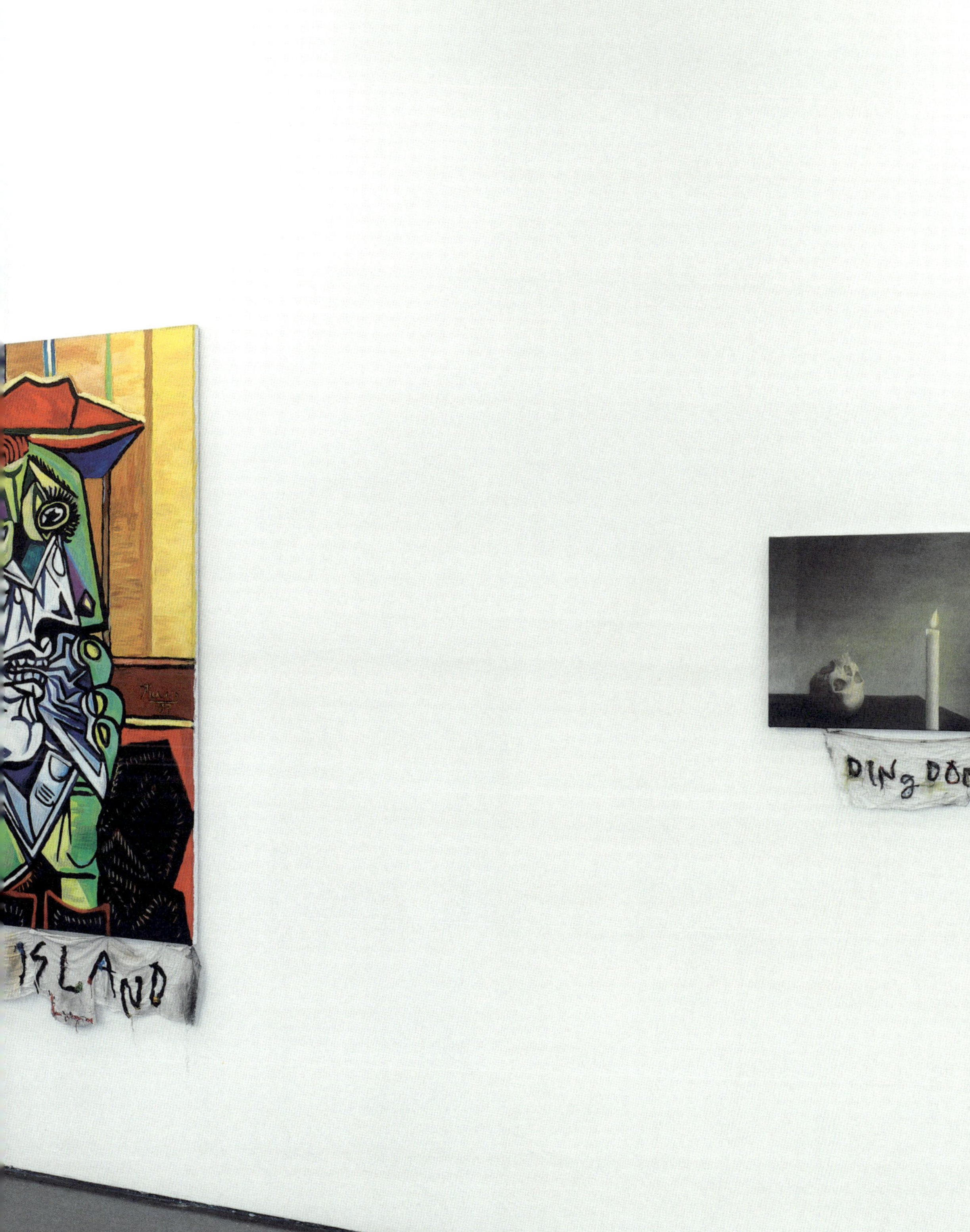
ISLAND
DING DONG

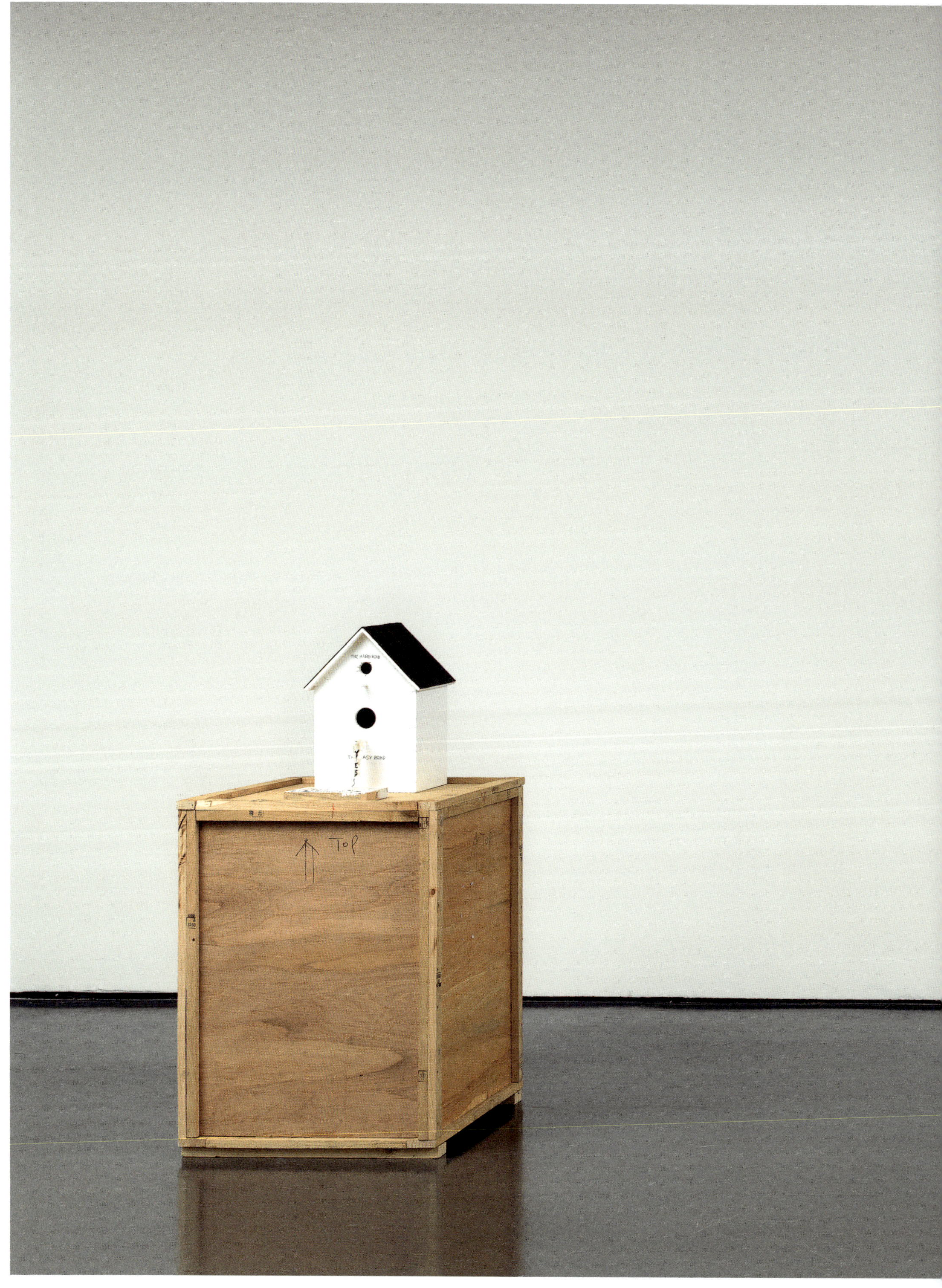

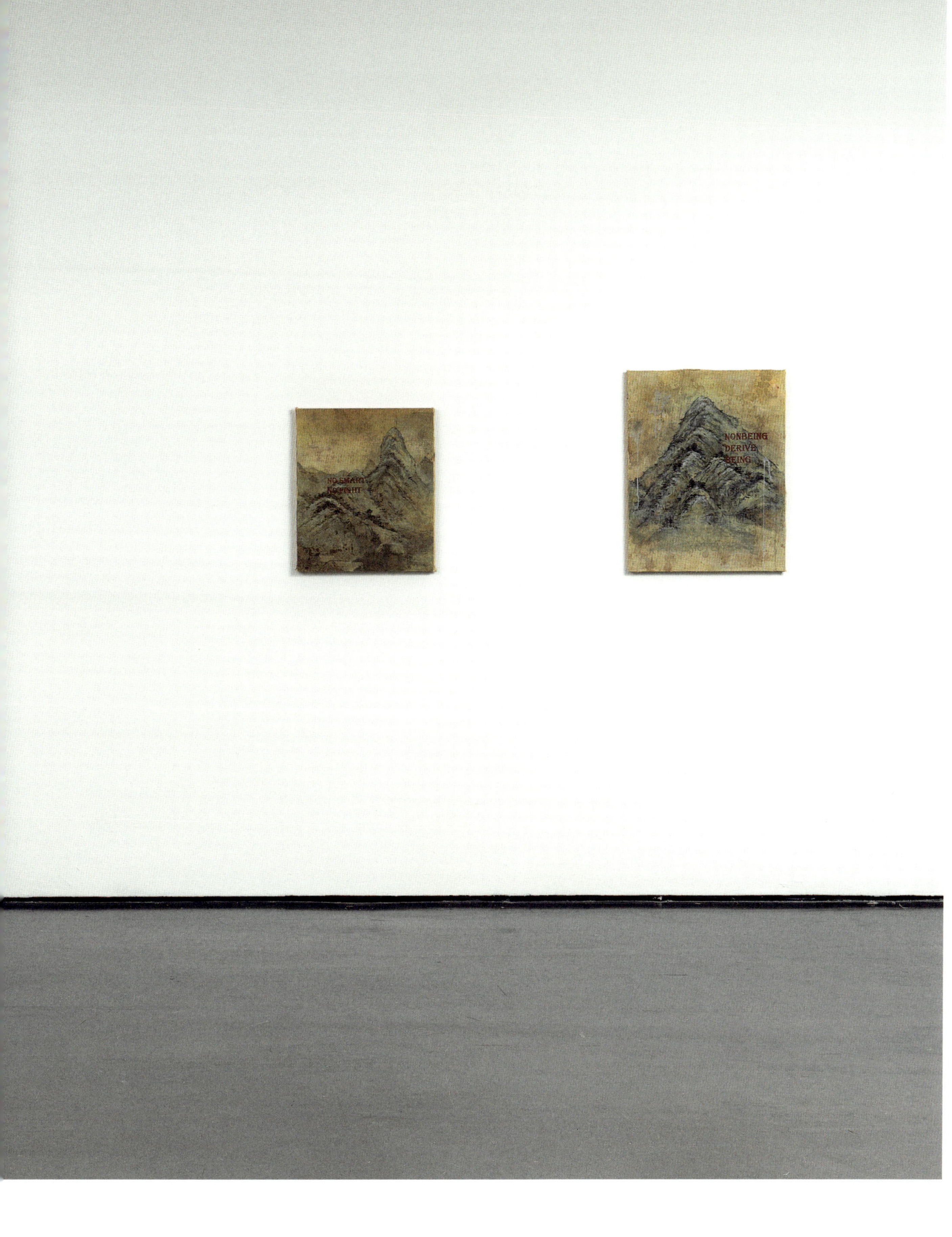
NO SMART
NO FIGHT
NONBEING
DERIVE
BEING

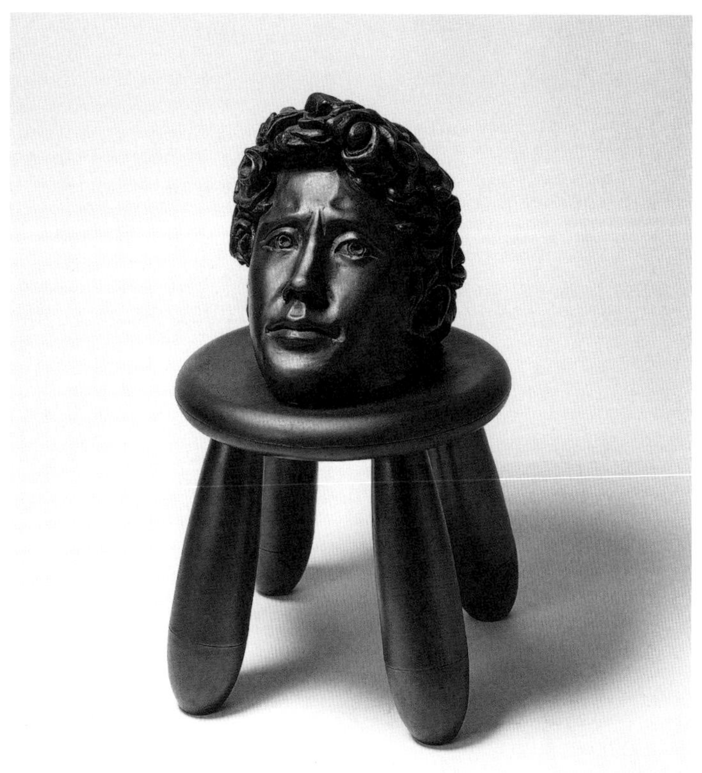

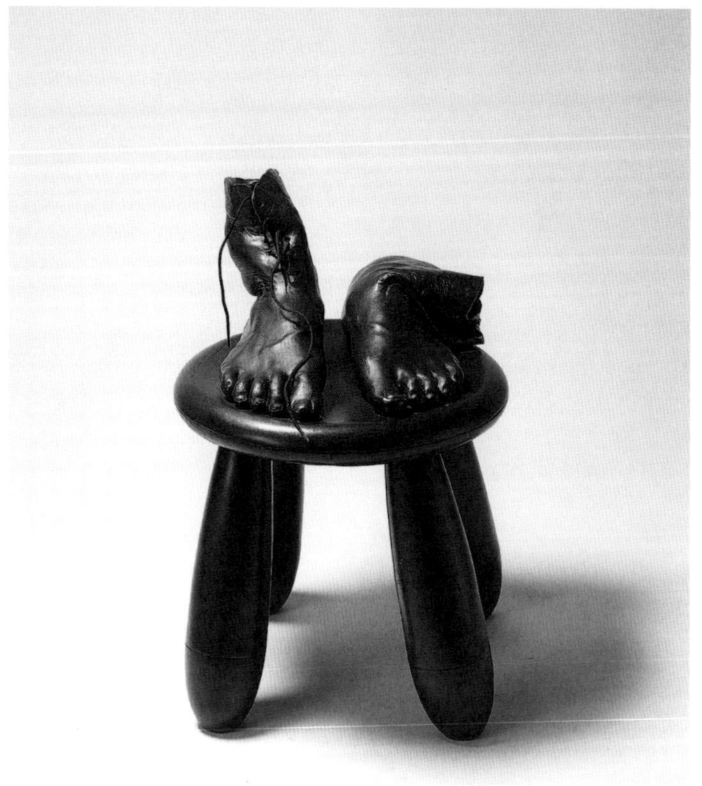

pp. 64–69 · Installation views at Kunsthalle Düsseldorf (2015)
Self-Portrait 1 · 2014 · Bronze
Self-Portrait 2 · 2014 · Bronze

Sumi Kang
The Aesthetic Value of a Flower from East/West: On Cody Hyun Choi's Visual Art

1. Effects—Side Effects

I T is a precarious project to try to identify an artist's work with her or himself. Too much empathy with the artist's private life can result in compromising the autonomy of his/her artworks creating possible misinterpretations. On the other hand, asserting the aesthetic achievement of an artist's work as the ultimate criterion for evaluation can also lead to the mistake of idolizing or depreciating the artist's life, which becomes a function only of his/her work. In the case of certain artists, however, one should willingly take these kinds of risks. Such artists include those who consider their art as an object of hysteria in the psychoanalytic sense: projecting and objectifying their own life in it with a commitment that borders on fixation. These artists consistently exploit the tension between the world and the self, thereby elevating that relation into a special kind of perceptual status. To borrow the terms of Freudian psychoanalysis, the subject becomes "hysterical" not by virtue of the pressures of an exterior object but because s/he projects his/her own repressed mental energies and emotions into it. What is at stake here is an unconscious psychological process of venting—of the kind that seems to have afflicted Anna O. in the clinical report by Josef Breuer. Anna O.'s hysteria was not caused by the care she offered to her sick father, but, on the contrary, arose from her obsession with attending to him.[1] One might say that the relationship between an artist's private life and his/her art is "hysterical" (using the term as a psychological metaphor) when s/he completely attaches him/herself to art and projects his/her own life to it. But we need to make some subtle distinctions: could his/her artistic product be the result instead of self-pity or paranoia as the self is deprived of an exterior world? Or is it a visual exposure of symptoms that represent the dynamics between the subject and the objective world surrounding it and the phenomena that arise through the process of utilizing, deconstructing, and transferring the "self" in art as the most fundamental, empirical effect of experience and perception? The former contention might

---

[1.]

See Josef Breuer and Sigmund Freud, *Studies in Hysteria*, trans. Nicola Luckhurst (London: Penguin Books, 2004), 25–50.

give rise to overly subjective art or art that could be the by-product of a pathological symptom. On the other hand, the latter suggestion is quite reasonable, helping us to understand the correlation between extreme "objectivity" and self-destruction.

The discussion that follows takes up with this idea of the symptom, for "Cody Choi" and "Cody Choi's visual art" formed a dyadic relationship from the beginning of the artist's career in the nineteen-eighties and have been producing effects and side effects occasioned by the relations between the hysterical subject and his art objects ever since. In other words, Choi's choric neurotic questions regarding "desire for others" and "my place" in life—"What am I to others"? "What do others want from me"?—instigate and galvanize his artistic practice, produce success or failure, and nurture and diversify his work, making it sometimes more obscure, sometimes clearer. My argument turns on the suggestion that these effects and side effects of life and aesthetic reality issue from an overriding question of *identity* to which the artist's work will ultimately respond. The center of this discussion is informed, then, by the individual Cody Choi and some of his works.

2. Golden Boy and Thinking Identity

I WANT to begin my consideration of Choi's "selfhood"—the undeniable source and the indispensable catalyst of his art—with two recent works: *Self-Portrait 1* and *Self-Portrait 2*, both made in 2014. They are bronze sculptures of moderate scale—*Self-Portrait 1* is the severed head of an Adonis-like Western boy with glaring eyes, placed on a small stool; *Self-Portrait 2* consists of a pair of foot-shaped shoes (or shoe-shaped feet) located on the same stool, but looking rather disheveled. As bizarre as it may appear, the bronzes must be understood as a product of a contemporary artist's imagination. But in order to comprehend the complicated context of why and how an individual "Cody Choi" presented these works to the world, further investigation is needed into the meaning and significance of the "self-portraits," from their titles to the specific forms they inhabit. The severed head of *Self-Portrait 1* is an appropriation from Michelangelo's famous *David* (1501–04). Likewise, the foot-shaped shoes or shoe-shaped feet of its companion piece derive from René Magritte's painting *The Red Model* (1934); while the form of the stool is cast from a child's plastic stool—a mass-produced IKEA product. Choi converted the stools into pedestals, placed on them the replica forms taken from Magritte and Michelangelo, and then cast each ensemble in bronze. The process is reminiscent of Marcel Duchamp's *Bicycle Wheel* (1913), a combination of a bicycle wheel and kitchen stool that marked the introduction of the "readymade." As we will see, Duchamp's defining gesture has signal implications for Choi's work.

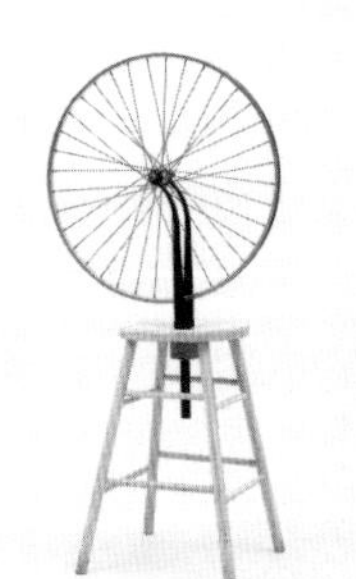

However, if these two bronze sculptures are, in fact, "self-portraits" of Choi, their implications surely extend beyond the horizon of art historical appropriation or the tactical re-appropriations so prevalent in the art world in the second half of the twentieth century. The original artworks borrowed for Choi's sculptures are iconic representatives of the Western Renaissance and the modernist avant-garde, respectively. Clearly, the images, tastes, aesthetic judgments, and compositional arrangements that inform these works—in sum, their aesthetic epistemology—far removed from the individual "Cody Choi" or any self-portrait he—or we—

might conceive. Born in the early nineteen-sixties, Choi grew up in Korea, but was forced to move to the US against his will in an emigration that caused him to suffer from "anger, frustration, and schizophrenia." He had to adapt himself to a new American way of life and negotiate the dual identity of a "Korean-American." When he returned to Korea after more than twenty years as a mid-career artist, he found himself once again "tremendously confused" and "sad that Korea was not the Korea [that I used to know] any longer."[2] He did not feel at home anywhere and was constantly living in an uprooted state. For the Choi who underwent these experiences, a sculpture created from a masterpiece of Western art coupled with a commodity mass-produced by a multinational company would not seem to be appropriate to serve as his self-portrait. The fact that Choi nonetheless calls them "self-portraits" obliges us to investigate further.

The art historian John C. Welchman, who has made some profound observations about Choi's artistic practice in the US, observed that in the nineteen-nineties Cody Choi "fabricated his own visceral legend" by "waging surrogate war with the titanic period icons of Western visual culture—classical Greek sculpture, Michelangelo, Auguste Rodin."[3] Following Welchman's suggestion, we realize that Choi has been engaged in tenacious reflection—beginning in the early nineteen-nineties and continuing until *Self-Portrait 1* and *2* in 2014—on the dynamics of a deformed and distorted life in which the identities of others (even those fragmented and unsuitable to the here-and-now) happened to become part of his own identity (the identity eventually becomes to represent "I," the object of judgment and recognition of others). In this process, Choi's works went through qualitative transformations rather than self-repetitions. Breaking away from the "legend" of his youth in the nineteen-nineties, Choi matured into an experienced individual and artist. From the perspective of cultural criticism, he now contemplates the bitter irony that he had no choice but to present artworks that are the result of the influence on him of the outer world instead of expressing an autonomous "self." He presents a self-portrait assembled from debris and fragments either severed from Western art history or dislocated from the production and consumption apparatus of global capitalism.

Self-Portrait 1 and *2* are artistic self-manifestations of Choi's life during the past thirty years. They are imbued with the artist's multiple negotiations between his own subjectivity—male, Asian, immigrant, foreign student, minority, art school teacher, artist—and formations and others both exterior to and interleaved with these constructs. They bear witness to the artist's need to suppress some parts of himself in order to survive in the framework delivered by capitalist desires, especially the hierarchical aesthetic order of Western art and the high-end art world. In this light, probing the life of the artist—though excluding unnecessary biographical facts or topics of mundane interest—is a crucial method for understanding Choi's art.

Born into a wealthy family, he could get anything he wanted, the finest and the best, until he reached adolescence. During this period, however, Choi suffered from anxiety and neurosis brought on in large part by the obsession and abuse of his mother who was struggling with bipolar disorder caused by the premature death of her two young daughters, Choi's elder sisters.

2.

Cody Choi, "Some Confessions for the Writers from Cody Choi," unpublished artist's note, 2014; other quotations are from this note or my conversations with the artist.

3.

John C. Welchman, "Culture/Cuts: Post-appropriation in the Work of Cody Choi," *Art After Appropriation: Essays on Art in the 1990s* (Amsterdam: G+B Arts International, 2001), 245.

In the early nineteen-eighties he entered one of the most distinguished universities in Korea to study sociology, but his studies were soon disrupted when his family suddenly had to flee to the US due to the failure of his father's business. In the US he found himself in radically new circumstances, obliged to shift his social status from a day laborer to an employee of a design company, from an unemployed person to a student in a theological college. After much meandering he finally enrolled at the Art Center College of Design, Pasadena where he met Mike Kelley, a strong and controversial figure in American contemporary art. Kelley's advice "to study the clash of cultures and postcolonial culture as subjects for art" became a turning point in Choi's artistic practice. Soon after graduating, his work caught the eye of Jeffrey Deitch, a leading art dealer in New York during the nineteen-eighties and nineties, and Choi emerged as a successful artist. During the late nineteen-eighties the art world in New York was dominated by postmodernism, poststructuralism, postcolonialism, multiculturalism, and philosophies of difference and alterity. In this environment, Choi was indeed seen as a "golden boy" who was able to appropriate alternative and heterogeneous discourses of philosophy and literature—especially theories of post-colonialism—that resisted the grand episteme of modernism, merging them with his practice and effectively delivering them through visualization. It was only a matter of time before he was invited to important exhibitions to present a series of works that are now categorized as "Cody Choi's early representative works."

Although he was born and raised in Seoul, a "small town in Asia" that represented both an epistemological other and an aesthetic periphery from a Western perspective, Choi adapted to Western culture successfully, transforming himself into plural identities. His position as a self-evolved artist was somewhat unique in the art world of the time, for his presence activated a multicultural symbol in which Asian exoticism and the American dream coexisted in reality. The works he created during this time—*Searching for a Missing Child* (1986), *Made in USA* (1989), *Golden Boy Poster (Heidegger in Bagesvaerd Church)* (1986-91), *Dialectic Shampoo* (1992), *The Thinker* (1996), *Scamps, Scram* (1993), *Pepto-Bismol Hit and Overlay, Rambo* (1989-90), "Box Animal Face" (1993-94)—suggested a new formal language of neo-conceptualism reflecting his critical thinking as an artist. He had all the reasons and many of the "values" needed to stand for a while in the art world's limelight, the more so as his work engaged with many of the conditions set out in postmodern cultural theory and the discourses of contemporary art. Welchman, for example, described the basis of Choi's work as "the sense of loss, anxiety, and schizophrenia that the decentered self experiences in the gap between Korea and the USA."[4] The most important aspect of all this, arises from the fact that Choi, as a cultural symbol himself, took on an objective stance from which to observe himself and his work. In works based on this "objective perception," Choi voluntarily objectified the cultural and political situations that he was facing in reality, which in turn enabled him to achieve a measure of self-criticism. The term "golden boy" is, in fact, taken from Choi's work *Golden Boy Poster*, a composite photograph with a red background and patterns that look rather Chinese, in which Choi, an Asian man in his twenties, stands in front of a rooster surrounded by a golden halo, holding a bottle of Pepto-Bismol, the common American remedy for stomach problems, as if he were selling it—as well as himself—in the capital market.

4.
Welchman, "Culture/Cuts," 257.

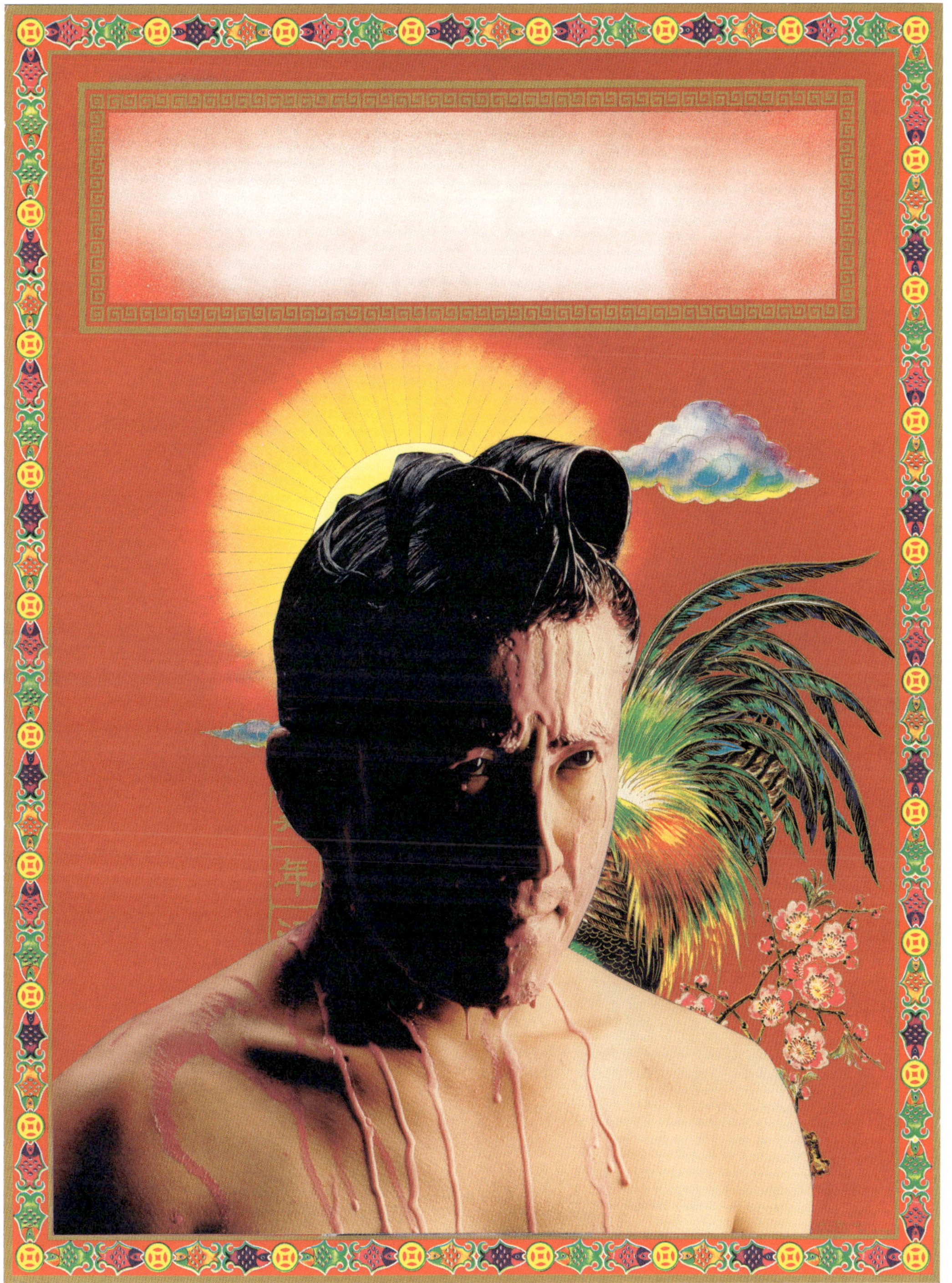

Dialectic Shampoo · 1992 · C-print

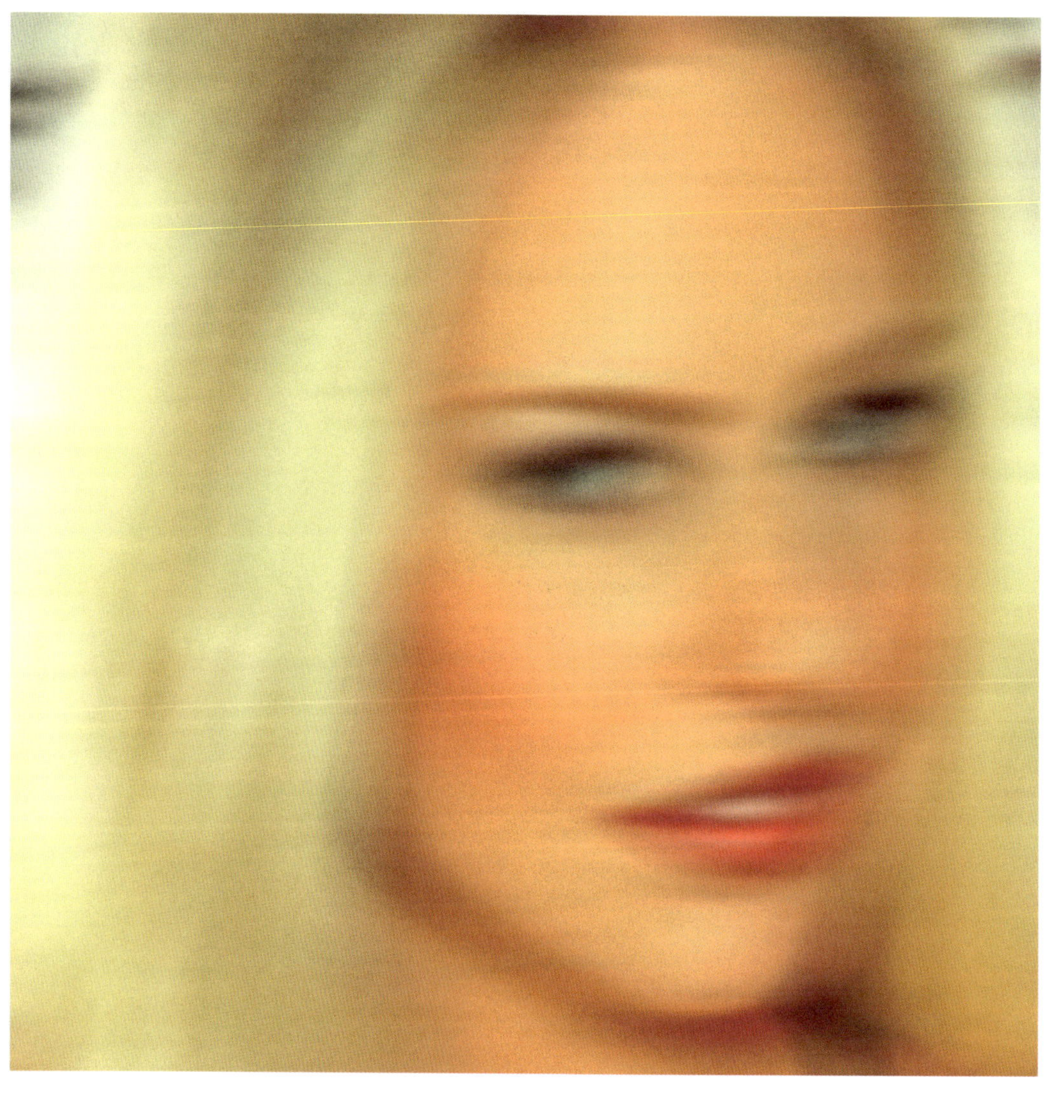

Made in USA 2 · 1986/2003 · Print on canvas

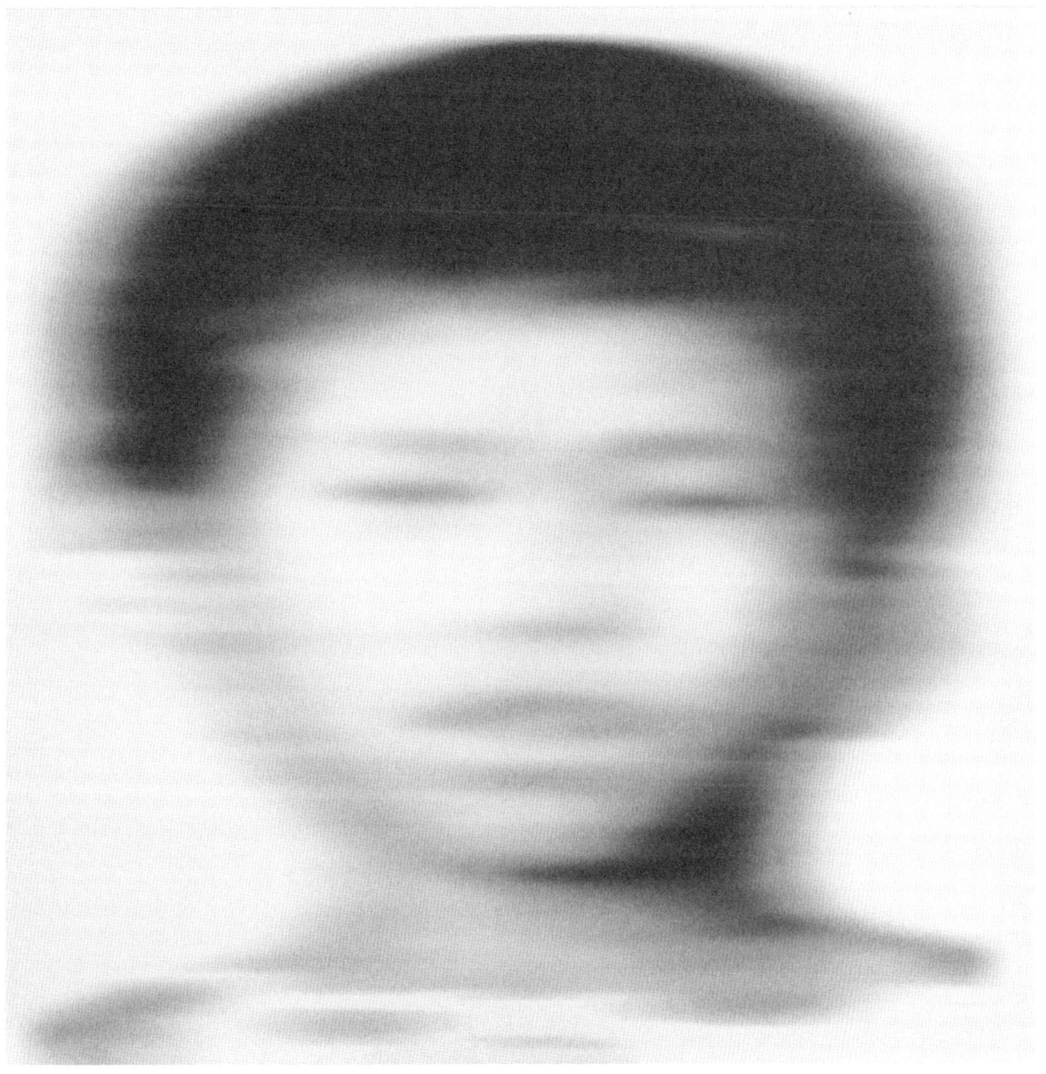

Wanted Lost Child 2002 · 1986/2002 · Print on canvas

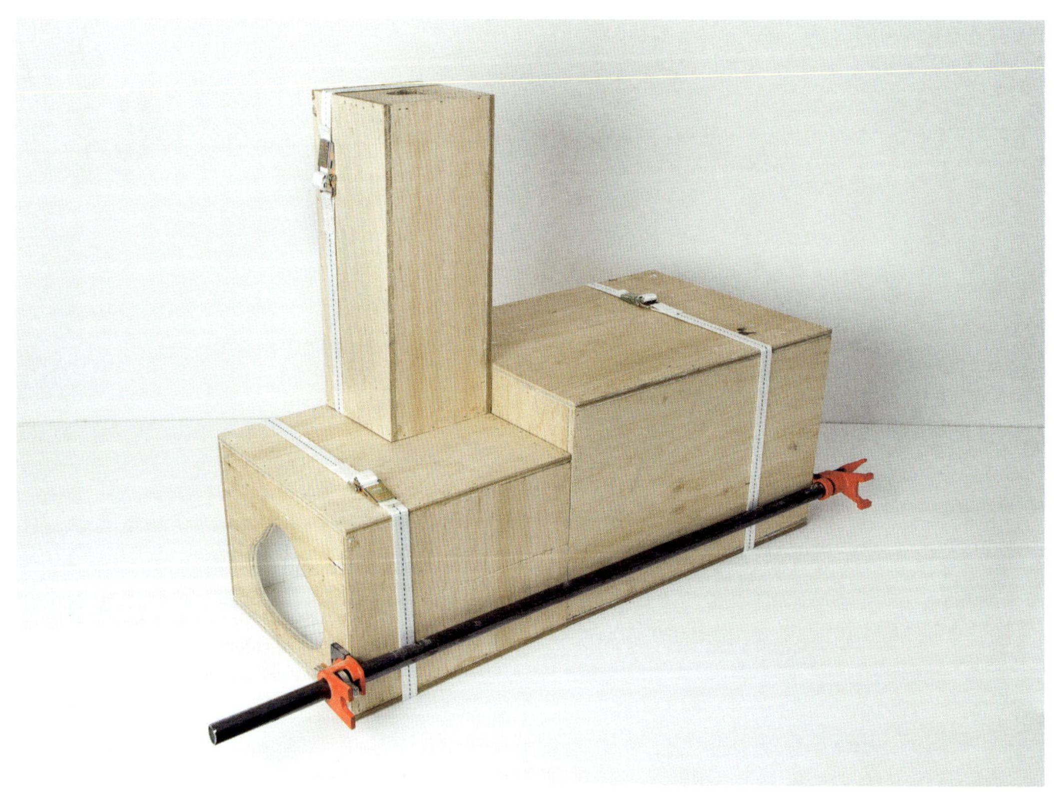

Box Animal Face 4 · 1993/2014 · Wood, steel, banding strap

If the image of the "golden boy" offered ostensible public identity for Choi that he managed to construct through his active involvement in the American art world by virtue of a subtle mirage of sociability, Asian "looks" and artistic talent, his hidden identity, which was plagued by neurosis, damaged from culture shock and beset by the social, political, and economical conflicts he had experienced in reality (and crudely reproduced), was "the thinker." Like *Golden Boy Poster*, Choi's "thinker" also refers to a series of works, "The Thinker," a group of large sculptures accompanied by a performance that was one of projects that helped to secure his reputation as the "young Korean-American artist Cody Choi" paving the way for a successful artistic career. Yet, evaluating "The Thinker" series as a premonition of Choi's joyful success and also as a good aesthetic object—both visually and intellectually—would be too superficial. Modeled on the shape of Auguste Rodin's *The Thinker*, Choi's variants are made of toilet paper soaked in Pepto-Bismol—a medicine familiar to the artist as he had to ingest a bottle of the pink liquid every day due to the chronic stomach disorder he developed after moving to the US. Choi's dyspepsia was, quite literally, the product of an "unhappy consciousness"[5] that emerged from the rupture created when body and mind collided with the world outside them. The nature of the materials that comprise the sculpture—including a wooden crate-cum-pedestal—are as anti-aesthetic and anti-artistic as the artist's creative attitude. During the exhibition, Choi created a performance during which he squatted, naked, in a hole cut out of the box as if seated on a toilet (or imitating the posture of Rodin's—and his own—sculpture). "Scamps, Scrams" and "Box Animal Face" share a conceptual space with "The Thinker." In "Scamps, Scrams," seven differently sized, body-perforated boxes harvest the energies of seven body parts including head, breast, genitals, and so on. This performance-sculpture presents the human body in its raw state removed from all formalities and customs. In these series, Choi shoves, amputates, hides, exaggerates, adorns, undresses, insults, mocks, or covers up his own body. How, then, can we come to terms with the "self" that he strives to show and speak for through these struggles? It is a surrogate corporeality engendered by the experience of consistently rearticulating an identity that knows only that it has lost, and cannot reclaim, what was once original to it. It shouldn't be necessary to refer to Gilles Deleuze and Félix Guattari's ideas about the logic of "becoming," the "body without organs," and "unconsciousness as a production machine"[6] to understand that the personhood at stake here reaches for the insides of himself,[7] with the desire of others connecting the head (thinking) to the rear (excretion) and dividing appearance (thinking gesture) from inner energies (the seven energy boxes).

From a cultural perspective, Choi is both a multiplex being and a singular one; while, conceptually speaking, although his is an identity determined by modern society—secured by "steel casting"[8] in Max Weber's term, that is solidified by nationality, locality, and family

---

5.

Borrowing from G. W. F. Hegel, I follow T. J. Clark's use of this formula in a discussion of the tension that modernist artists experienced regarding the problem of artistic creation; see T. J. Clark, *Farewell to an Idea: Episodes from a History of Modernism* (New Haven, CT and London: Yale University Press, 2001), 299–369.

6.

Gilles Deleuze and Félix Guattari, *A Thousand Plateaus: Capitalism and Schizophrenia*, trans. Brian Massumi (Minneapolis: University of Minnesota Press, 1987), 26–38, 149–51, 237–38.

7.

The title *Scamps, Scram* is difficult to translate into Korean. Choi explains that it refers to "the hate of one's own body and cursing it." This reflects not only a simple self-negation but also to an attempt to articulate oneself through the desire of others.

8.

See, Stephen Kalberg, "Max Weber on Contemporary American Culture: A 'Hard as Steel Casing'?" *Sociologia Internationalis* 36, no. 1 (1998): 1–14.

relations—he also adapted himself to a flexible identity—something akin to Zygmunt Bauman's "light cloak"[9] that varies according to cultural conditions and tastes—that his life required him to accept. Thanks to the experiences he underwent as an immigrant in the US, Choi developed a self, mantled by a "light cloak" that he put on and took off according to various social or cultural conditions. Still, deep down in his heart, he yearned to become a singular individual (*der Einzelne*): deep-rooted and determined to protect the self as distinct from others. As we investigate the oscillation between these poles and the schizophrenic effects/side effects arising between the social self and inner desires, it is clear that Choi's art is none other than the visual production of these symptoms. It arises from an individual who maximizes the effects of cultural and political multiplicities. It is an aesthetic indicator reflecting physical damage (stomach disorders, complexes, anxieties, et cetera) and the agony of the double denial—reluctance to prop up a self that is not yet an autonomous subject, while resisting the imitation of a dominant form, and thus abandoning the self—that an individual had to suffer during his self-formation.

3. Epistemic Sabotage: East/West

MAKING, teaching, and exhibiting actively in the nineteen-nineties, seemingly with a bright future ahead in New York, Choi also began to gain a reputation in the Korean art world. Represented by an influential gallery in Seoul, his exhibitions brought little-known aspects of contemporary art and cultural politics to Korea, and often had an explosive impact. Attentive members of the Korean art community had to pay attention to his work, for better or worse. The processes through which Choi addressed issues of identity, cultural difference, subculture and the subaltern—in short, what he termed the "topography of contemporary culture"[10] in studies infused with postmodernist and postcolonialist ideas—offered Korean artists, critics, theorists, and curators a signal series of concrete moments exemplifying an epistemological and aesthetic paradigm shift about which they had hitherto been largely ignorant. Unable to overcome the fundamental limitations and the structural "gaps" of the society he confronted as an émigré Asian in the international art world, Choi, however, returned to Korea in the early 2000s. Back "home" he was forced to endure another cultural shock no less intense than the once through which he lived as an immigrant.

Born into the patriarchal social system of the early nineteen-sixties, Choi grew up during the era of rapid industrialization and modernization of the nineteen-seventies and left Korea in the early nineteen-eighties when the country was under military dictatorship. Beset by schizophrenic symptoms of a new digital, global, and multicultural society, twenty-first-century Korea was no longer a motherland for him. Coming back from the US, his adopted foreign country, Choi could—and would—not reassimilate into a homeland that was no longer his home: he found himself at a loss as to how to establish a clear or settled position. The exclusiveness of Korean society—propped up by its "rules" and assumptions—forced him into

---

9.

Zygmunt Bauman, *44 Letters From the Liquid Modern World* (London: Polity, 2010), 47.

10.

See Cody Choi, *Topography of 20th Century Culture* (Seoul: Culturegraphy Press, 2010); and *Understanding Contemporary Culture: Topography of Contemporary Culture* (Seoul: Culturegraphy Press), 2010.

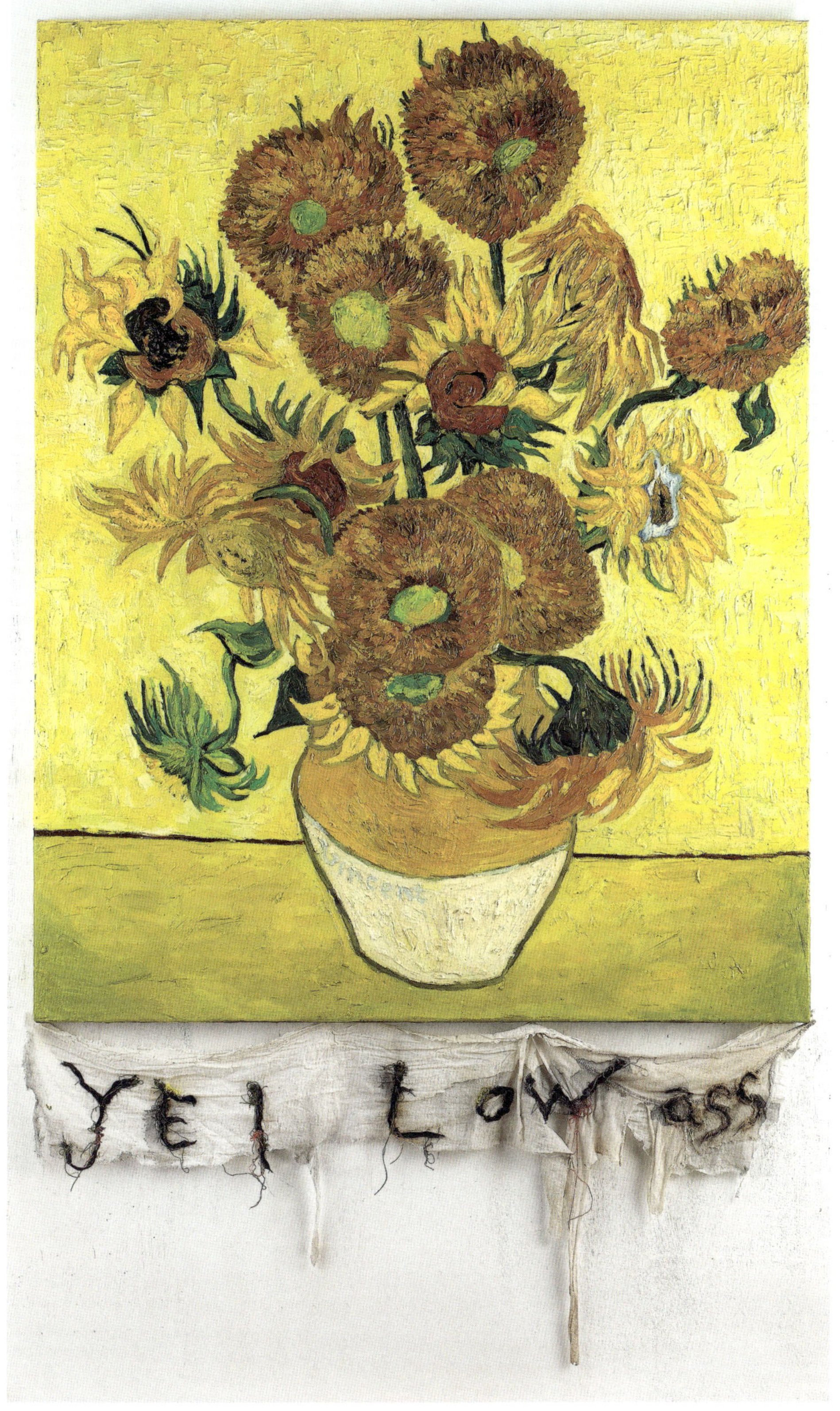

Episteme Sabotage–Yel Low Ass (Big) · 2014 · Oil on canvas, cloth, thread

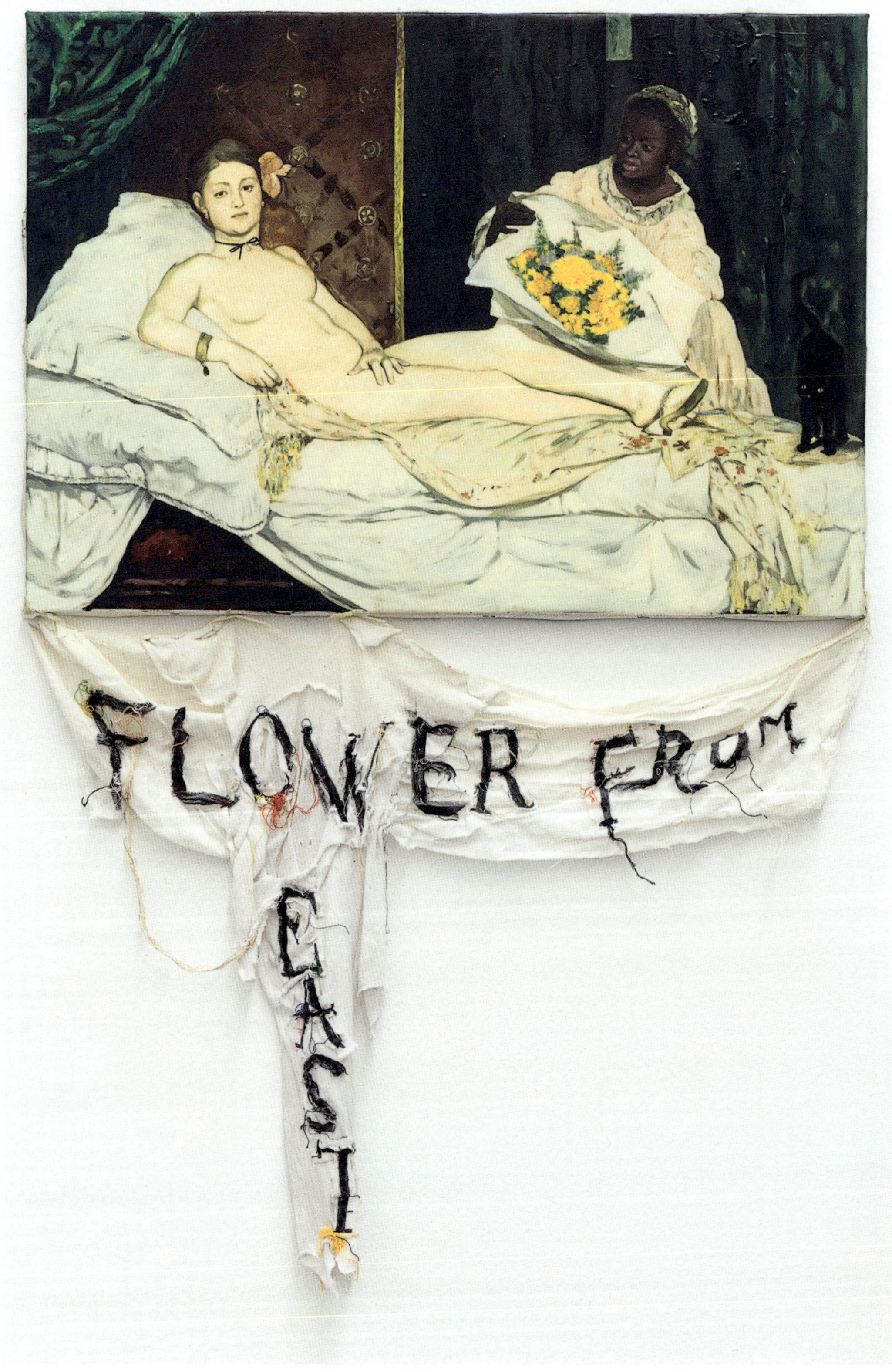

Episteme Sabotage–Flower From East · 2014 · Oil on canvas, cloth, thread

the position of a stranger who is familiar yet also *unheimlich* (uncanny). Further, the formal structure of the Korean art world, which operates through exclusive patronage systems and networks of influence, relegated him to virtual nonexistence. Choi claims that he did not give up the aspiration to stay "inside" an art world that has (or appears to have) stable and privileged authority and trust—all the more so because he is an artist who has been accorded no space inside the border laid down by the art world's gatekeepers. However, one should not mistake this for an opportunist desire or a shallow ambition to achieve something by capitulating to the establishment. As Choi's new "Episteme Sabotage" series (2014–15) demonstrates, he defends his right to be an artist because he knows that he can clearly reveal the "irrationalities between ontology and epistemology" particular to the art world by attaching himself to this role some-what hysterically). Clearly, Choi realized himself through the process of entering the world of "art" and building his own aesthetic values with fragments and leftovers gleaned from social and cultural environments that did not even permit him to choose between immigrant or per-manent resident, elitist or failure, existence or nonexistence.

Cody Choi's "Episteme Sabotage" is a series of critical-conceptual paintings: small sheets of cotton cloth, on which short phrases are embroidered, are attached to various imi-tations of masterpieces of Western art history. For example, "old cow" is affixed to a replica of the *Mona Lisa*, and "Yel Low Ass," a variant of "Yellow ass," a demeaning term for Asians, is embroidered on Van Gogh's *Sunflowers*. These works offer a platform from which viewers can critically reexamine the process through which the term "masterpiece" conditions their per-ception of painting. They form a proving ground to test the automatic acceptance of a work without exercising subjective judgment because a certain image has already been defined as a "masterpiece." *Episteme Sabotage-Flower From East* poses these questions with a unique twist. It features a replica of Édouard Manet's *Olympia* in which the flower bouquet held by the black maid is painted in yellow, the only difference from the original painting. A cloth embroidered with the phrase "FLOWER FROM EAST" is attached on the canvas. Does the "flower from East" refer to Olympia in Manet's painting? Or the flower from the East sent from an unknown customer to a high-class prostitute in Choi's appropriated version?

My interpretation is that while the flower could have satirical implications or symbol-ize a secret tryst, it might also represent a person. If we define selfhood as the cognition and perception of a total persona, embracing scientific knowledge and cultural or artistic sensibili-ties, but also the small tastes and pleasures of life—the "flower from East," from the viewpoint of a Western Olympia, can be seen as Choi himself, an intellectual, cognitive, and perceptive entity from the East. The encounter between the two might evolve into either "unconditional acceptance" or "rejection." In other words, Choi (East) may be unconditionally accepted or rejected by Olympia (West). On the other hand, attending to the title *Episteme Sabotage*, "flower from East" can be understood as an artist, the subject who rejects the episteme of the authority of Western art history and aesthetics, and Olympia as an aesthetic object to be rejected. The second interpretation is more important: Choi is skeptical about Korean artists' conditioned perception of (and blind acquiescence to) Western "masterpieces." The "Episteme Sabotage" series suggests an apparent intellectual rejection and criticism of this culturally conditioned reflex. By the same token, Choi also performs the role of the "flower from West" here in Korea. As suggested above, from the nineteen-nineties to the present, Choi took on the role of the other, sometimes willingly, sometimes unwillingly—a nuncio introducing heterogeneity to the more conventional epistemological and aesthetic orders of the Korean art world. It is by this means that he has been residing in art without conforming to Eastern or Western conventions, and without being fully accepted by either, and at the same time not accepting them himself. Herein lies Choi's aesthetic value: the flower from both East and West, the only aesthetic position that he can take.

4. Self Destruction—Self Organization

But what is the relationship between Choi's artwork and his criticism, and is it productive or unproductive? Walter Benjamin's description of the reader of a novel as an enthusiastic subject who "swallows up the material as the fire devours logs in the fireplace" might help us here. According to Benjamin, a novel is not a rigid structure like a building constructed by an architect, but an object that the reader is "to make … completely his own, to devour it" by deconstructing it.[11] In the process of devouring, the reader will discover an aesthetic joy, a new meaning, and an insight into his own vision of life. This is the kind of relationship I have now established with Choi's visual art as a critic. His works are artistic structures that produce certain meanings; voluntarily burning themselves through criticism like logs in the fireplace. The very nature of Choi's art makes this kind of relationship possible. For what comes first in his work are the pressures of an individual who has experienced a life meted out by social and political circumstances rather than the self-consciousness of an artist. Of necessity, Choi's works have been created through processes of persistent self-analysis and self-perception. The desire to deconstruct the hysterical self, the spirit that perseveres through instability and positionlessness, the ability to assemble those fragments—these are the coordinates that map out Choi's practice. They engender an aesthetics that is found and constructed yet burns and disappears. I hope I have illuminated this aspect of Choi's work: self-destructive yet self-organizing, a schizophrenic product of its own side effects.

11.

Walter Benjamin, "The Storyteller," in Walter Benjamin: *Selected Writings, Volume 3: 1935–1938*, ed. Howard Eiland and Michael W. Jennings, trans. Edmund Jephcott, Howard Eiland, et al. (Cambridge, MA: Harvard University Press/Belknap Press, 2006), 156.

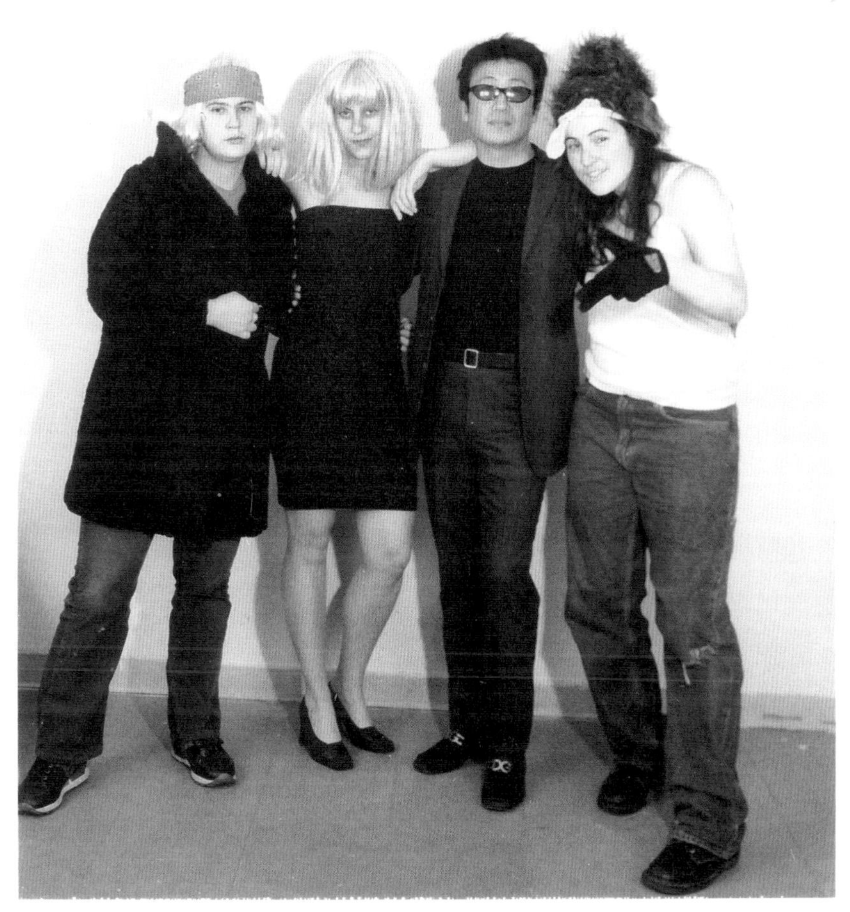

Neo-POCO *2001* • 2006 • Print on paper (Photo: Nancy Barton)

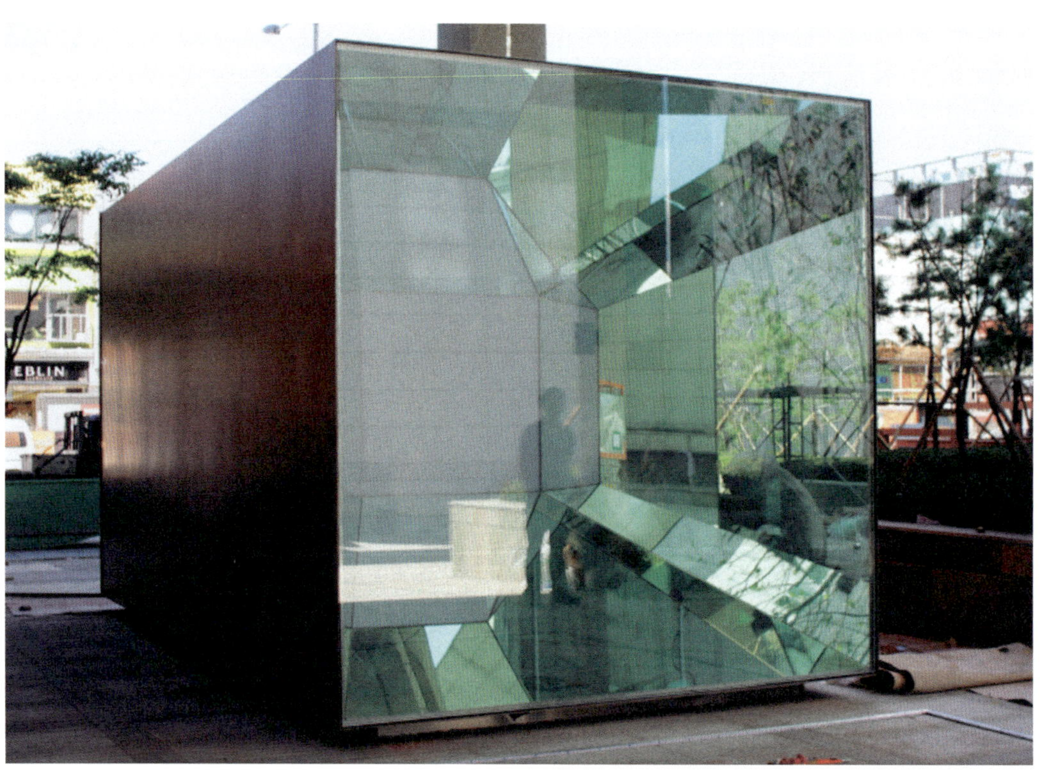

Luminous Cube · 2007–08 · Stainless steel, glass, LED

Gregor Jansen
Behind the Mirrors: Aspects of Reflection in the Work of Cody Hyun Choi

Luminous Cube

IN a public space, at Konkuk University Hospital in Seoul, stands a hermetic and yet open box. Consisting of steel, glass, mirrors, and LEDs it situates viewers in multiply reflected versions of themselves activated by the autonomous mirrored cube as both an exterior skin and as an interior space, and by the surrounding space of a pedestrian zone between the university hospital and the road. Cody Choi realized this sculpture, *Luminous Cube*, as a public project in 2007 and 2008. Visiting the site in 2012, I was astonished by the coldness and elegance of this object. I seemed to be isolated in front of it (standing outside), yet also reflected in its interior—so that my own selfhood, reflected in fragments, appeared split, fractured, and broken. This is not a Dan Graham cube beset by anticipatory borrowings. On the contrary, *Luminous Cube* strikes us by reflecting our being or existence as "foreign" individuals appearing behind the mirror.

Jabberwocky

IN 1871, seven years after the surprising success of *Alice in Wonderland*, Lewis Carroll escorted his heroine on another journey into the realm of fantasy, where logic is once more turned on its head. His story is an intellectual game with language, space, and time, turning on ideas and experiences of transformation and perception. In *Through the Looking-Glass*, Alice climbs through a mirror and enters a world that at first resembles the real world, except that everything is backwards. While in *Alice in Wonderland* the heroine follows a white rabbit into a deep hole, not thinking about how she might return. The White Queen speaks of "living backwards" and remembers most clearly events that haven't yet taken place. For example, she punishes the king's messenger, who has not yet stood trial and not yet committed any crime. *Alice in Wonderland* begins on a warm day in May, Alice's birthday, but Carroll's sequel starts on a snowy day in early November. Alice is playing with her cats in front of the fireplace and philosophizing about what the world would look like on the other side of a mirror. Then she climbs onto the mantelpiece and notices that the mirror above the fireplace actually leads to a parallel world. On the other side she finds a reflected version of her house, in which objects

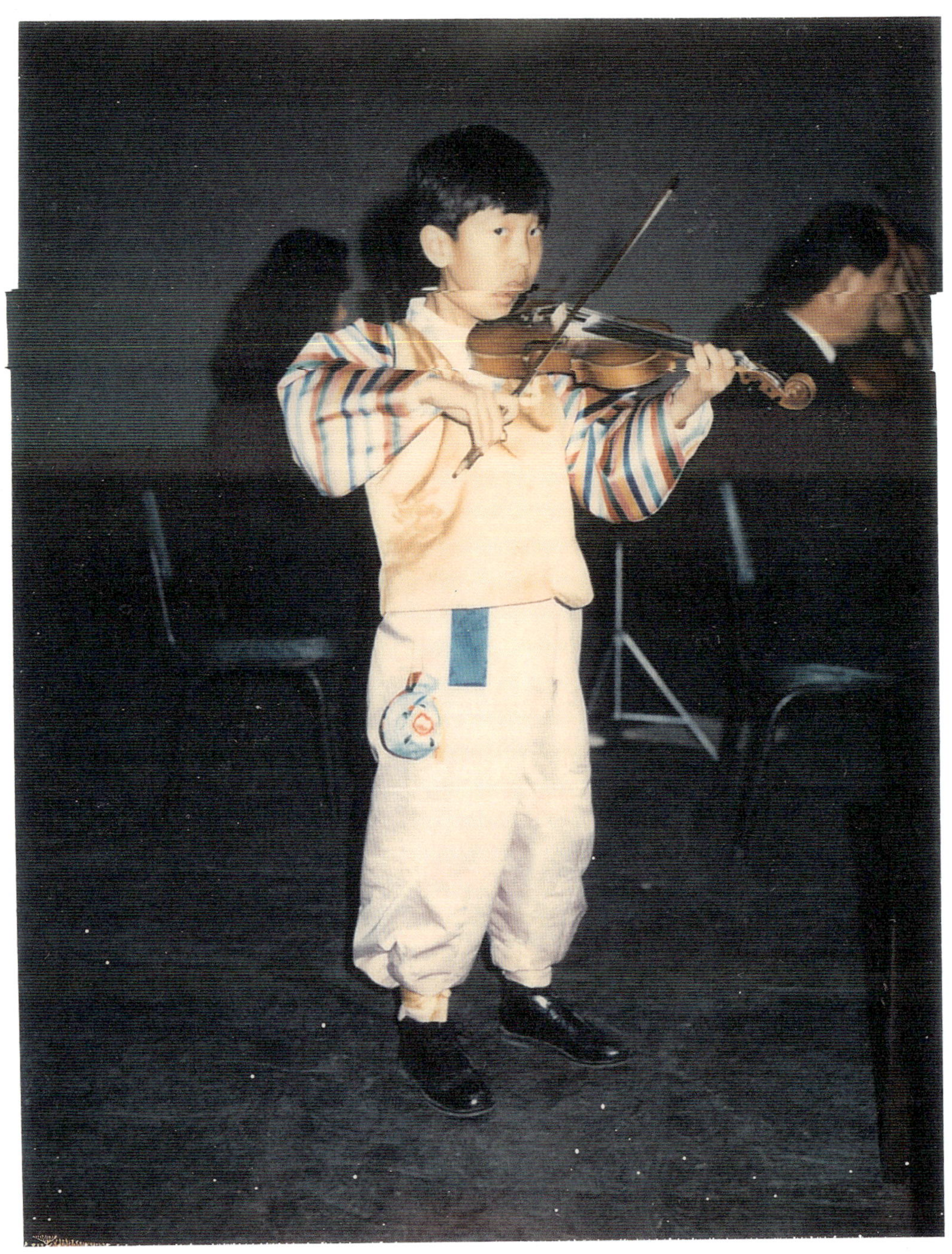

Neo-pocolonian · 2013 · C-print

such as pictures, clocks, and chess pieces have come to life. She also finds a book written in mirror writing containing the nonsense poem "Jabberwocky." She resolves to continue exploring the house and proceeds to the garden. The adventure begins.

To commence a text on a contemporary Korean artist Carroll's luminously offbeat fantasy fiction might seem puzzling—the more so since Choi's media-reflective, conceptual, postcolonial, and postappropriative work seems, at first, to have little or nothing to do with the famous children's book. But Choi's life "through the looking glass" is also a kind of exploration of a foreign, strange world, an at times painful adventure that, I want to suggest, begins with his sculpture *Luminous Cube*. After all, astonishing parallels and associations emerge when one relates the fictional story to the real one from this perspective.[1] In fact, a loose but salient sequence of motifs and references emerges that shines new light on Choi's fascinating and deceptively complex work.

Educational Complex

DURING his childhood and as a young man, Choi spent many hours watching movies at the cinema. His pastime was somewhat different, however, from the humdrum experience of filmgoers at movie theaters around the world. For Choi was able to watch movies that were unavailable to ordinary Koreans, since his father's wealth and business interests gave him access to American dramas and films not scheduled on television or in the national theater chains. In the nineteen-sixties, few Koreans had the opportunity to watch television or go to the movies due to endemic poverty after the Korean War. As Choi notes, "At that time I had my own TV in my room. Most of the TV programs were American dramas and films dubbed into Korean."[2] He thus absorbed many of the visual products of capitalism at the height of the Cold War. And, thanks to the dubbing, he was convinced that all Americans spoke Korean. One must also keep in mind the problematic relationship between North and South Korea with the superpowers of the United States and the USSR in the context of the US occupation of Japan after the Second World War and its presence in Korea during and after the Korean War—as well as imperial Japan's occupation of Korea for three and a half decades after 1910. The Korean conflict began in 1950, shortly after the Americans and the Soviets had left the occupation zones, and ended in the summer of 1953 with the signing of the armistice by the United Nations Command, North Korea, and China, but without the signature of South Korea's president, Syngman Rhee. With the establishment of a four-kilometer-wide Demilitarized Zone, the border between the two Korean states was also set along the thirty-eighth parallel as a result of the military governments after the Second World War (similar to the Soviet Occupation Zone in former East Germany). The fear of another invasion continues to affect politics in the partitioned nation to this day.

1.

Gayatri Chakravorty Spivak, for instance, emphasizes that it is politically necessary to try to understand identities—even if only temporarily and from a strategic point of view—in order to expose these identities as necessarily false. See, "Can the Subaltern Speak?" in *Marxism and the Interpretation of Culture*, ed. Cary Nelson and Lawrence Grossberg, (Chicago: University of Illinois Press, 1988).

2.

Cody Choi, email to the author, March 22, 2015.

ORN in 1961, Choi was strongly influenced by these political events, just as he was by the early death of his two older sisters. However, it is difficult to estimate to what degree the political balance of power and any "longing" for liberal-democratic, ultimately capitalist, society, were indelibly burned into the young man's cultural and visual memory. Or, in other words, how the "bachelor" experienced projections of the desiring machine of the Hollywood dream factory, and the American mantra of "life, liberty, and the pursuit of happiness." Thus, it was a seemingly "logical" decision as well as a portentous experience for the young Choi when he later made his way to the United States—a promised land with endless possibilities. There was only one destination for him: Los Angeles. After Choi spent a brief period studying sociology in Seoul, his family was forced to flee the country and immigrated to California in 1983. Thus, he arrived on the other side of the mirror more or less against his will, and the strange world that he had previously seen in movies was now real and unreal at the same time. Yet, nothing from the movies corresponded with reality. He suffered from schizophrenia. Everything was reversed by the cruel refractions of emotional perception. Choi's dream—and his real desire—to live in America was confronted by the experience of having a different, unanticipated status: he was an Asian and an immigrant. The Korean in LA was shocked, then frustrated and depressed. He fell ill, plagued by gastric ulcers. Art was his sanctuary, at first at Rio Hondo College in 1985, and later at Art Center College of Design in Pasadena, where he earned his bachelor's degree in 1990. His body had long since arrived in America; his heart and his stomach were there, but he was somehow unable to speak. Recognizing his problem with communication, Choi was fortune to find a mentor and friend, Mike Kelley, a sensitive but unabashed deconstructor of symbolic orders, whom he met in 1987.[3] It was during the years of their acquaintance that Kelley's objects and installations gained widespread recognition. Kelley's subtle commentaries on collective fears and socialized desire, were localized in working and emergent middle-class life and American religiosity, especially the conflicted Catholicism Kelley inherited from his family in suburban Detroit.[4] The friendship between the two artists afforded Choi a new trust in himself and helped him overcome his shyness. Kelley guided him toward postcolonial theory and ideas about cultural difference, and encouraged him to focus on—rather than try to discard or abandon—his own fears. Choi's first works in the late nineteen-eighties and early nineteen-nineties show the mirror image of the Americanized Korean. For looking into the mirror in reactive jubilation, as a holistic corporeal experience, and as a crucial "stage" in the formation of the ego (as described by Jacques Lacan), is contrasted with the fragmentation of the body and the series of painful, symbolic amputations to which it have rise.

3.
"In 1987, I met Mike Kelley who was not yet the famous artist he became, at Art Center, Pasadena. Mike was the only teacher who understood and sympathized with my anger and cultural difficulties; but he was different from other teachers. He caught my heart and always gave me advice. The other teachers only mentioned Western art and Western aesthetic and academic ideas ...!" Cody Choi, email to the author, March 10, 2015.

4.
See, Elisabeth Sussman, ed., *Mike Kelley: Catholic Tastes*, exh. cat., Whitney Museum of American Art (New York: Whitney/ Abrams, 1993).

Gerhard Richter's Mirror Metaphors

MIRRORS and the phenomenon of mirroring are a common thread that runs through Richter's oeuvre. If painting is a subjective act, the mirror is passive: it reflects what happens in front of it and calls on the viewer to act. Instead of contemplation and numinousness—as modernist art more or less dictates—mirrors oblige us to confront our own image. Richter allows viewers to determine the meaning of their own images and their relationship to them. The mirror is reminiscent of the banal photographs that Richter began using in 1962 as templates for his figurative pictures; for the photograph and the mirror represent two methods of capturing a moment. However, while the photograph preserves a moment, the mirror is not a permanent medium. Instead, in painting, it is a clear symbol for *vanitas*: the intrinsic is fleeting, it appears and disappears. We directly experience our own impermanence. Although Richter's work is suffused with mirror metaphoricities, these tropes also point beyond his long-established painterly virtuosity. What began with his *Four Panes of Glass* in 1967, continued in numerous *Gray Paintings* and culminated in 1981 in an exhibition at the Kunsthalle Düsseldorf: *Georg Baselitz, Gerhard Richter: Mirror* (1981), the work shown there (and which remains in the museum collection today) measures 225 × 318 cm and was one of his largest works at the time. Never before had a painter questioned his own work (as well as that of his colleague, Baselitz) more coolly, clearly, conceptually, or brilliantly. In numerous other paintings, to be sure, the mirror shows what is located outside of the picture. And this, of course, is also the case with Richter: it is always objects that lie outside the boundaries of the frame that are reflected.

Culture Cuts and Strips

THIS is why it was important to me to include Richter's mirror in the Choi survey exhibition at the Kunsthalle Düsseldorf, just as I had previously brought together Choi with Jeff Koons and Takashi Murakami in 2000 at the central entrance area of of an international (and transnational) exhibition.[5] In this way, a curatorial concept was realized within a broader framework. The relation of Choi and Richter, however, is somewhat different as they combine neo-conceptual approaches.[6] Even though their oeuvres seem diametrically opposed, the reference to Richter in Choi's "digital paintings," which he began in 1999, is more than a convenient allusion. Whether borrowing from Rodin, Michelangelo, or Richter, Choi makes use of appropriation in the traditional sense in an incorporation and digestion of "masterpieces" from Western art history. The metabolic breakdown that results in each case is blatantly—and ironically—accentuated in works from the nineteen-nineties using the staple pink stomach

---

5.
For the exhibition *Continental Shift* at the Ludwig Forum für Internationale Kunst, I invited Murakami and Choi, among others, to exhibit works alongside the permanent installation *Made in Heaven* by Jeff Koons.

6.
There are several other relations: Koons and Choi were also affiliated with the Jeffrey Deitch gallery in New York; while the parallel Asian backgrounds of Murakami and Choi were important for my exhibition concept about Japan and Korea which featured their work alongside American Pop Art from the collection of Peter Ludwig. The aim was to make clear—but also to "stymie"—the new predominance of Asia on the threshold of the twenty-first century which challenged the predominance of the West—the US, in particular—in the second half of the twentieth century.

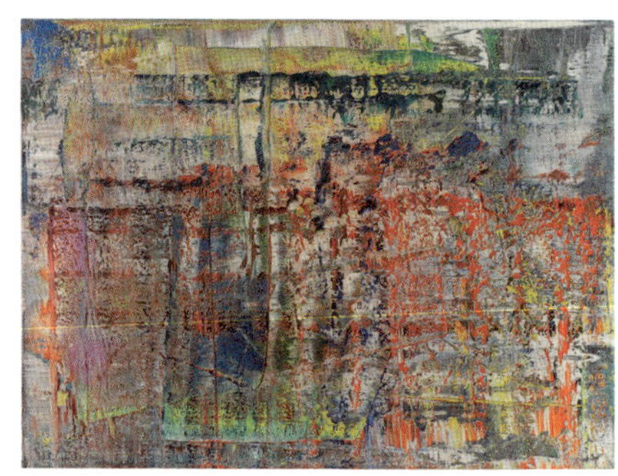

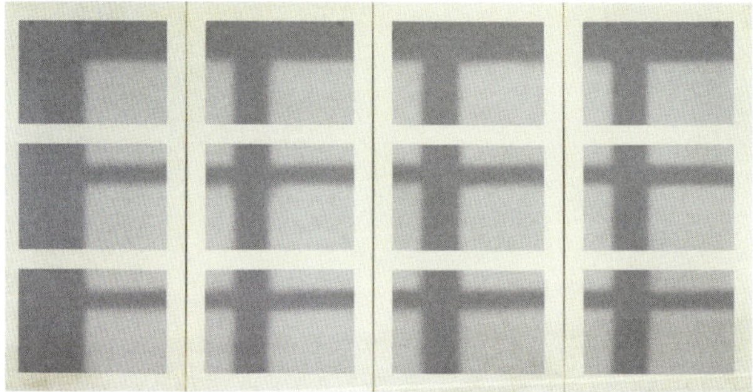

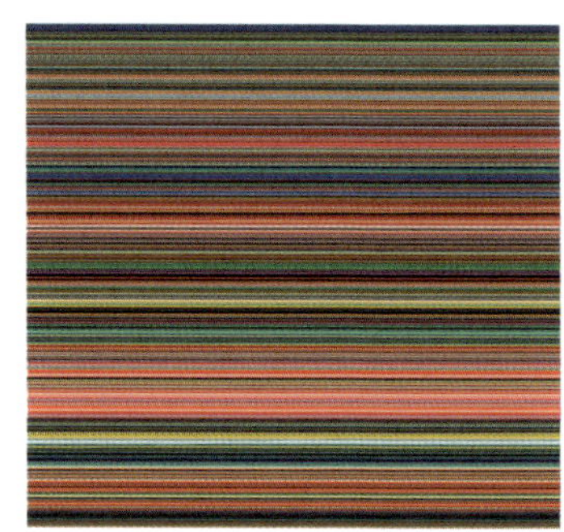

Gerhard Richter · *Abstract Painting* · 1990 · Oil on canvas

Gerhard Richter · *Window* · 1968 · Oil on canvas

Gerhard Richter · *Strip* · 2011 · Digital print on paper between Alu Dibond and Perspex (Diasec)

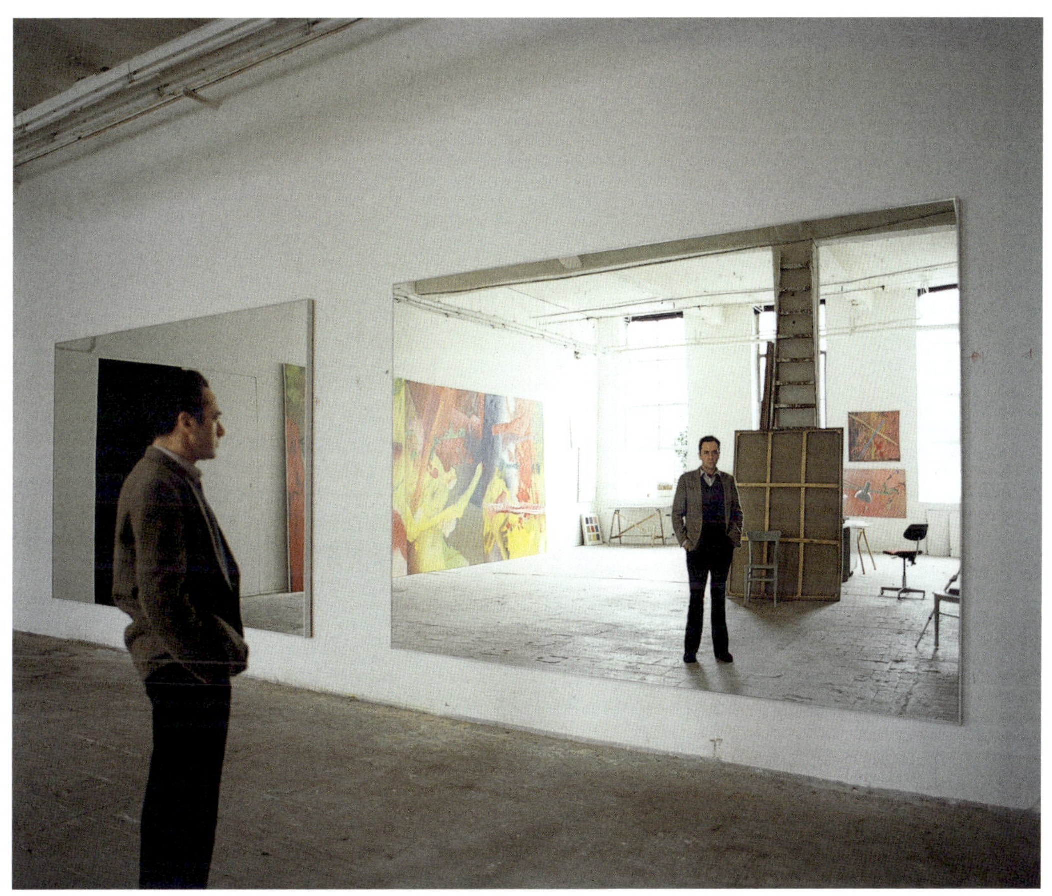

Gerhard Richter · Mirror · 1981 · Mirror

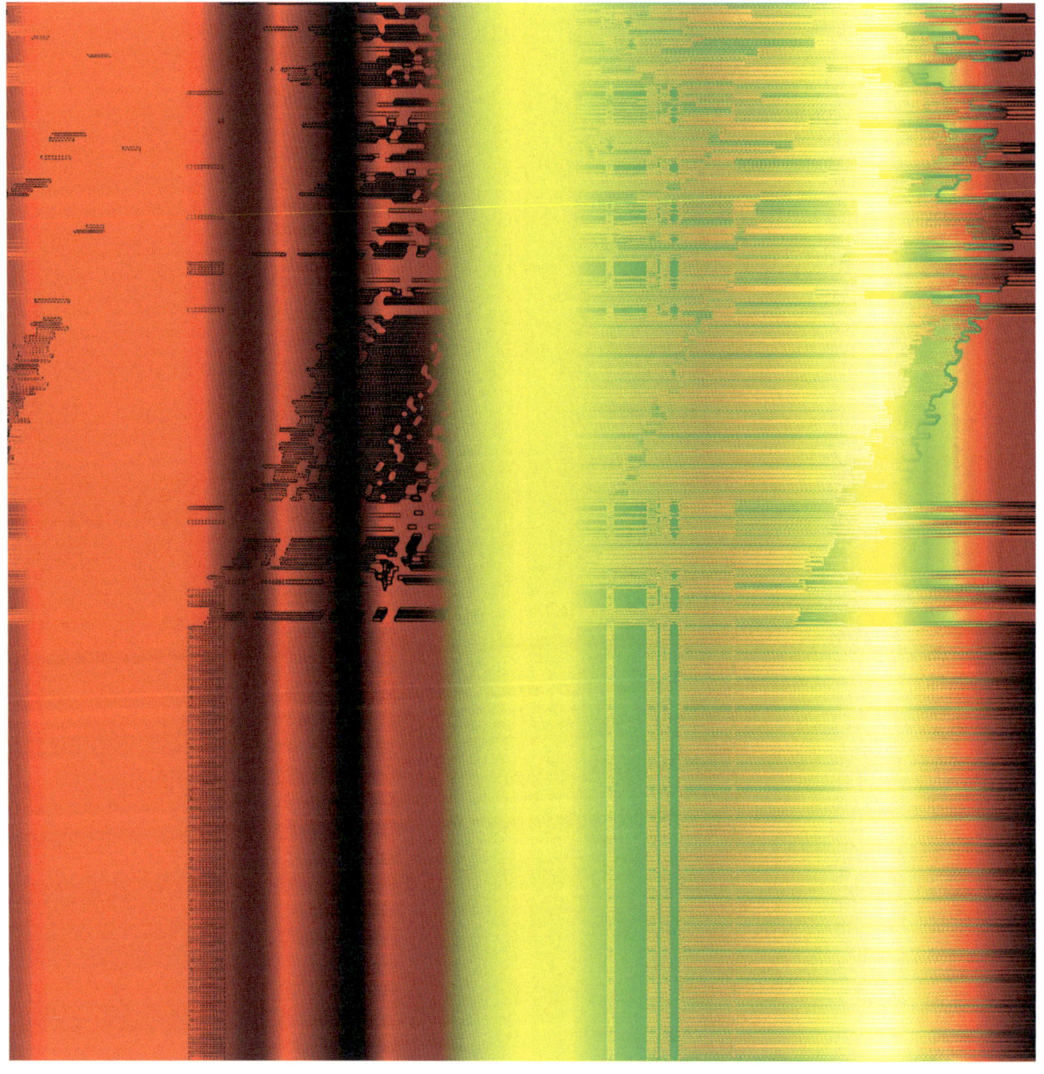

Abstraktes Bild 1999-17 · 1999 · VUTEk ink on mesh, mounted on canvas

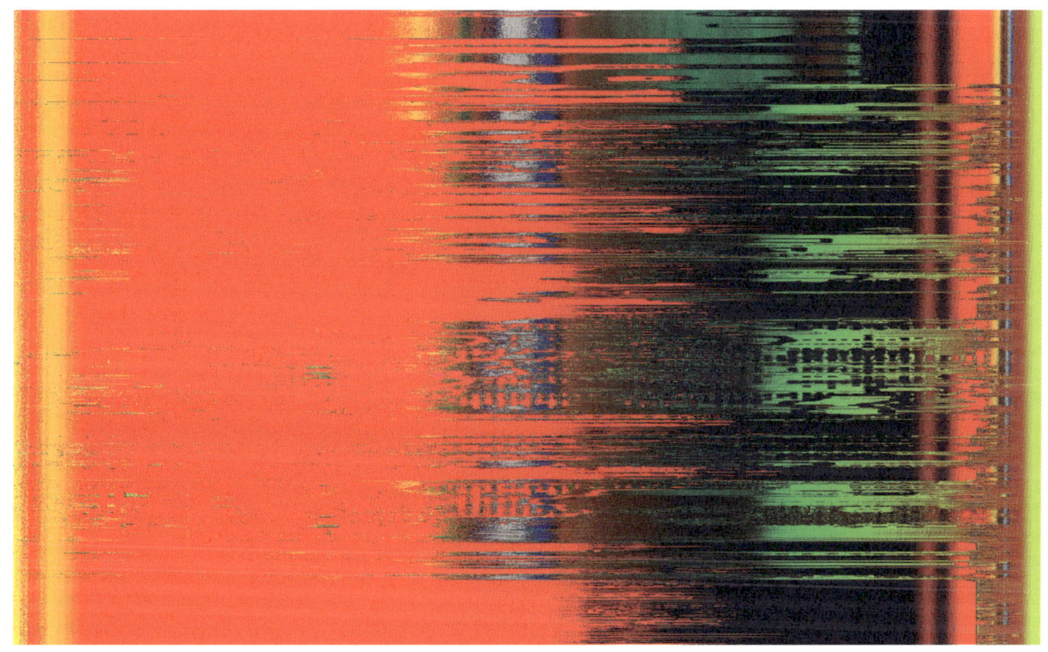

Abstraktes Bild 09-7-r 1999 · VUTEk ink on mesh, mounted on canvas

medicine Pepto-Bismol and toilet paper. Begun a little later, Choi's "Database Paintings" (1999–2000) continue this process by different means, offering deceptively naïve depictions of "exotic" fauna and other imagery developed in New York using his son's computer painting program. In Richter's anti-painterly abstraction he found yet another new worldview—though one that could no longer play a role in his art following his definitive return to his homeland of South Korea in 2004. Logically enough, Richter also took up with abstract digital pictures in 2011 having experimented with numerous related methods and techniques. His "Strip" series, for example, is based on paintings whose colors are digitally analyzed and reproduced as horizontal lines. Just as Choi used Richter's "Abstract Paintings" and separated them into digital stripes, Richter reused his *Abstract Painting* (1990) in digital form. Richter reinterprets his abstract painting by filtering it through a computerized imaging process: he divides the abstract composition into smaller and smaller segments, which are extended by mirroring them on the horizontal axis, and then recombining the parts. The result is a combination of apparently randomly found stripe motifs and Richter's ordering manipulation. Both artists arrive at the same solution from completely different processes—one through disintegration and redefinition, and the other through abstraction as a figurative process for the derivation of the pictorial. In one case we witness a form of sociopolitical deconstruction of values; in the other advanced formal analysis and visual reconstitution.

The Broken Mirror[7]

AFTER returning to his homeland over a decade ago and writing two books on twentieth-century art theory, Choi's works became more reflective, simpler, and more open. No longer working digitally, he has instead engaged with traditional methods and iconographies. Choi seems to have stepped back in front of the mirror in order to reveal more of his own, physical self—as fractured and reflected by himself. "By himself" refers to his initially jubilant reaction when he switched back to his former cultural system after his return from the United States. At the same time, his works from the past decade seem like a broken mirrored reality that can only be entered, exited—or simply passed-through—by a fragmented self. The focused, metabolic bodily experience that distinguished Choi's early work is no longer possible. He observes his new old environment; he addresses the problems of the "American way of life" and the loss of tradition in the capitalist coopting of Western liberal-democratic structures—but his criticism is expressed uncomfortably, sometimes cynically. His concepts and statements are disguised and ambiguous; they direct the gaze to the wounds of the new value system and rub salt into them. Like advertising slogans, they promise a fleeting moment of individuality and happiness. Upon closer examination, however, his ideas shock the viewer with an ambiguous indecisiveness that recognizes the artist as an object influenced by remote but systemic declensions of power. Or, to put it differently, in his own works Choi emphasizes the shift in values of a society of which he is a part and yet to which he does not feel he

---

7.
The exhibition *Der zerbrochene Spiegel: Positionen zur Malerei*, curated by Kasper König and Hans-Ulrich Obrist was at the Deichtorhallen Hamburg, October 15, 1993 to January 2, 1994.

belongs, whose values he participates in producing while simultaneously "failing" to do so, whose mirror he both constructs and shatters. In a new, global world of cultural, economic, military, and climatic upheavals, crises, and catastrophes, in a world marked by migration, changing affiliations and shifting conditions, states and their associated cultural systems such as language, art, and identities are becoming increasingly provisional, and their inhabitants increasingly "stateless."

Luminous Cube was a product of, and response to, these contingencies. Choi developed various perspectives inside a structure that appears simple from the outside, as in a hall of mirrors. Set up to solicit non-Euclidian perspectives, the inner nonperspective of the cube encourages an allover perspective.[8] He also understands the work as a commentary on the pluralist position of the cyber generation, for whom perspectival multiplicity has became natural and self-evident. But Choi and his generation, like all Koreans who grew up before the internet, was raised with only one perspective, which has confused and preoccupied him throughout his life.

Concepts of Mind

THIS dilemma has always been the topic of Choi's work, though with a renewed emphasis in the last ten years. For him, art becomes a game of images and words, a form of Conceptual Art (in the best sense of the word) in which visual aspects nonetheless play a prominent role. He emphasizes the artisanal, the painterly, and the appreciation of art—or, as in his neon works, that which is clumsy or nondesigned, like the calligraphic twists of his own handwriting. The neons are, quite literally, signature pieces; they return again to the self, and are, in a traditional sense, authentic and masterful. Here, as earlier, Choi alludes to naked or "bare" life, his existential vulnerability and simultaneous, conceptual reflection.[9] This is very wrong and at the same time very right: we cannot see beauty without accepting and at times only dully reflecting the tragedy of the modern—or rather, postmodern—mirror stage as a broken image of the self.[10] Like Choi, we are in a phase of indecisiveness that programs its judgment on the status of art as an anthropological quality in the social realm of perception, including self-perception.[11] What art and human beings are, what both can be, is inseparable—art and human beings are a symbiosis!

In the middle of an ink painting of a landscape without culture—without Western culture, to be more precise—a historical, Asian landscape scene, accompanied by words in capital letters which seem indebted to a nihilistic philosophy:

8.
These remarks and those following draw on an email from Choi to the author, March 10, 2015.

9.
See Giorgio Agamben, *Homo Sacer: Sovereign Power and Bare Life*, trans. Daniel Heller-Roazen (Stanford: Stanford University Press, 1998).

10.
One theory states that video art has been so successful because it ignores the moment of the viewer and continually illuminates the dull surface—a question of presentation and *immersive* contemplation and anticipation of perception.

11.
See Hans Belting, *An Anthropology of Images: Picture, Medium, Body*, trans. Thomas Dunlap (Princeton: Princeton University Press, 2011). The concept of the image that is discussed here was developed out of the interrelationship between mental and physical images. It also refers to the media on which they appear, in which images embody themselves and thus determine the physical experience of contemporary viewers. In this sense, every visual history is only the other side of a cultural history of the body.

WEALTH, DEBAUCHERY,
GOOD, EVIL,
RIGHT, WRONG,
BEAUTY AND UGLINESS
THESE ARE ALL
CONCEPTS OF MIND.

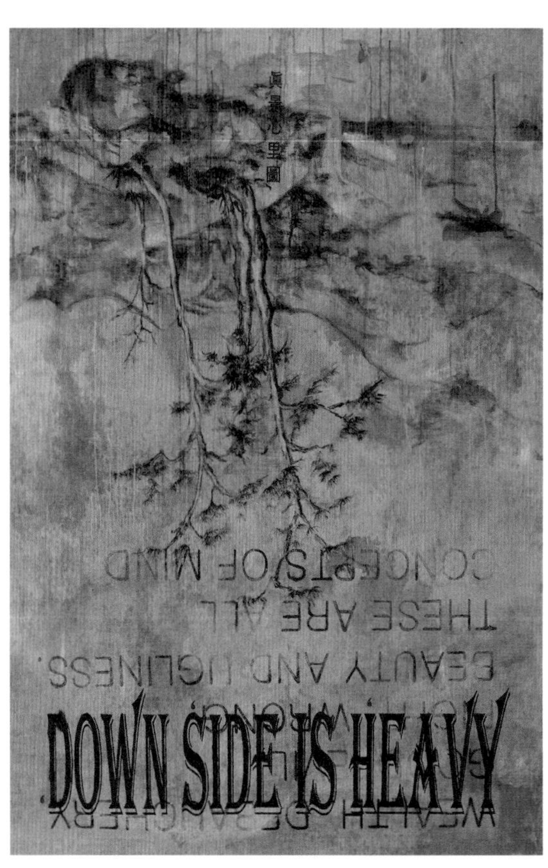

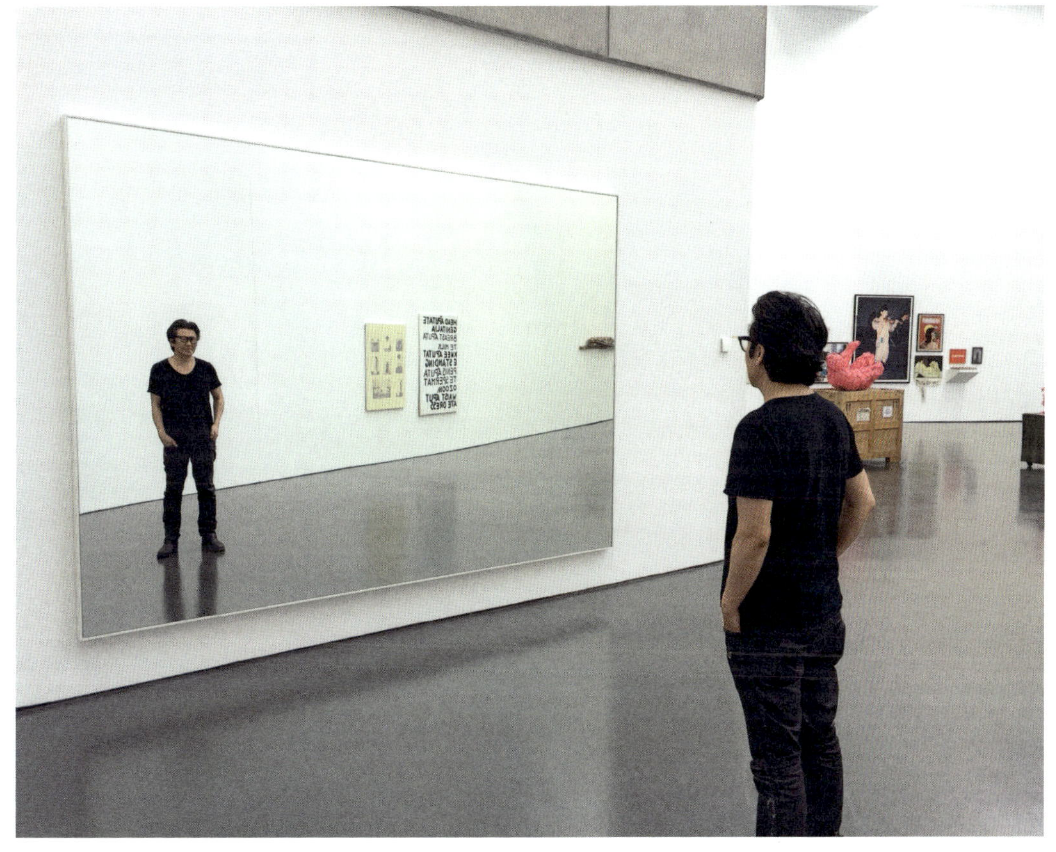

Installation view at Kunsthalle Düsseldorf (2015)
Cody Choi standing in front of Gerhard Richter's Mirror (1981)

Works

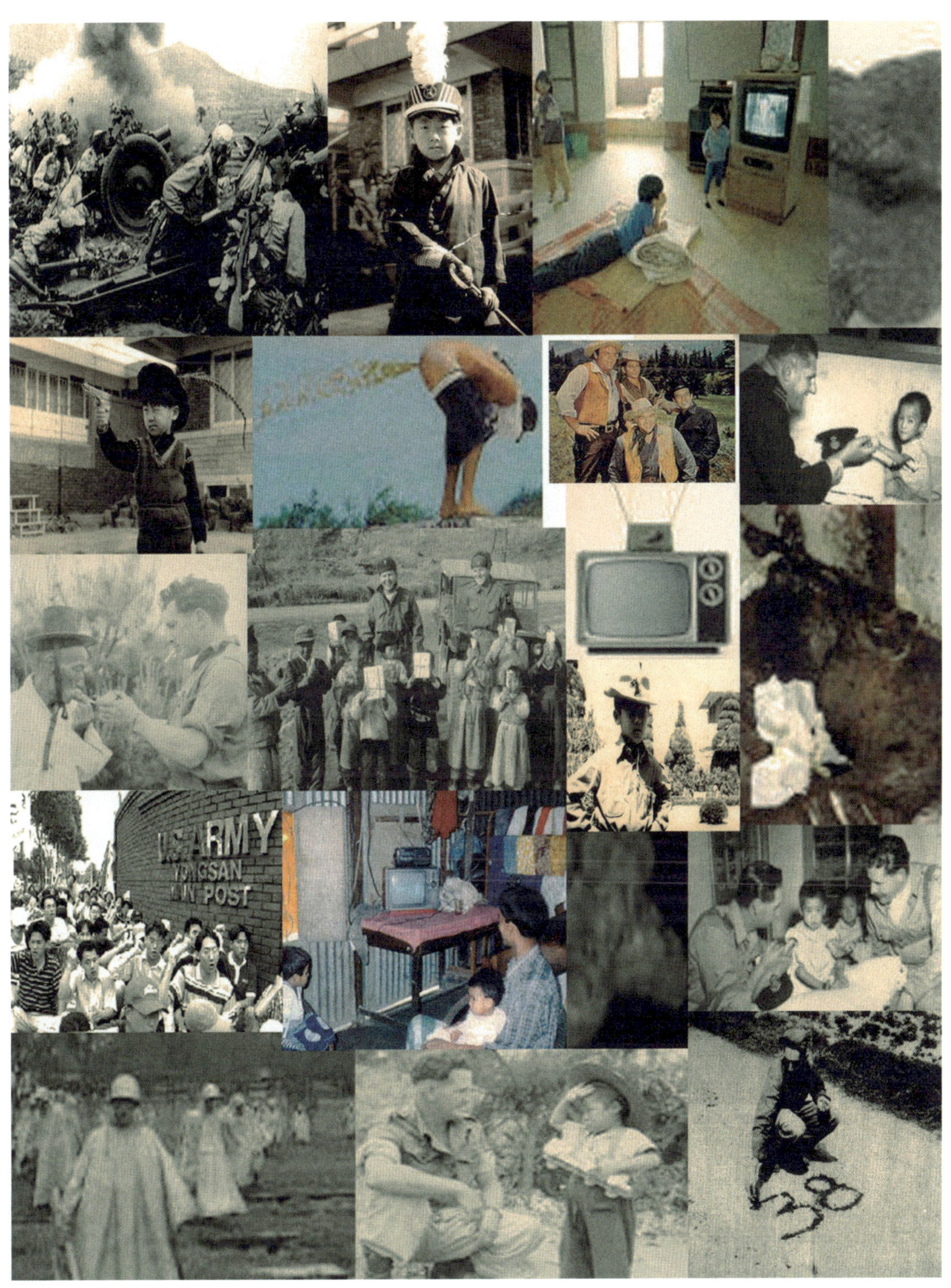

Dyseptic Universe · 1986–1992 · Photo collage, C-print

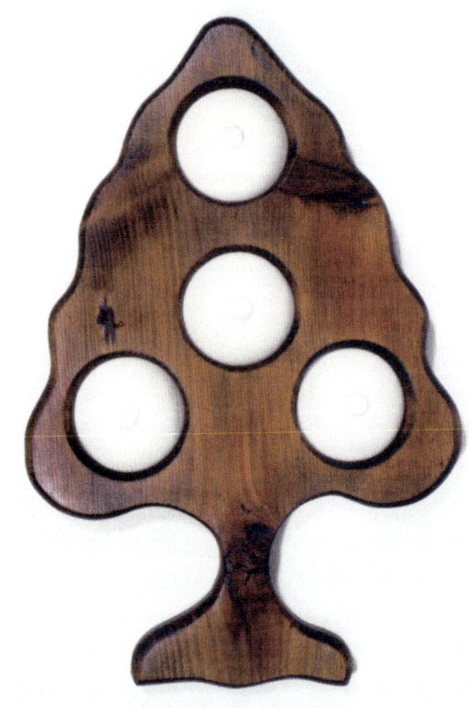

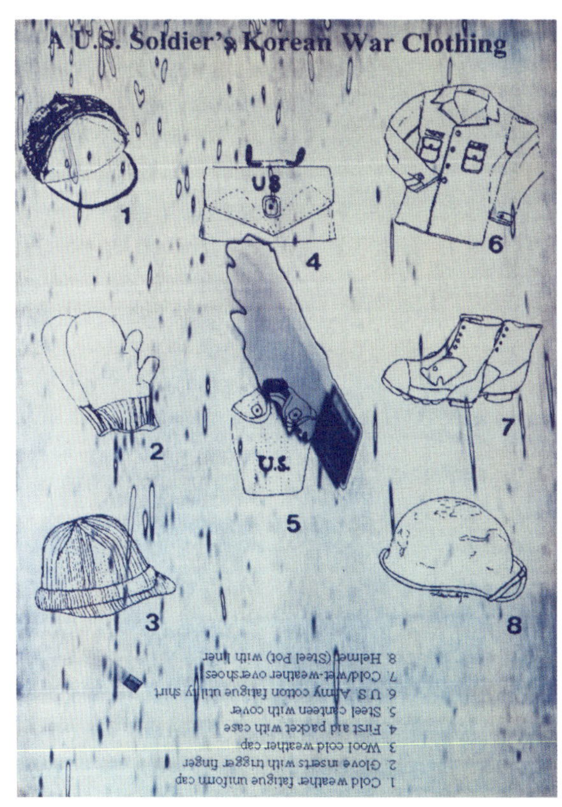

Christmast Tree · 1989–92 · Sponge, wood

War Cloth 2 · 1992/2006 (reprint) · Collage, digital print on paper

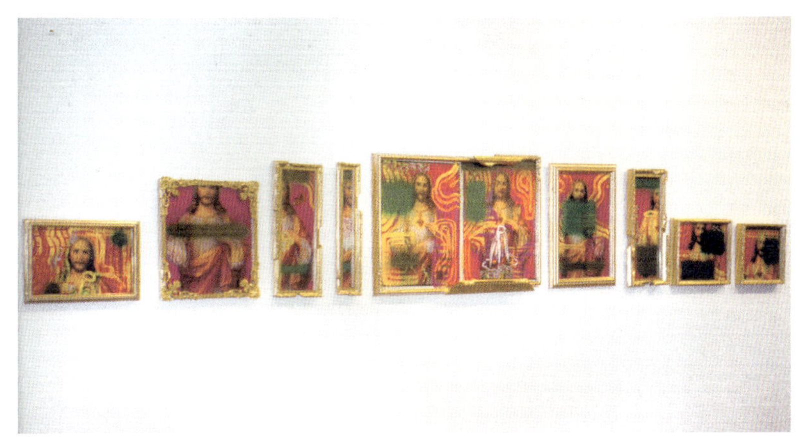

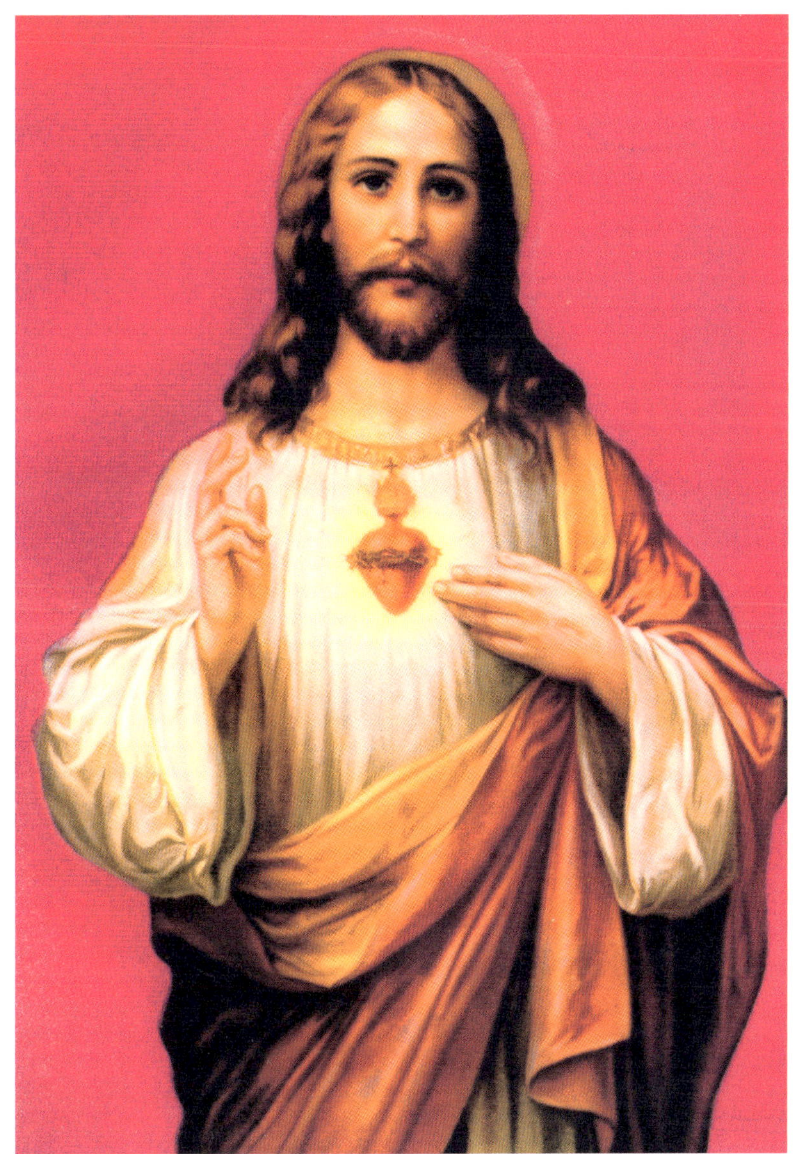

Yesue 7 · 1992 · Acrylic, print, frames
Yesue · 1989–1992 · Acrylic, liquid plastic, print

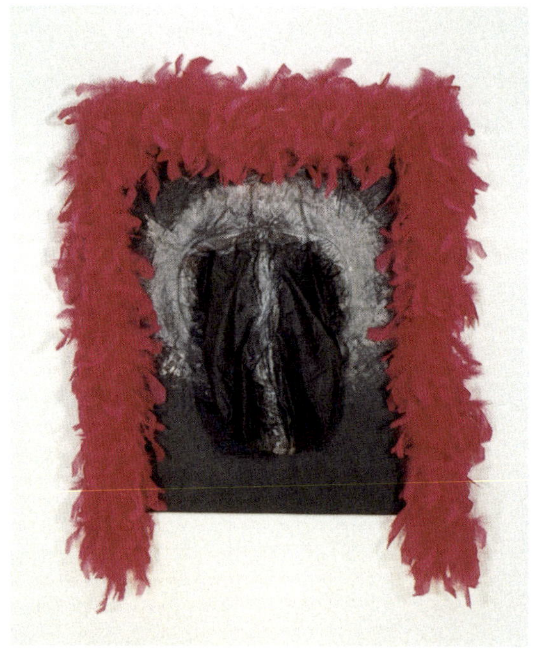

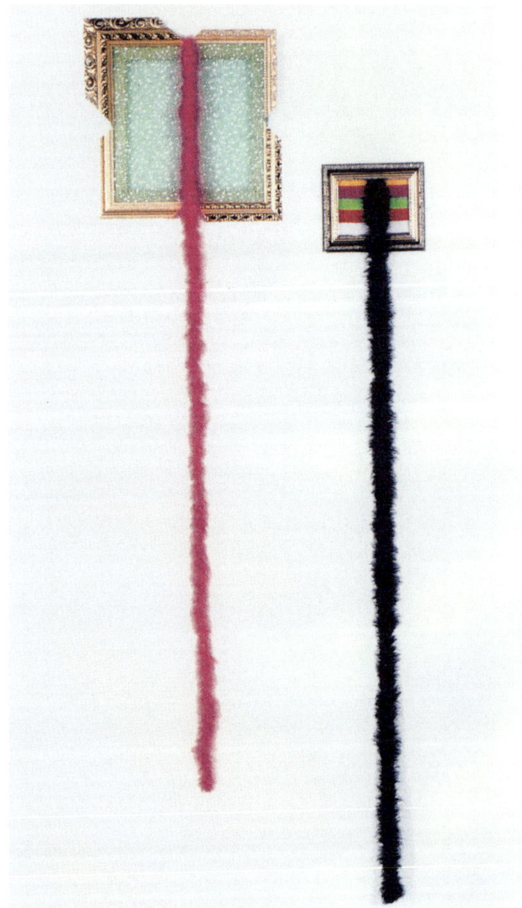

Christo · 1989–90 · US Army poncho, feather, wood
Dream and Tails 1–2 · 1989–92 · Wood, acrylic, cloth, dye feather

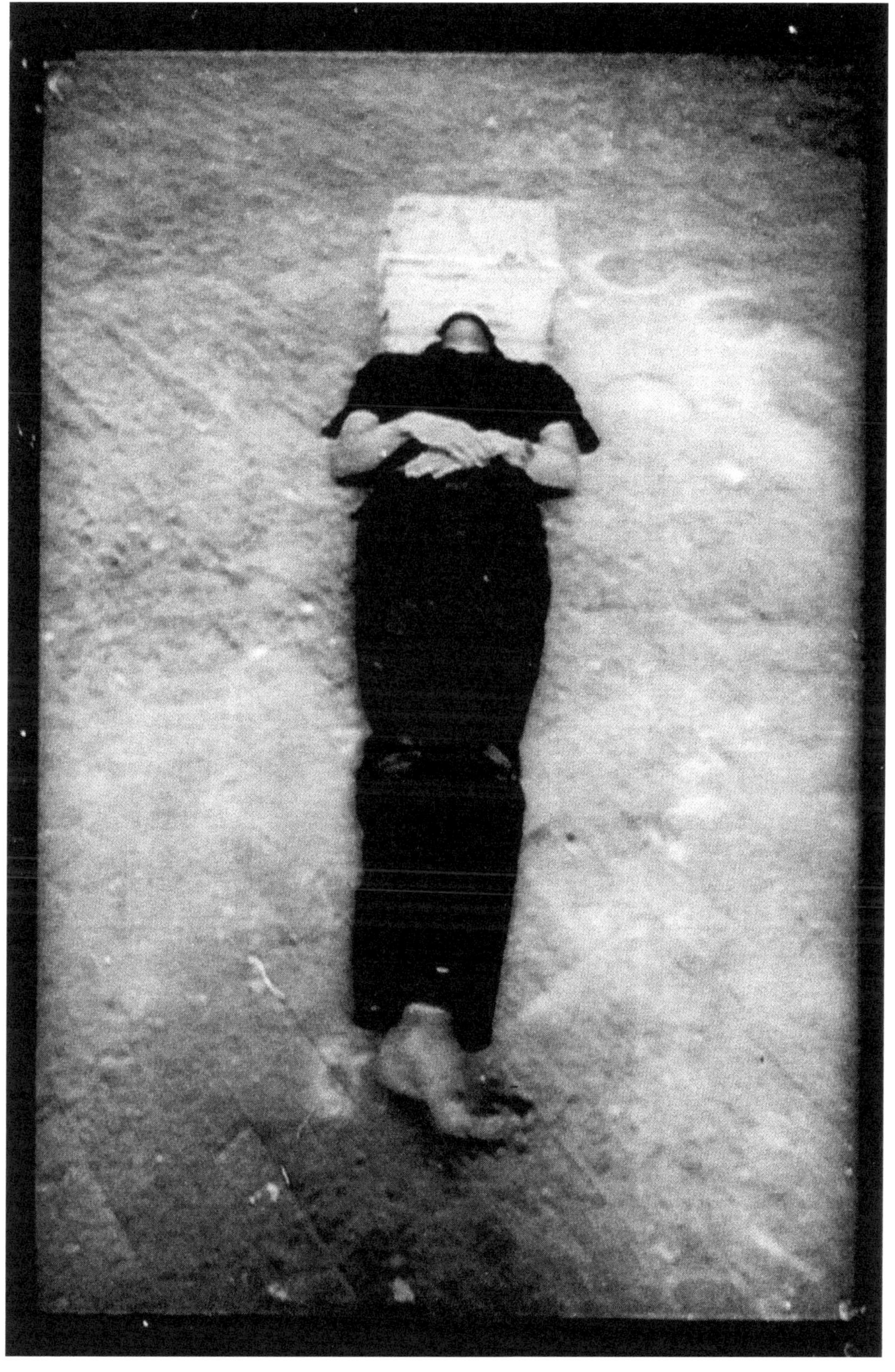

Untitled Photo 01 · 1992 · C-print

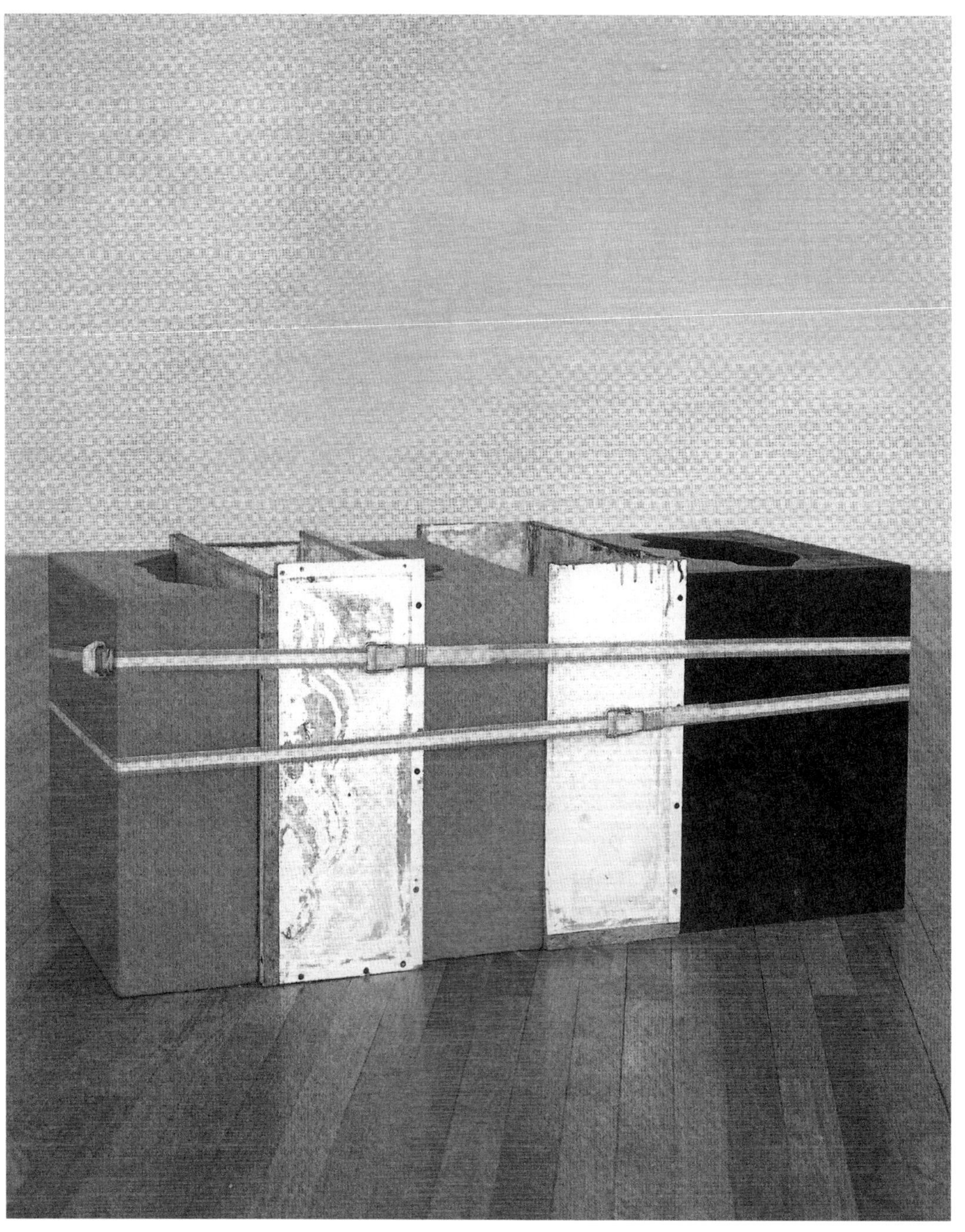

Box for Mold, Mold for Box · 1995 · Cement, wood, Pepto-Bismol, banding straps, lacquer, wax

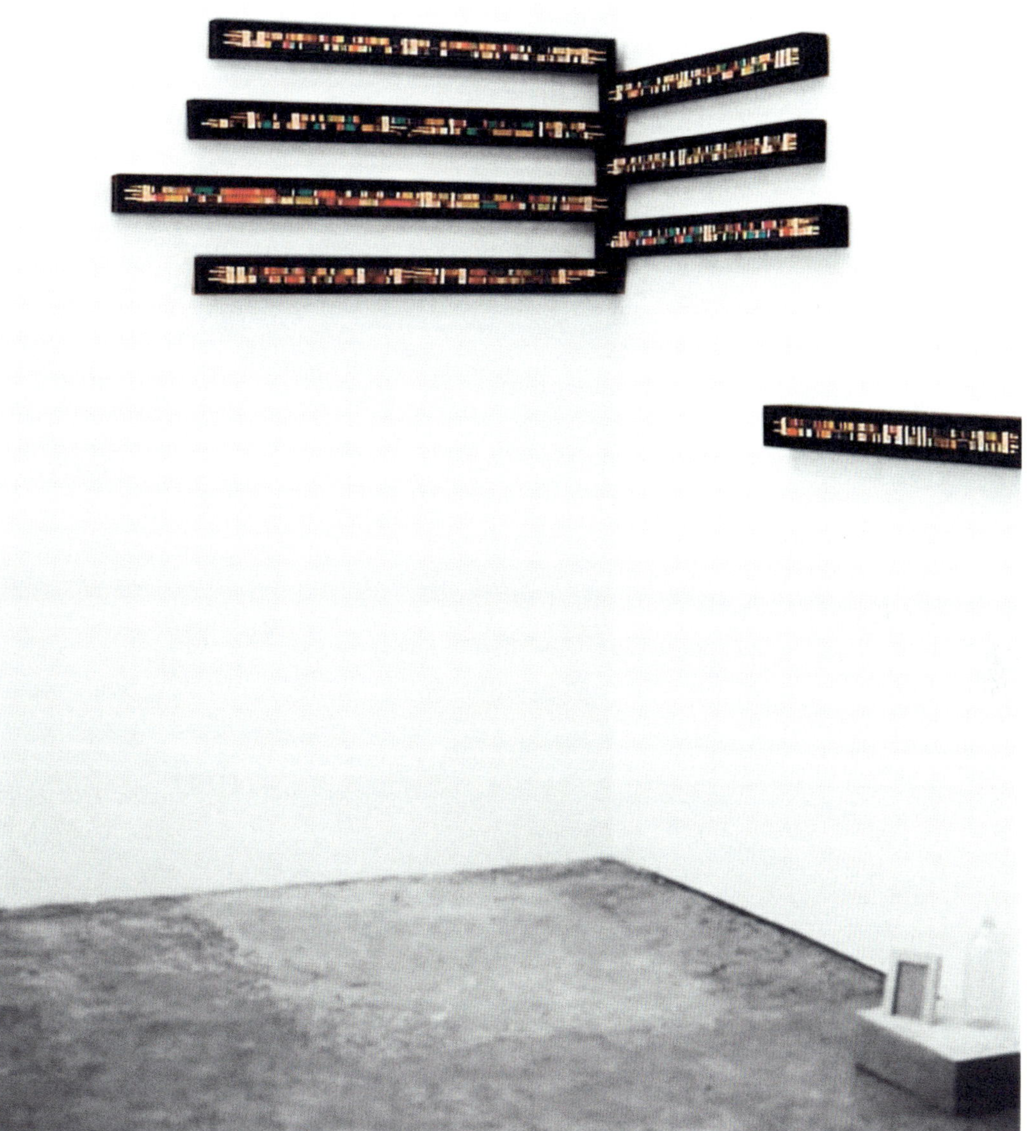

The Cliché · 1996 · Acrylic paint on paper, wood, plastic, linen

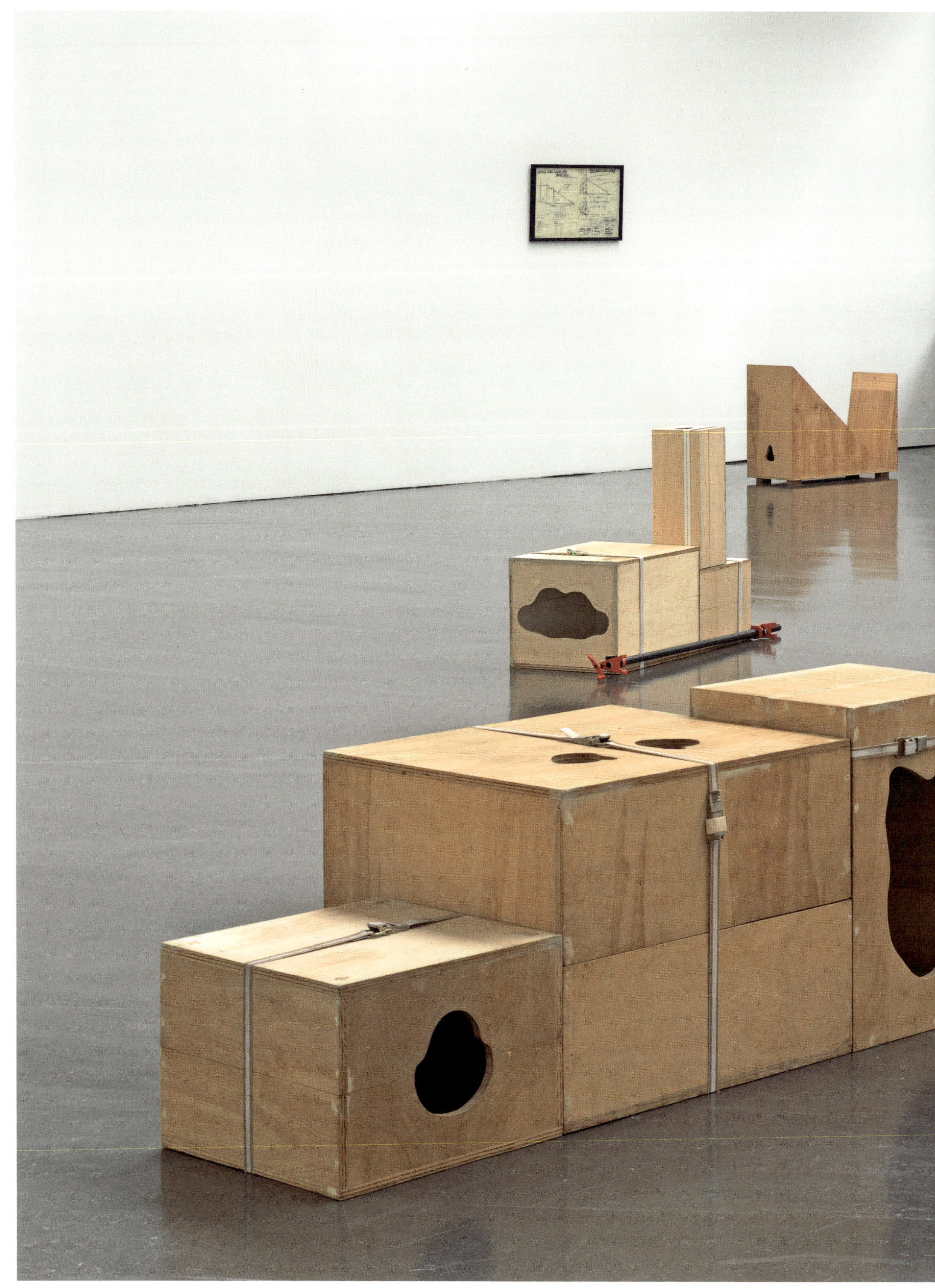

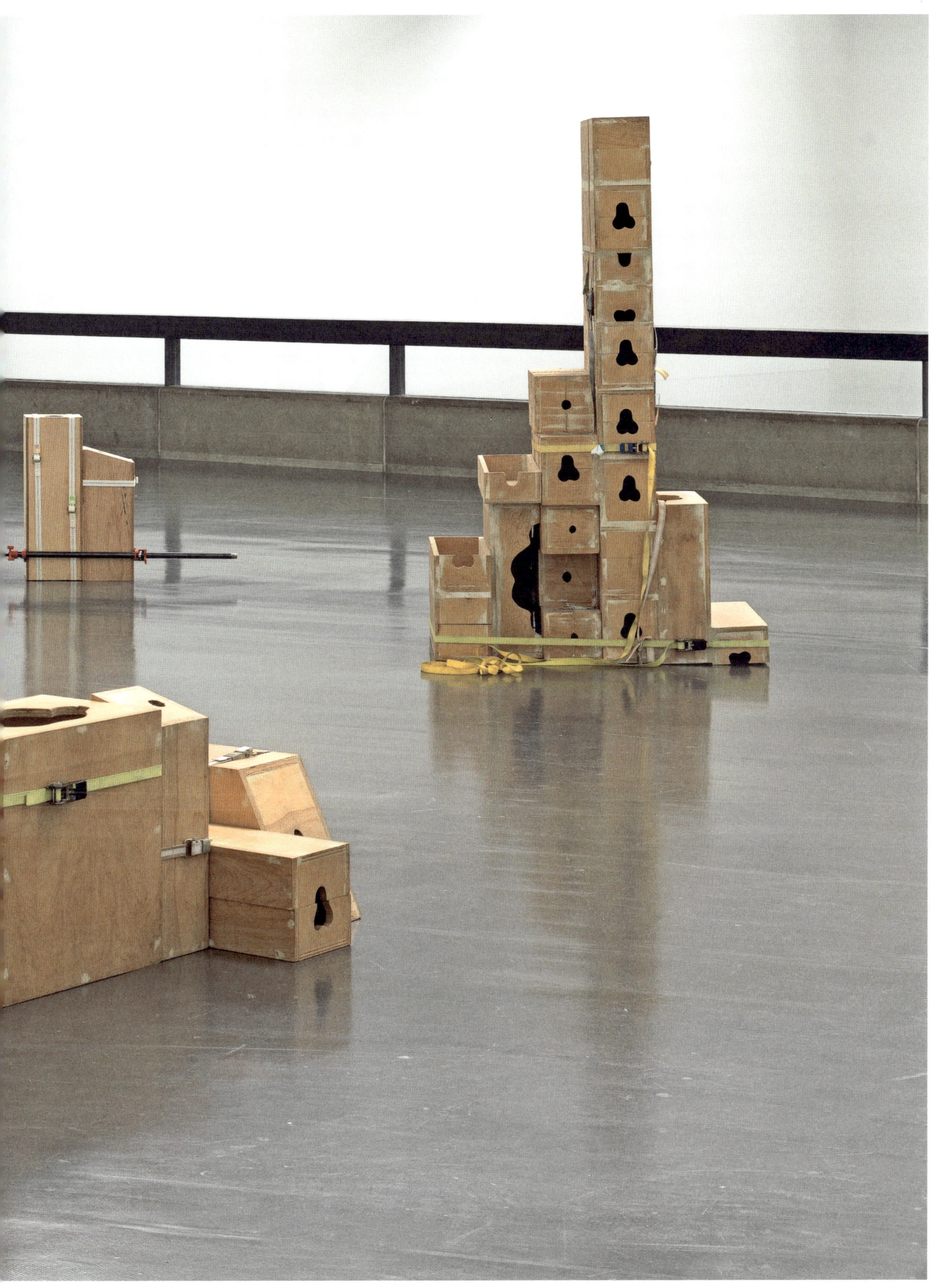

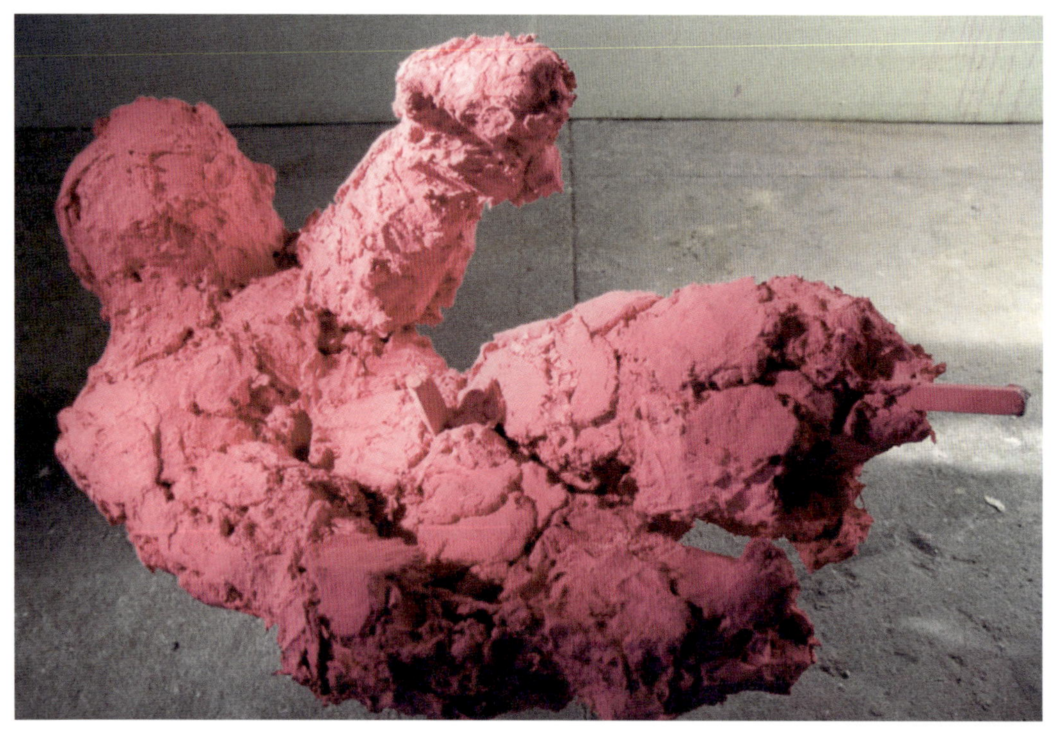

pp. 108–109 · Installation view at Kunsthalle Düsseldorf (2015)
Untitled · 1996 · Pepto-Bismol, wood

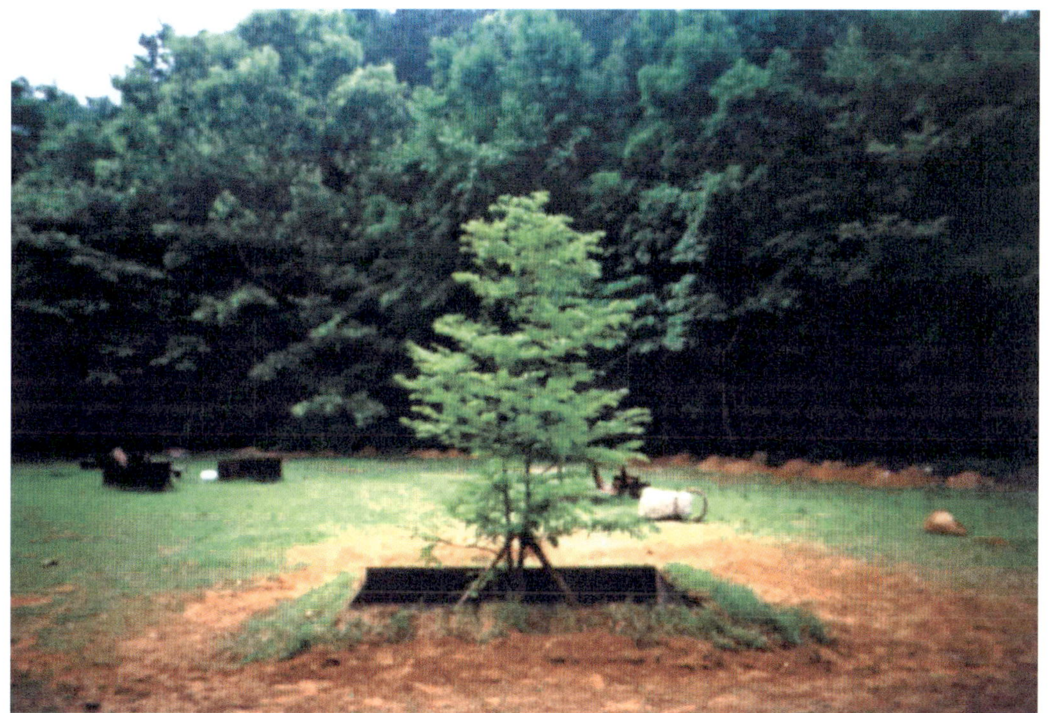

Soil Project (Planting the Tree under the Ground/Farwell to the 20th Century) · 1998–2000 · Tree, soil, labor

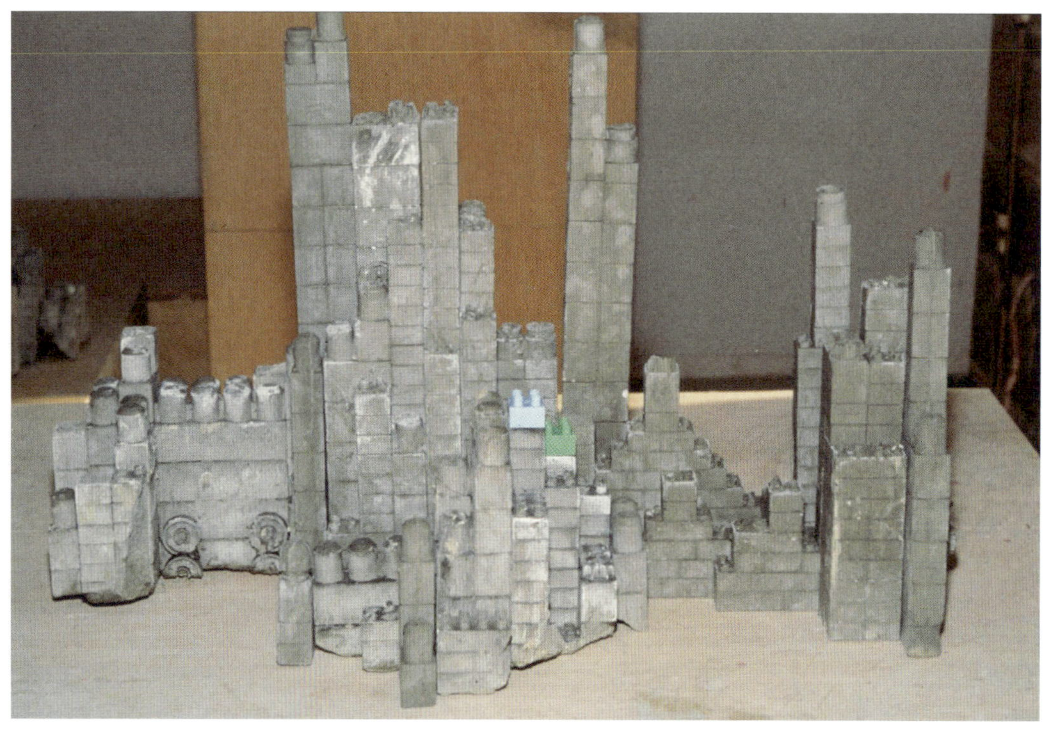

Left Over 6 · 1998–99 · White cement casting out of Lego blocks sculpture

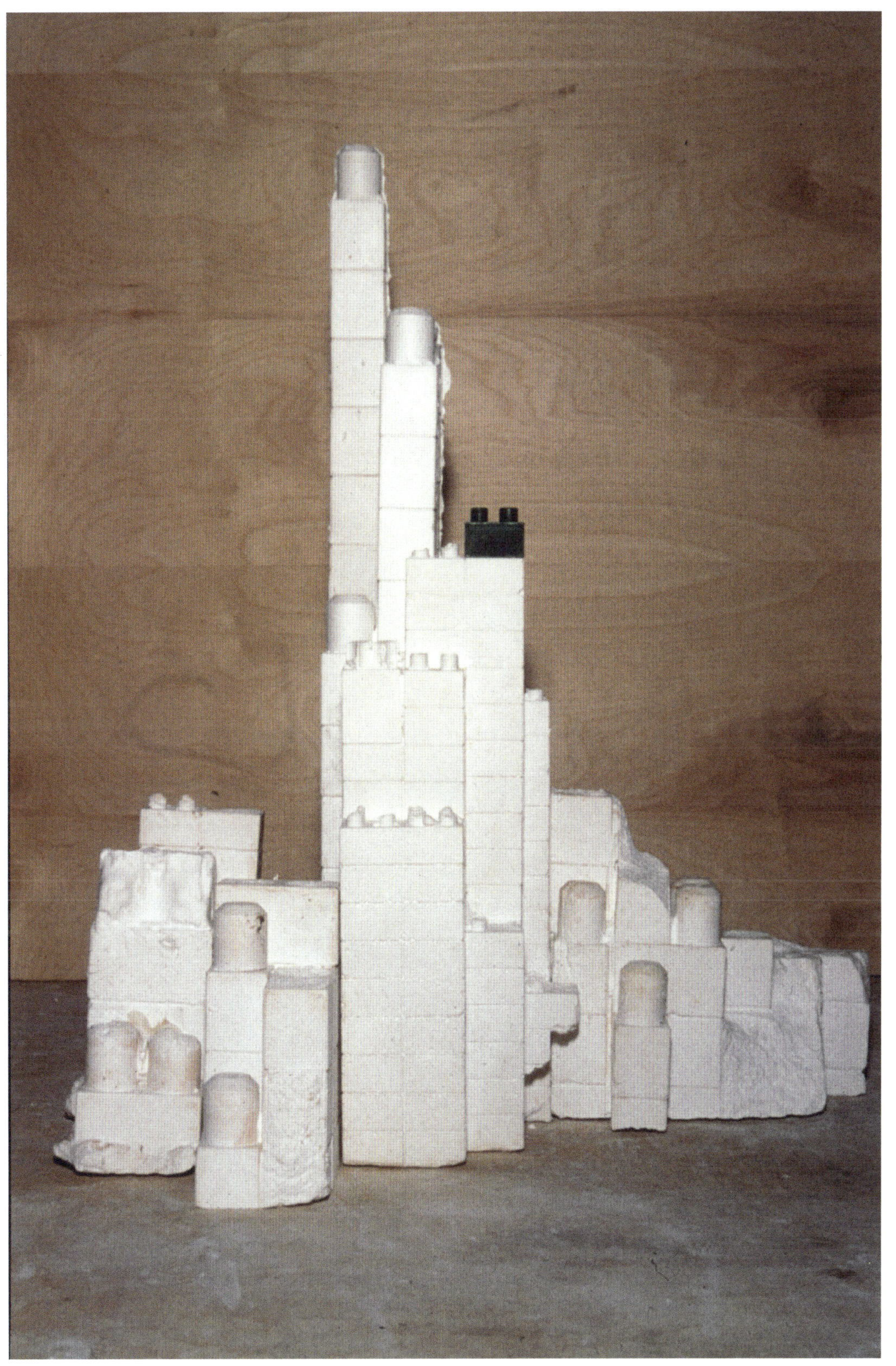

Left Over 4 · 1998–99 · White cement casting out of Lego blocks sculpture

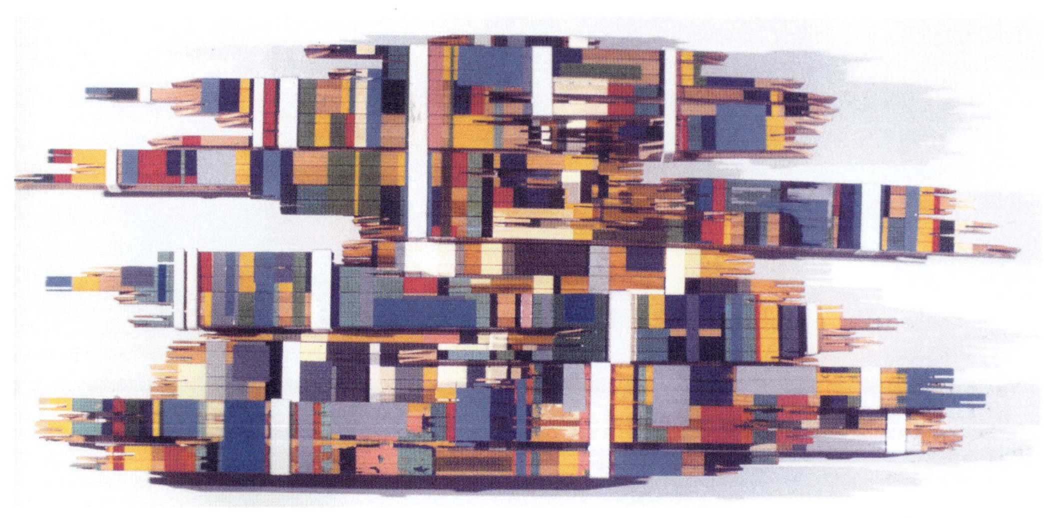

Edge Painting/Fat Free · 1996–97 · Acrylic, wood, cloth

Installation view at the exhibition *Continental Shift* at Ludwig Forum für Internationale Kunst (2000) showing (f.l.t.r.):
Database Base Painting Series #1, Fcat2 · 2000 · VUTEk ink on mesh, mounted on canvas
Database Base Painting Series #1, Fcat1 · 2000 · VUTEk ink on mesh, mounted on canvas

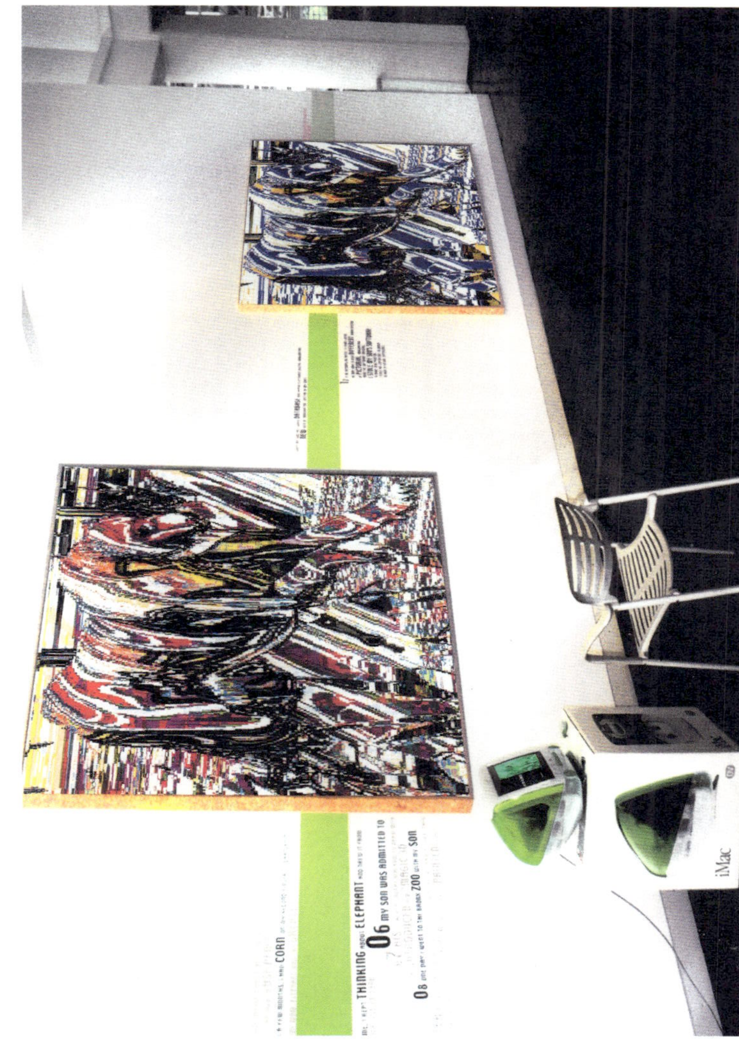

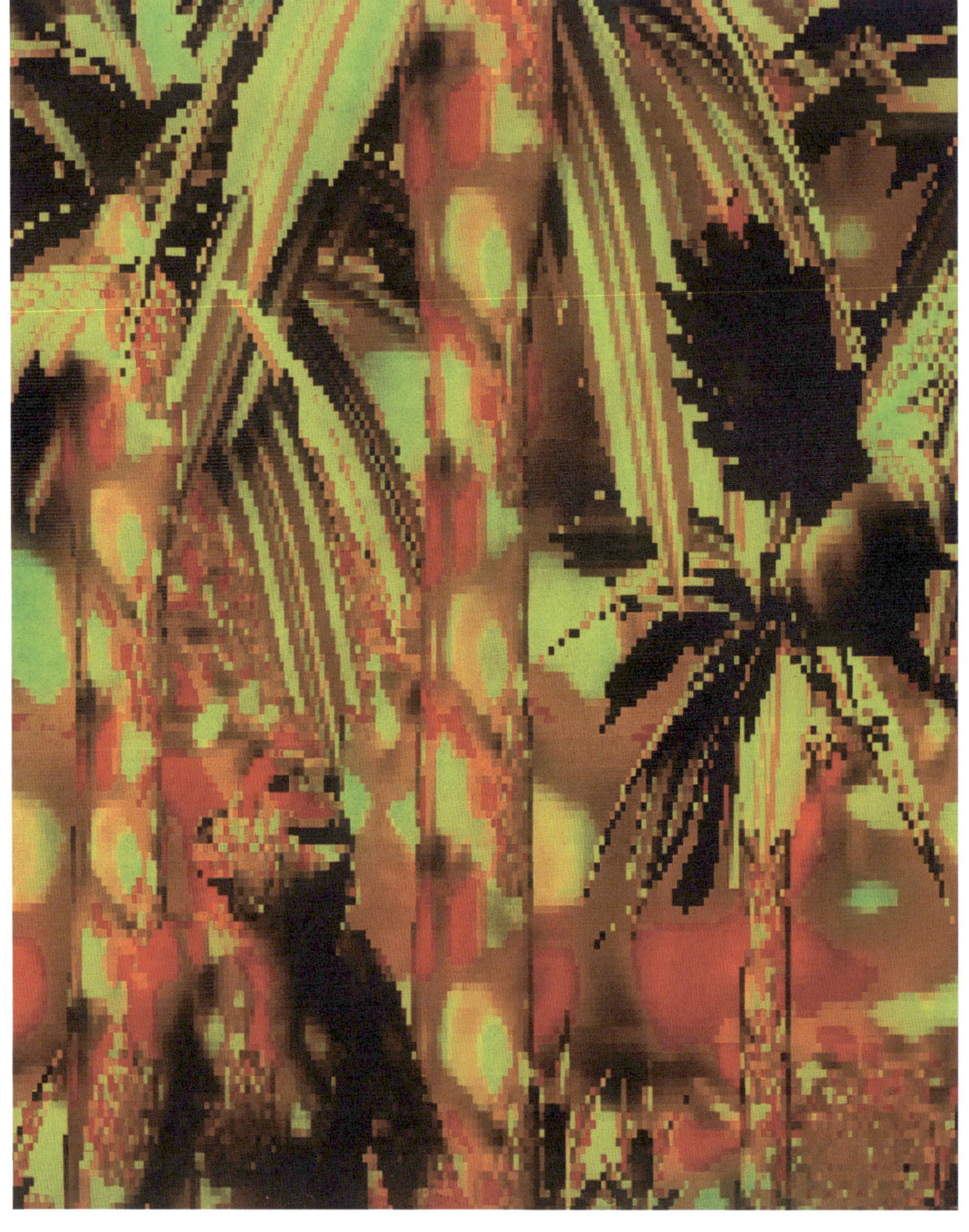

Animal Totem #11 · 2000-03 · VUTEk ink on mesh, mounted on canvas
The Museum of Contemporary Art, Los Angeles · Gift of Mike Kelley

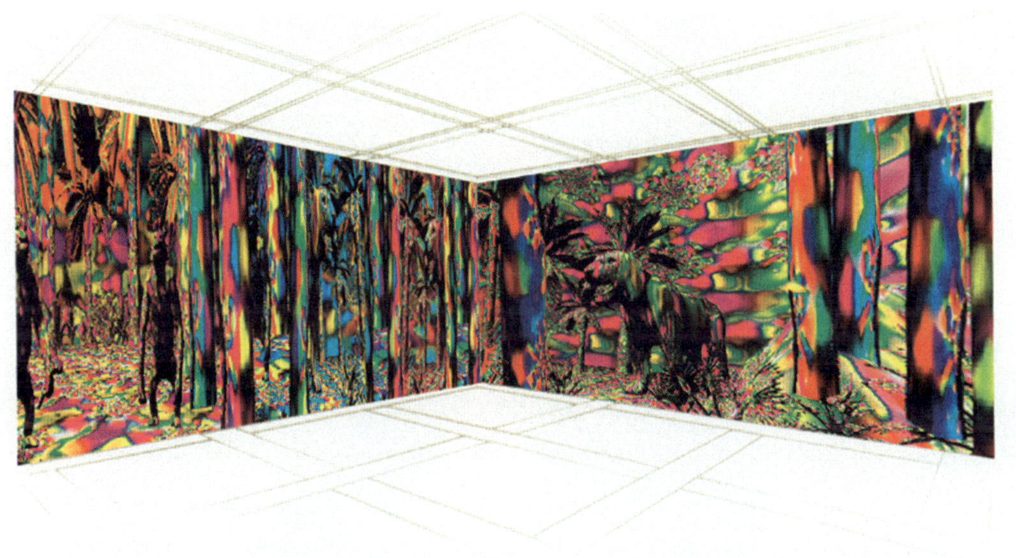

Jungle/Database Painting · 1999 · Virtual installation draft

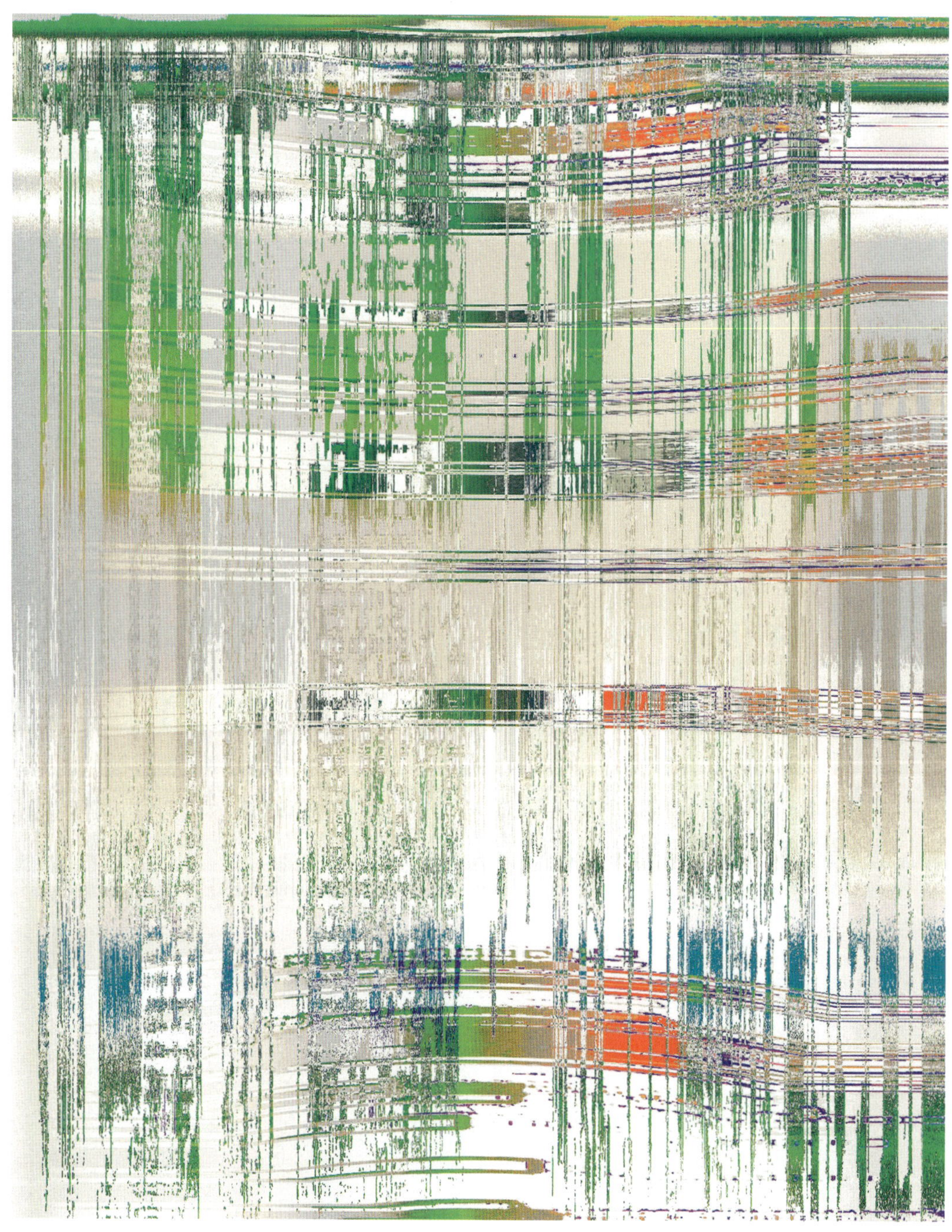

Abstraktes Bild *09–6* · 2001 · VUTEk ink on mesh, mounted on canvas

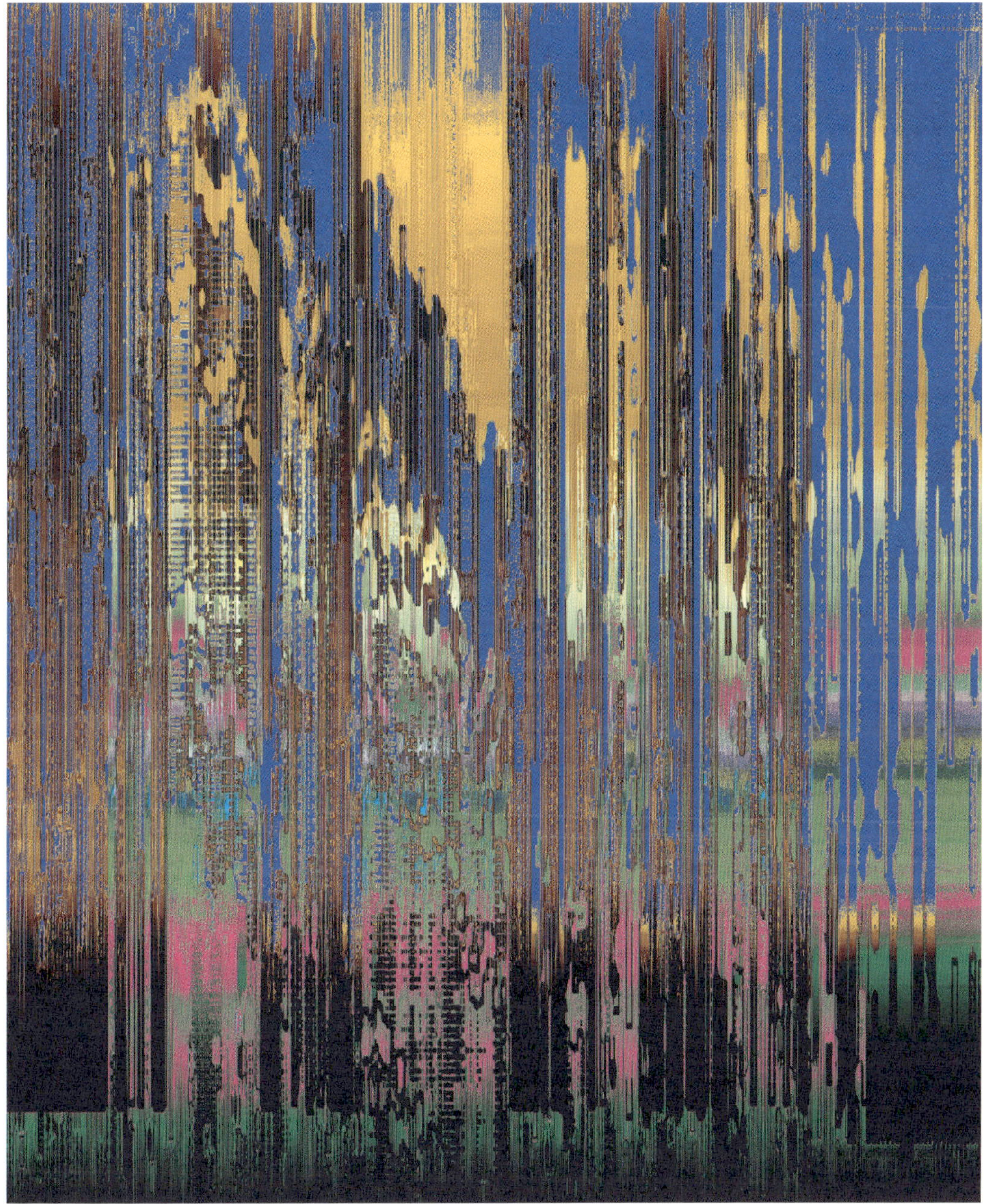

Abstraktes Bild 22–01 · 1999–2003 · VUTEk ink on mesh, mounted on canvas

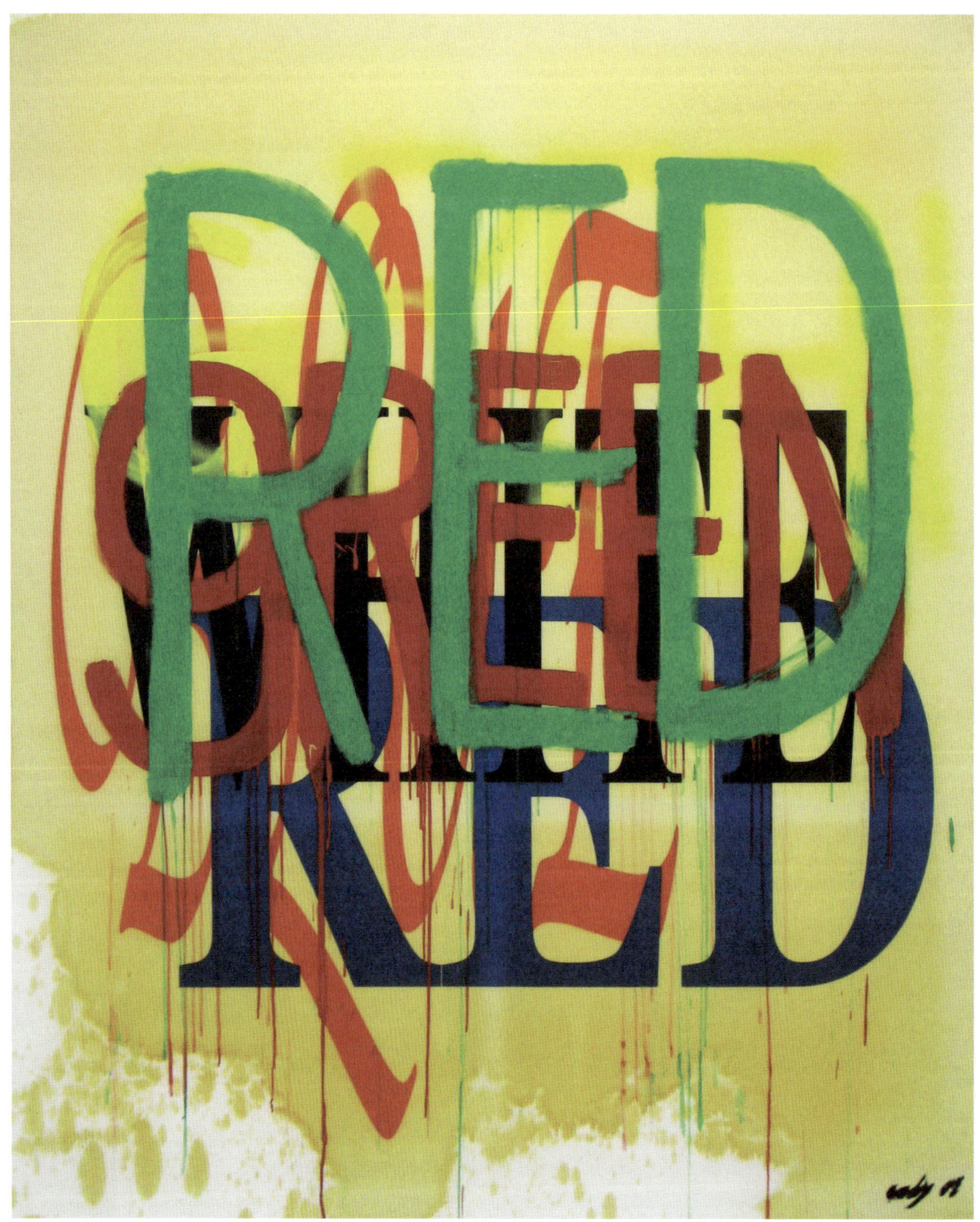

Delirium Trigger – RED · 2008 · Oil, VUTEk ink on canvas

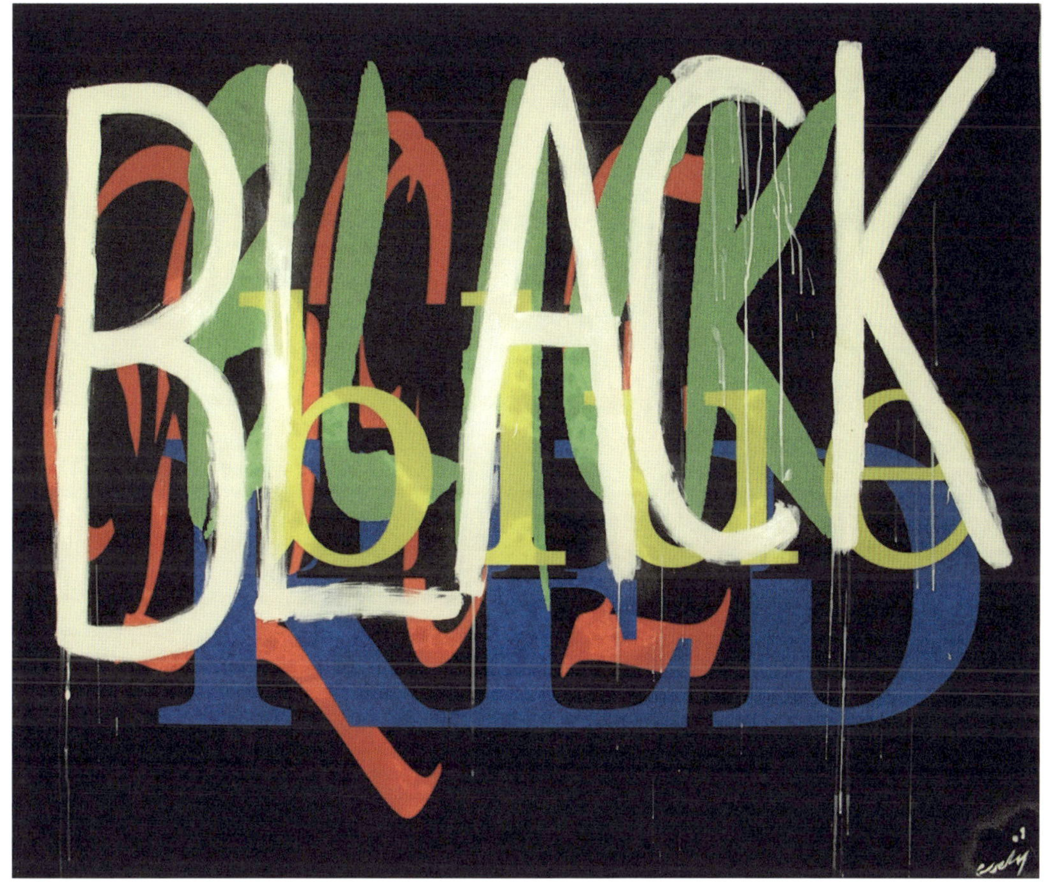

Delirium Trigger – BLACK · 2008 · Oil, acrylic, VUTEk ink on canvas

Zero Consciousness 3 · 2009–10 · Paper collage

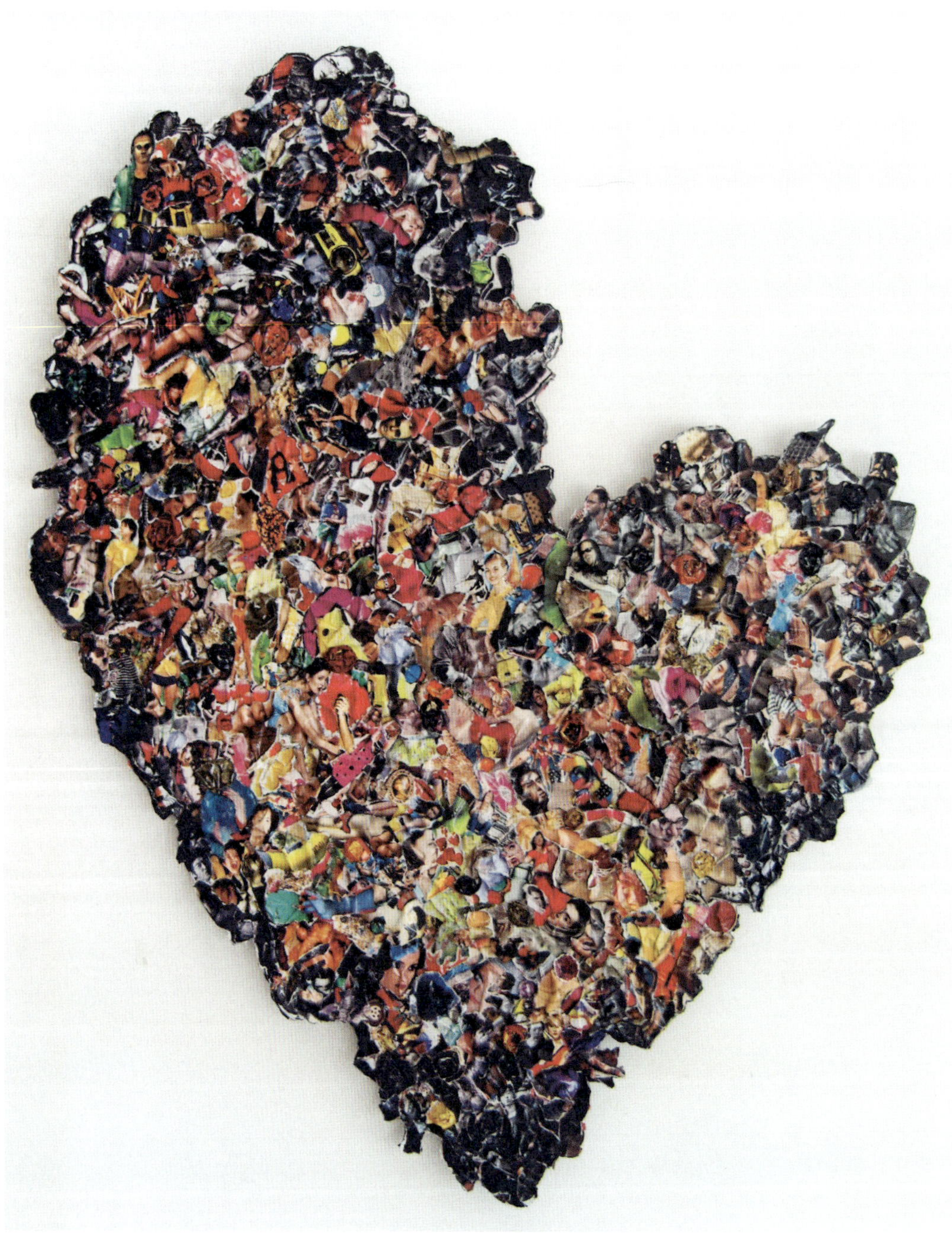

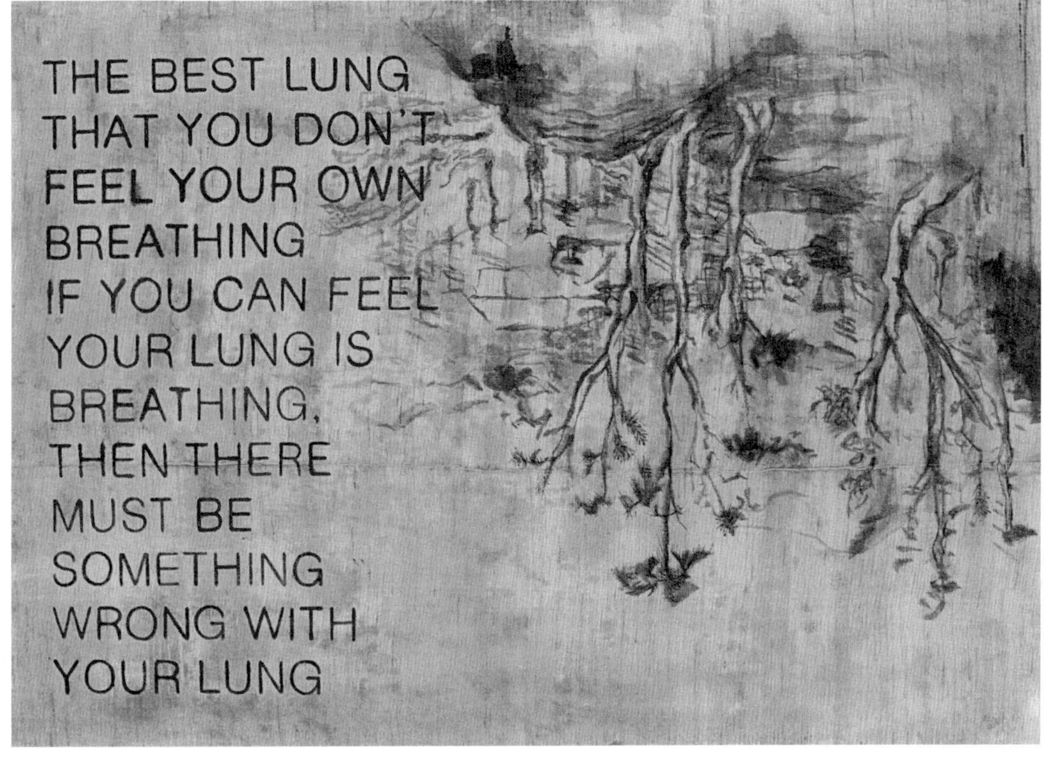

The Best Lung That You Don't Feel Your Own Breathing · 2011–13 · Chinese ink stick, cashew paint, shell powder, bone glue, hemp cloth

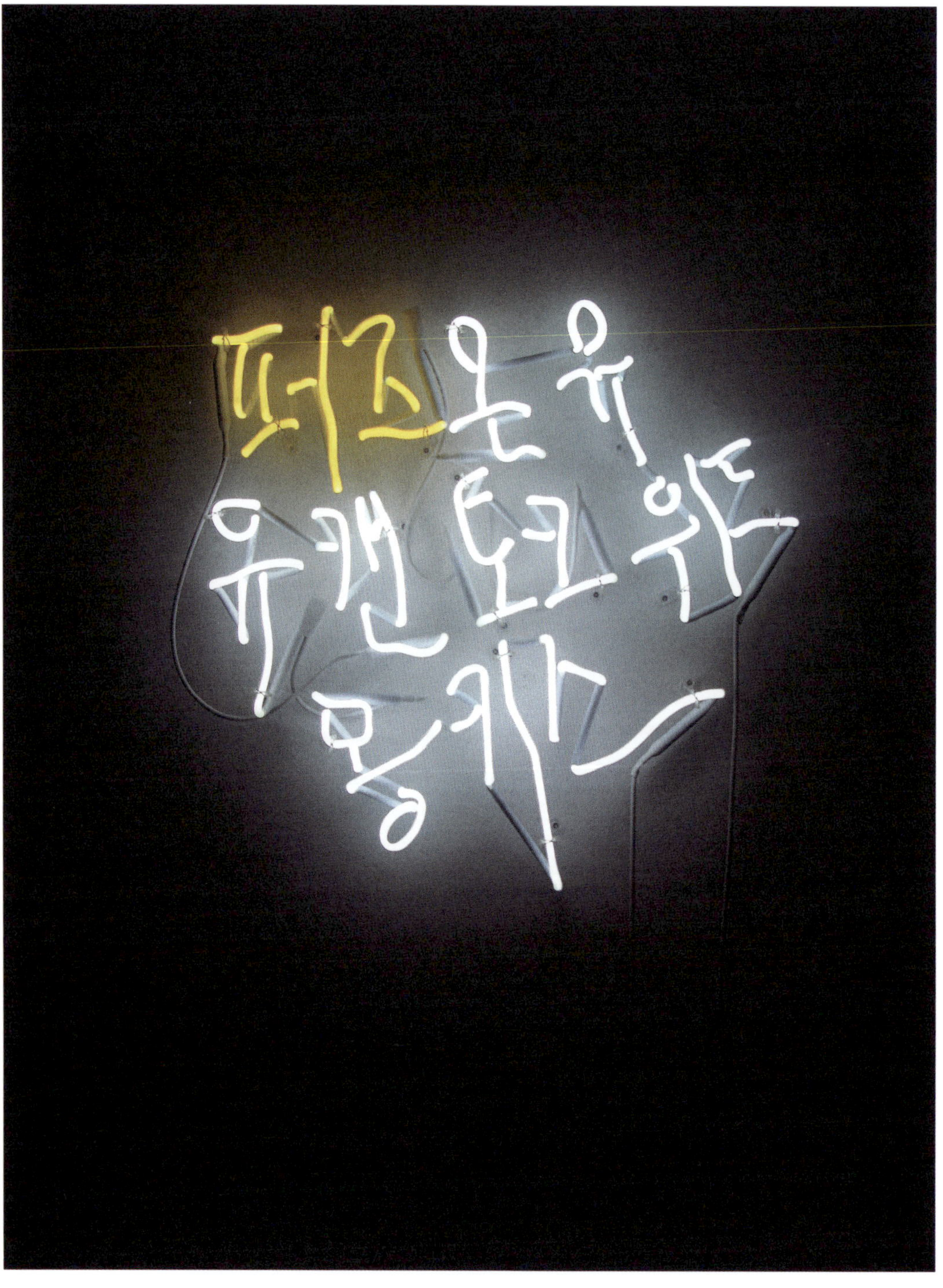

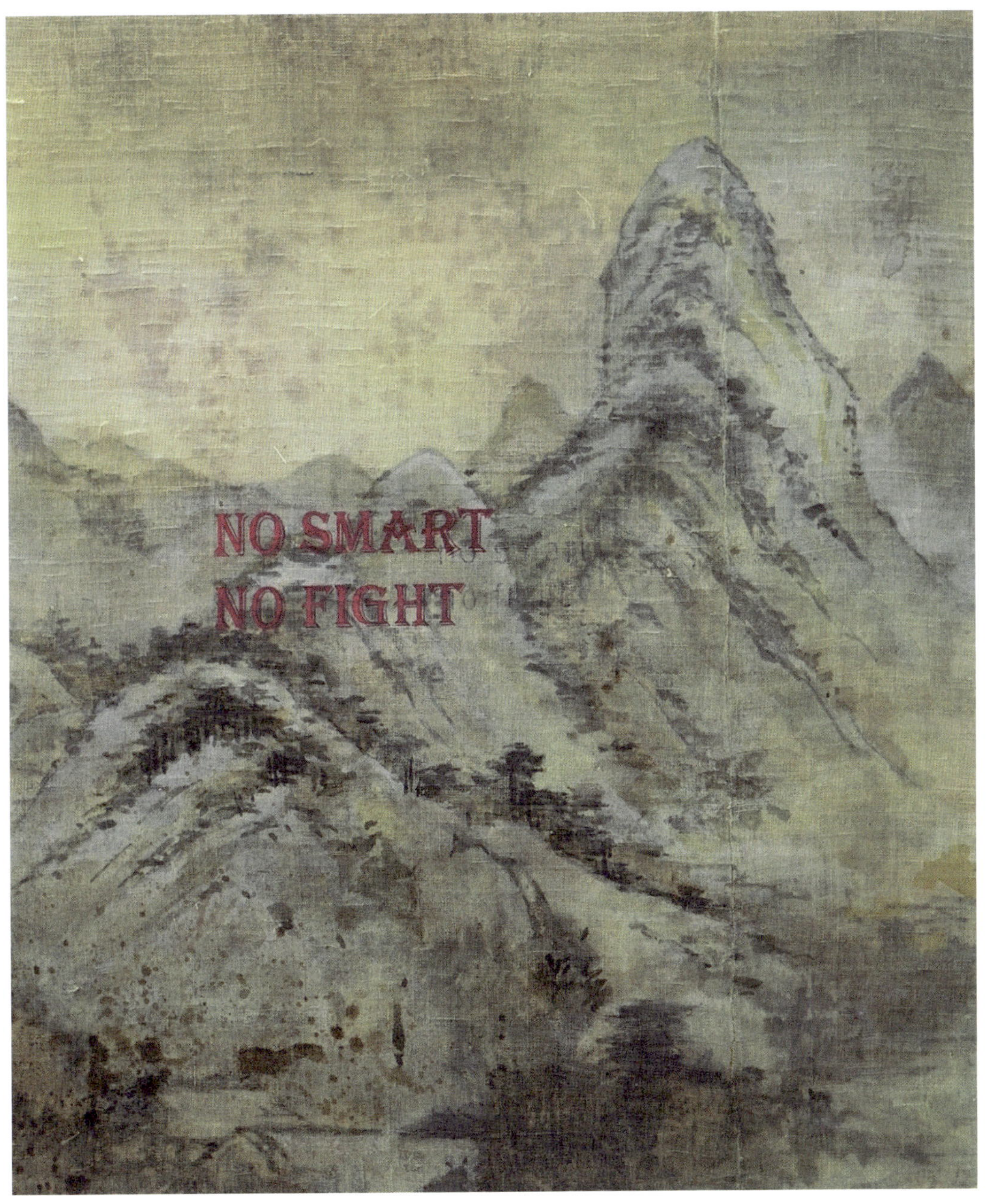

No Smart No Fight · 2011–13 · Chinese ink stick, cashew paint, shell powder, bone glue, hemp cloth

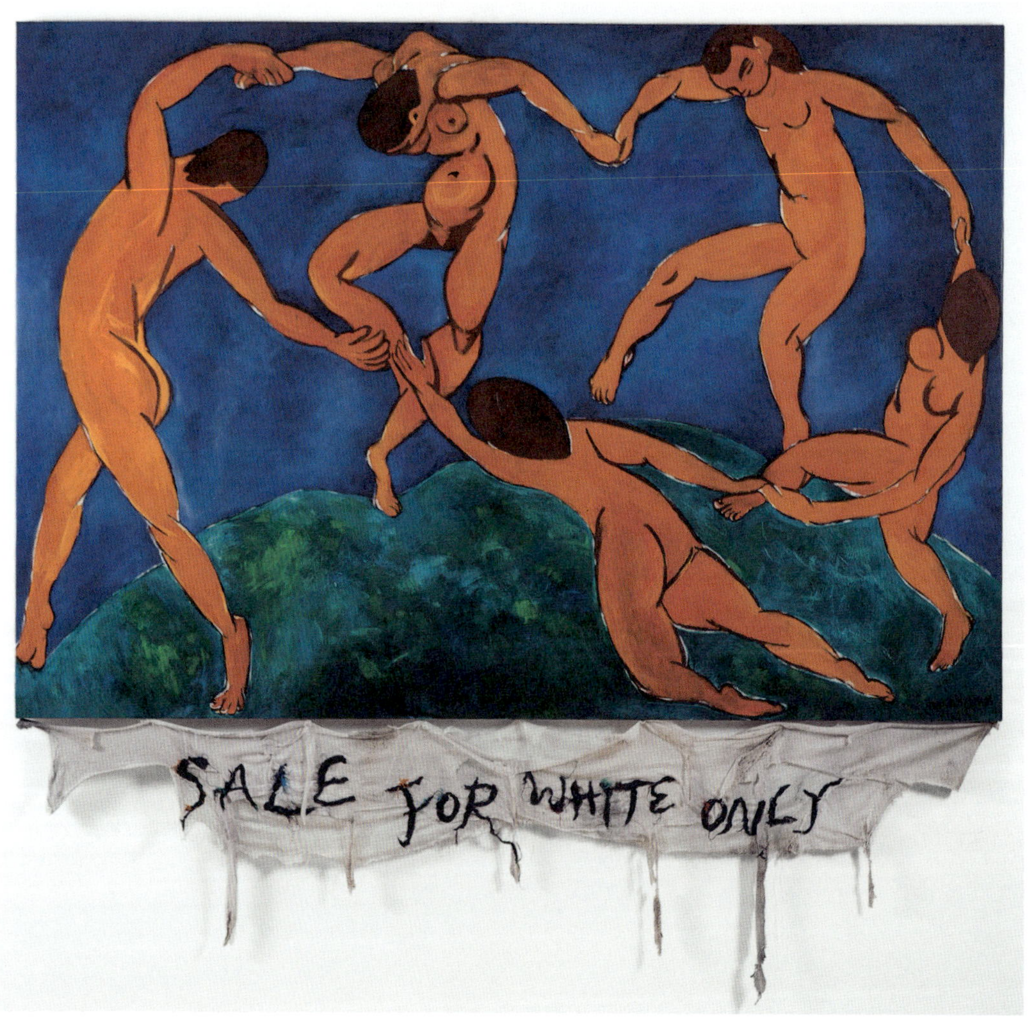

Episteme Sabotage – Sale for White Only · 2014 · Oil on canvas, cloth, thread

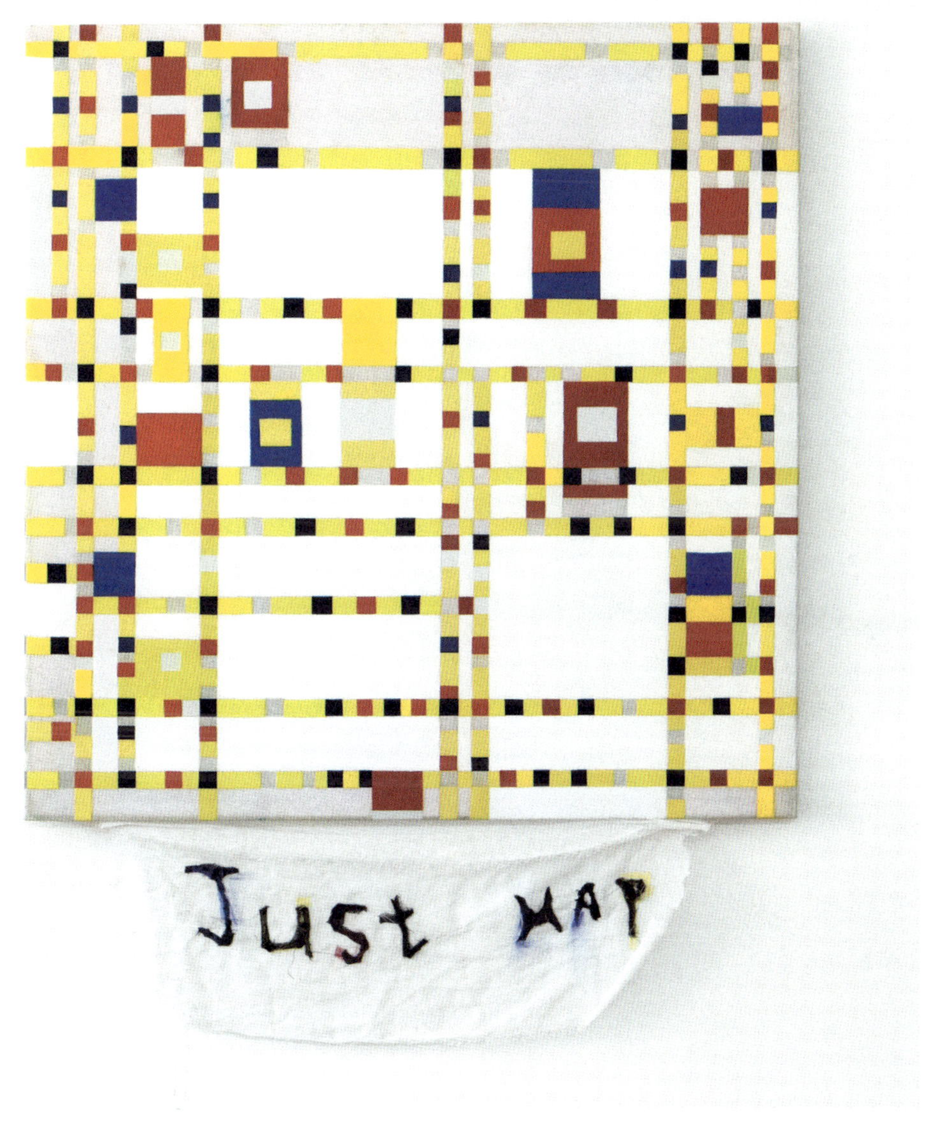

Episteme Sabotage – Just Map · 2014 · Oil on canvas, cloth, thread
Courtesy Stiftung Museum Kunstpalast, Düsseldorf

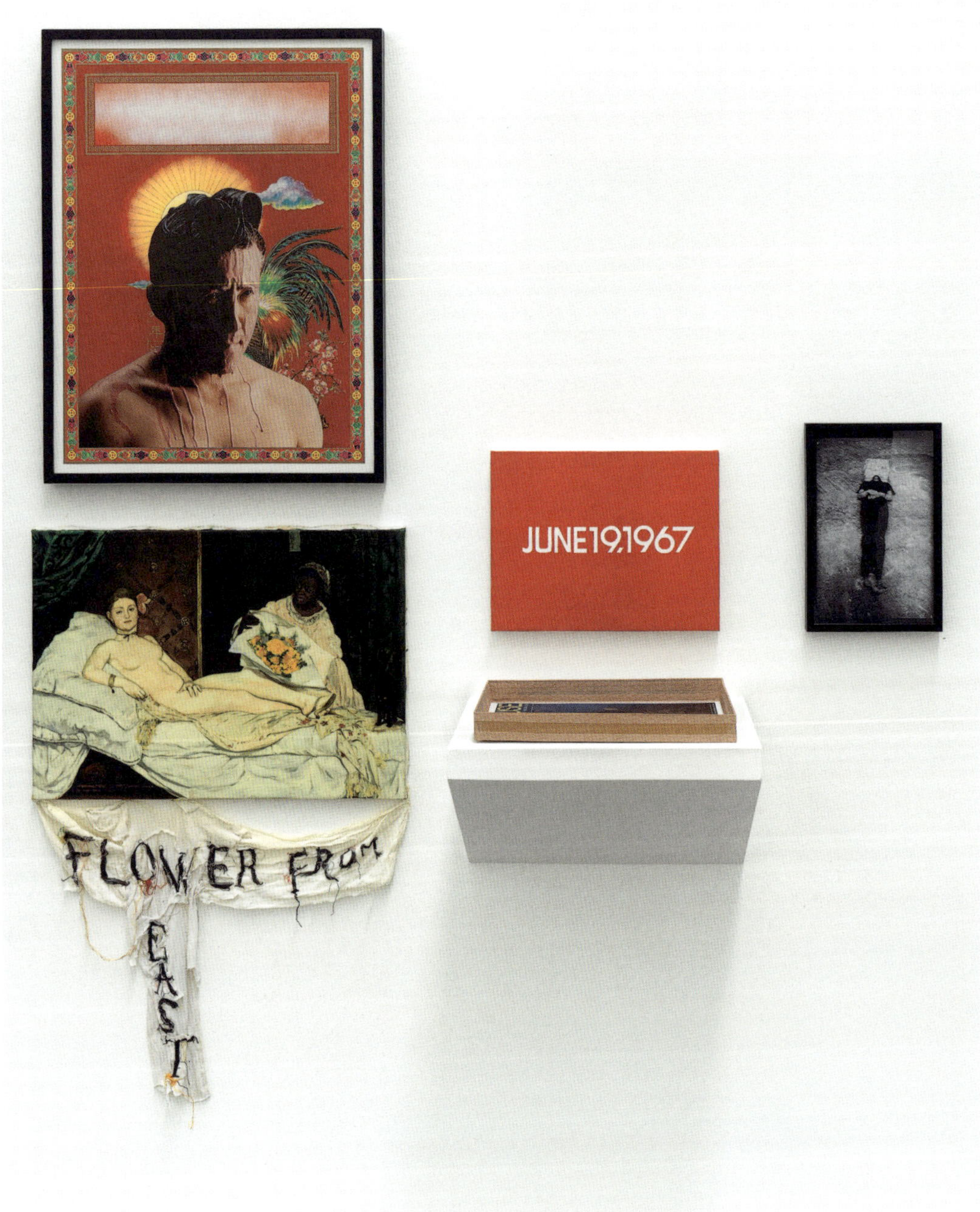

FLOWER FROM
EAST
JUNE19,1967

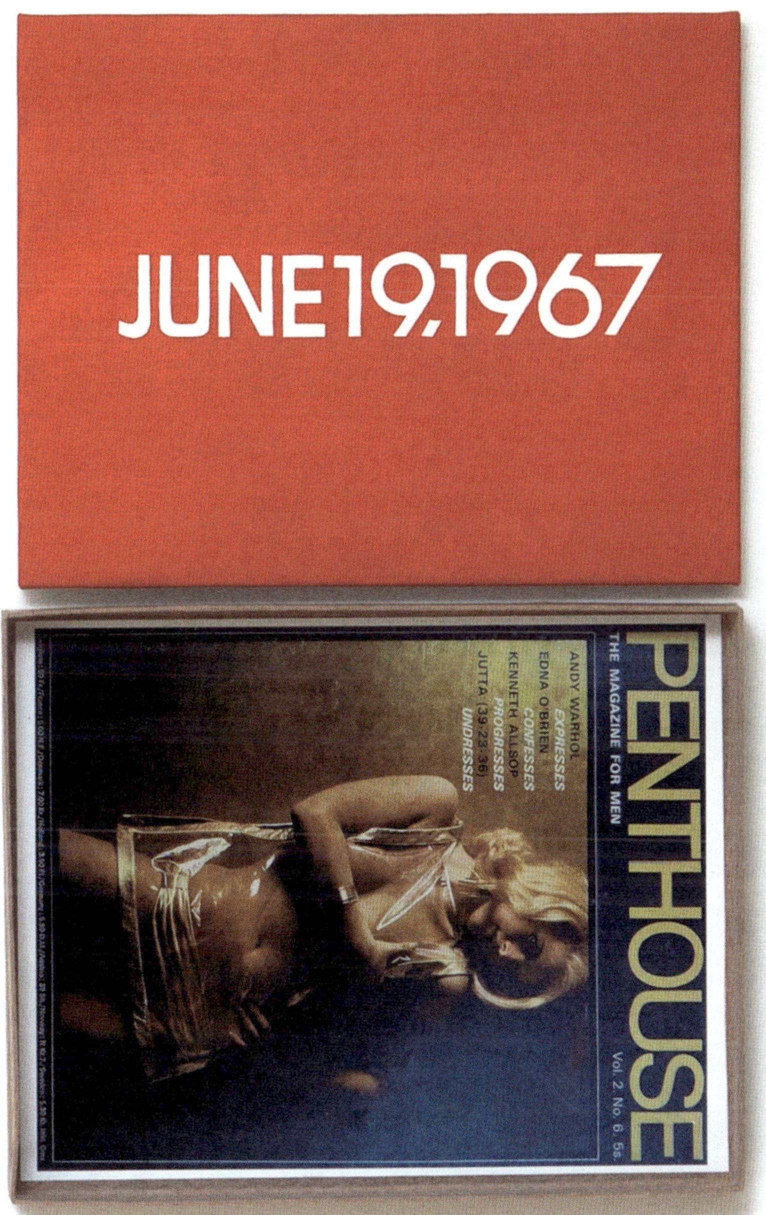

JUNE 19,1967
PENTHOUSE
THE MAGAZINE FOR MEN
ANDY WARHOL
EXPRESSES
EDNA O'BRIEN
CONFESSES
KENNETH ALLSOP
PROGRESSES
JUTTA (39-23-36)
UNDRESSES
Vol. 2. No. 6. 5s.

Episteme Sabotage – *Penthouse* · 2014 · Acrylic on canvas, magazine cover

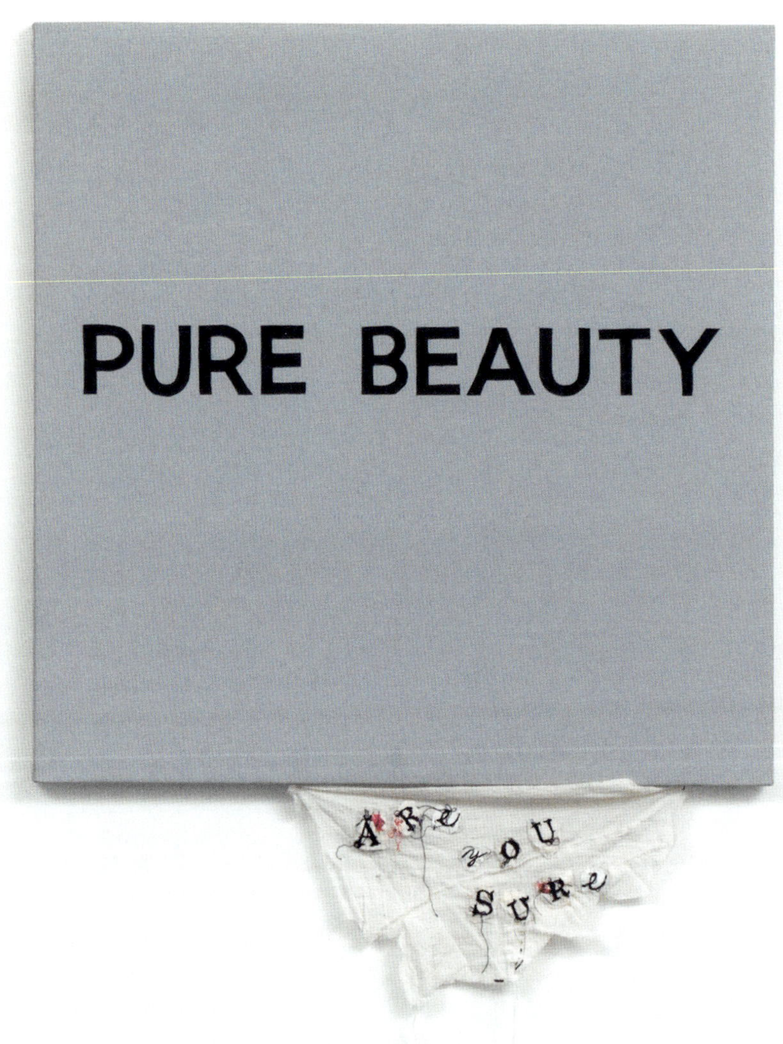

Episteme Sabotage – *Are You Sure* · 2014 · Oil on canvas, cloth, thread

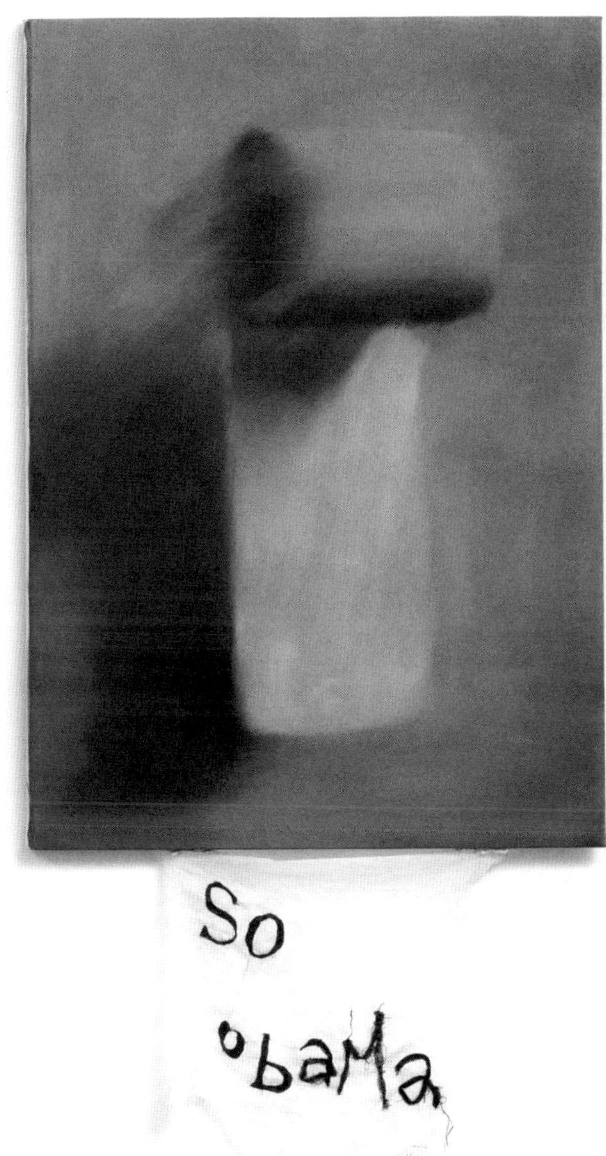

Episteme Sabotage – *So Obama* · 2014 · Oil on canvas, cloth, thread

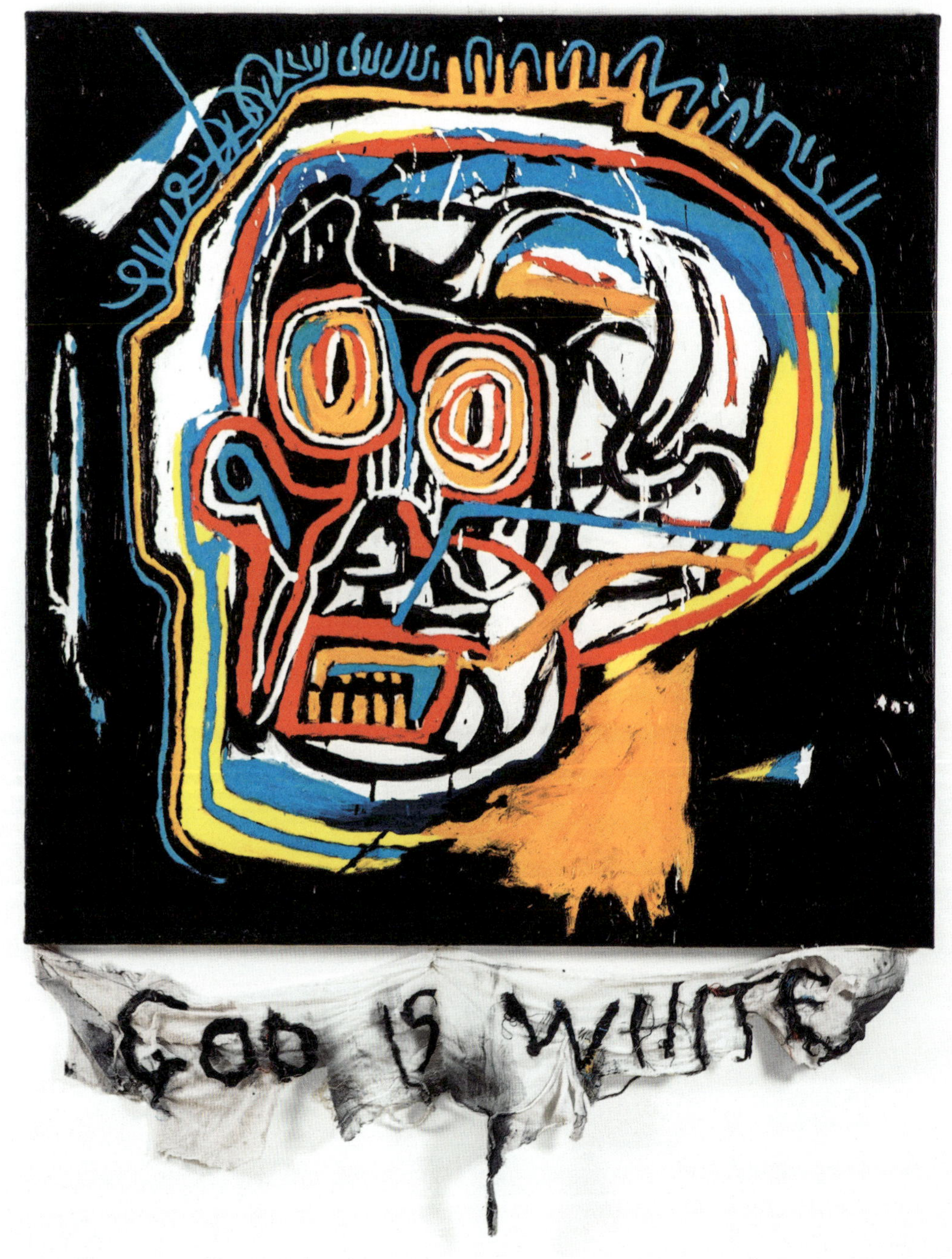

Episteme Sabotage – God is White · 2014 · Oil on canvas, cloth, thread

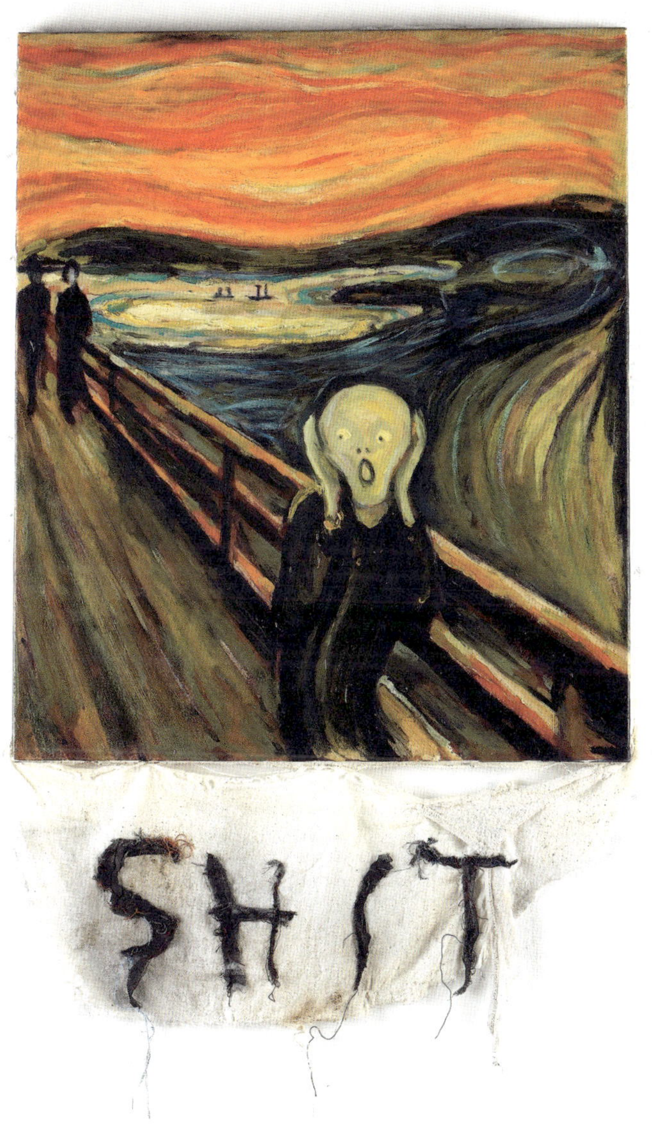

Episteme Sabotage – *Shit* · 2014 · Oil on canvas, cloth, thread

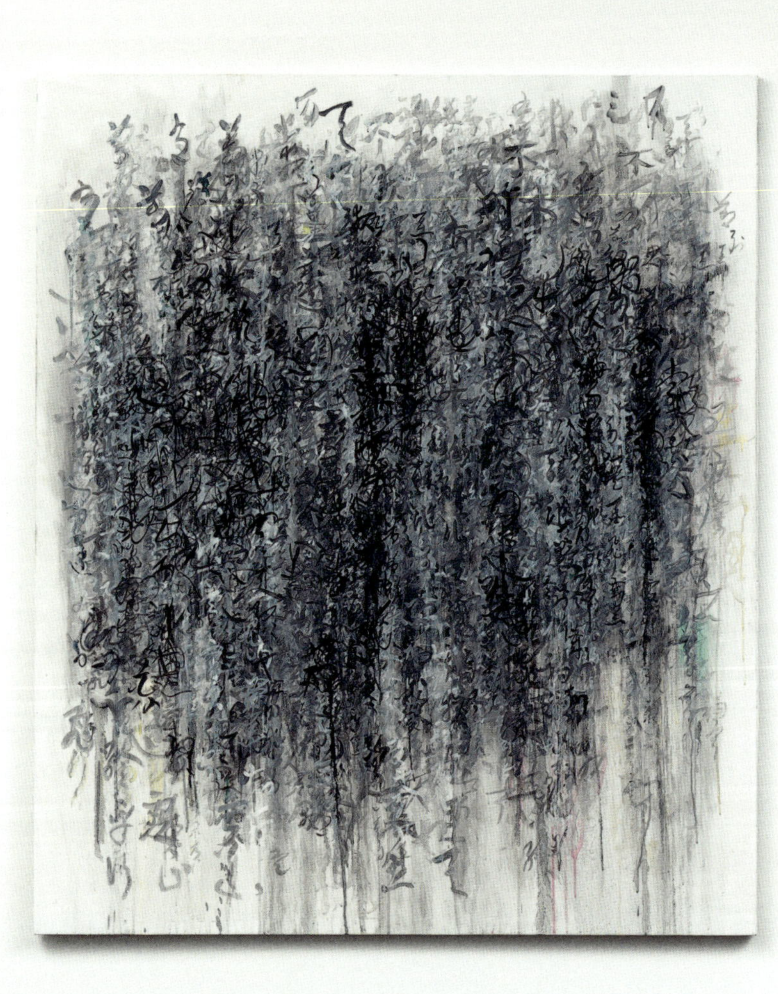

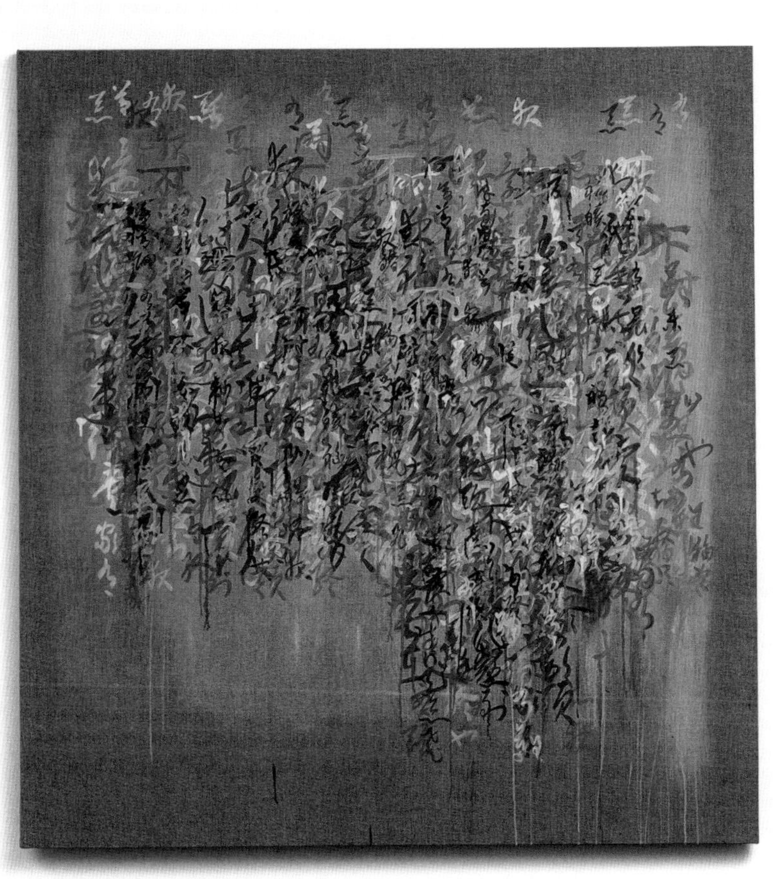

Ideographic Disappearence 1 "Myung shim bogam," literally: "bright heartmind precious" · 2015 · Oil on canvas
Ideographic Disappearence 2 "Myung shim bogam," literally: "bright heartmind precious" · 2015 · Oil on canvas
Installation view at Kunsthalle Düsseldorf (2015)

Cody Hyun Choi

Born (25.11.1961) in Seoul, lives and works in Seoul and New York

AWARDS AND GRANTS

2011
Excellent Book Select, Ministry of Culture, Sports and Tourism, Seoul, Korea

1994
International Studio and Curatorial Program (ISCP) Grant, New York, USA

1993
International Studio and Curatorial Program (ISCP) Grant, New York, USA

1990
San Marino League, Fine Art Association Scholarship Award, San Marino, California, USA

1989
Pasadena Art Alliance, Fine Art Scholarship Award, Pasadena, California, USA

1988
Art Center One Hundred Scholarship Award, Pasadena, California, USA

1987
Hallmark Cards Inc. Minority Scholarship Award, Kansas City, Missouri, USA

1987
Art Center One Hundred Scholarship Award, Pasadena, California, USA

EDUCATION
1986–90
Art Center College of Design, Pasadena, California, USA

1980–83
Korea University, Department of Sociology, Seoul, Korea

SELECTED SOLO EXHIBITIONS/ SOLO PROJECTS

2016
Cody Choi, Culture Cuts
Musée d'Art Contemporain de Marseille, Musée de Marseille, Marseille, France

2015
Cody Choi, Culture Cuts
Kunsthalle Düsseldorf, Düsseldorf, Germany

2011
2nd Chapter of Post-Colonialism
PKM Gallery, Seoul, Korea

2009
Luminous Future
Konkuk University, Seoul, Korea

2008
Cody Choi: Passage in Peking
PKM Gallery, Peking, China

2006
Cody Choi: Passage
PKM Gallery, Seoul, Korea

2003
Multiplying Difference: Post-Ready Made
PKM Gallery, Seoul, Korea

2000
New Pictorialism, Data Base Painting– We Are in Jungle
Kukje Gallery, Seoul, Korea,

1998
The End of the 20th Century Soil Project
Kaywon University of Art and Design,
Uiwang-si, Gyeonggi-do, Korea

1996
The Thinker, December
Deitch Projects, New York, USA
*Not Conservative in Conserve (Becoming
a Gesture of the Real)*
Kukje Gallery, Seoul, Korea

1993
Blow My Top
Mee Gun Gallery, Seoul, Korea

1992
Dip the Pink
Total Art Museum, Yangju-si,
Gyeonggi-do, Korea
Cody Choi
Mee Gun Gallery, Seoul, Korea

SELECTED GROUP EXHIBITIONS
2014
*Busan Biennale, Voyage to Biennale: 50 Years
of Contemporary Korean Art in Overseas
Biennales*
Busan Museum of Art, Busan Cultural
Center, Busan, Korea

2012
A Tribute to Mike Kelley
MOCA, The Museum of Contemporary
Art, Los Angeles, California, USA

2011
The New Epicenter: Chapter 2 Post-Human
Woomin Art Center, Cheongju, Korea

2010
2010 Media Art Festival, Digifesta
Gwangju Biennale Exhibition Center,

Kwangju, Korea
Oh! Masterpieces
Gyeonggi MoMA, Gyeonggi Museum
of Modern Art, Korea

2008
6th Busan Biennale
Busan Museum of Art, Busan, Korea
Meme Trackers
Song Zhuang Art Center, Peking, China

2007
Art Beijing 2007
National Agricultural Exhibition Center,
Peking, China

2006
The 6th Shanghai Biennale, Hyper Design
Shanghai Art Museum, Shanghai, China
Paper Tainer
Paper Tainer Museum, Seoul Olympic
Park, Seoul, Korea
Web Tree
Gallery Samji, Seoul, Korea

2004
Standing on a Bridge
Arario Gallery, Cheonan, Korea
Digital Sublime: New Masters of Universe
Museum of Contemporary Art, Taipei,
Taiwan
Corner/de-Corner: Bruce Nauman + Cody Choi
PKM Gallery, Seoul, Korea

2002
*The 2nd Seoul International Media Art Biennale,
Luna's Flow: Media_City Seoul 2002*
Seoul Museum of Art, Seoul, Korea
Snapshot
Beaver College Art Gallery, Glenside,
Pennsylvania, USA

2001
Ghost World
CAIS Gallery, Seoul, Korea
Digital Dreams, Analogue Desires
Arko Art Center, Seoul, Korea

2000
Snapshot
The Contemporary (Museum), Baltimore,
Maryland, USA
New York University Faculty Exhibition
80 Washington Square East Gallery,
New York, USA
*Continental Shift-Aachen/Heerien/Liega/
Maastricht*
Ludwig Forum für Internationale Kunst,
Aachen, Germany
Bonnefantenmuseum, Maastricht,
Netherlands
Musée d'Art moderne et d'Art
contemporain, Liége, Belgium
Stadsgalerij Heerlen, Heerlen,
Netherlands

1999
Mug Shots: Performing Persona
Atrium Gallery, University of
Connecticut at Storrs, Connecticut, USA
A Room with a View
Sixth@Prince Fine Art, New York, USA

1998
Body in Painting
Hanlim Museum, Daejeon, Korea
Daelim Cultural Foundation, Seoul,
Korea
Food Matters
Center Gallery, Bucknell University,
Pennsylvania, USA
ES Vandam Gallery, New York, USA
The Space/Incoded
Kukje Gallery, Seoul, Korea

1997
First Look
New York, USA
New York University Faculty Exhibition
80 Washington Square East Gallery,
New York, USA

1996
Images of Self
Schick Art Gallery, Skidmore College,
Saratoga Springs, New York, USA
*L'art au corps: le corps exposé de Man Ray à
nos jours*
Musée d'Art Contemporain de Marseille,
Musée de Marseille, Marseille, France
Imaginary Anatomy
Pasinger Fabrik, Munich, Germany
Mr. Edison's Black Box
The World Wide Web, Phenix.com, Paris,
France
*Exhibition for New York Asian Woman's
Center Auction*
New York Asian Women's Center, New
York, USA
Not a Metaphor
Art Projects International, New York,
USA
New York University Faculty Exhibition
APEX ART Gallery, New York, USA
Fun House Exhibition Part One and Two
ES Vandam Gallery, New York, USA
I.S.P. Open Studio
International Studio and Curatorial
Program, New York, USA
Border Crawl
Kukje Gallery, Seoul, Korea

1994
I.S.P. Open Studio
International Studio and Curatorial
Program, New York, USA
Selected Group Exhibition
American Fine Arts, New York, USA

Flesh and Ciphers
Here Art Foundation, New York, USA
I.C. Editions
Susan Inglett Gallery, New York, USA

1988
Organic Realism
Annex Gallery, Pasadena, California, USA

Exhibition Organizer/Book Editor
2002
Media_City Seoul 2002, International
Exhibition Organizer, Seoul, Korea
1998–2000
Lusitania Press, Contributing Editor,
New York, USA

Publications
Author
Choi, Cody. *Topography of 20th Century Culture*. Korea: Culturegrapher, 2010.

Choi, Cody. *Topography of Contemporary Culture*. Korea: Culturegrapher, 2006.

Choi, Cody. *Topography of 20th Century Culture for Understanding Contemporary Culture*. Korea: Ahn Graphics, 2006.

Co-Author
Park, Woo Chan, Keun Joon Lim, Suk Jae Lim, Hyun Hwa Kim, Mee Kyung Kim, and Cody Choi. *Abstraction, Changed the World*. Exhibition catalogue. Korea: Gyeonggi Museum of Modern Art, 2013.

Park, Woo Chan, Jung Hee Lee, Bo Yeon Lee, Mee Kyung Kim, Cody Choi, and Sang Yong Shim. *Understanding of Modern and Contemporary East Asian Art*. Exhibition catalogue. Korea: Gyeonggi Museum of Modern Art, 2013.

Choi, Tae Man, Sang Chul Kim, Myung Woo Nho, Jin-Sup Yoon, Linda Inson Choy, Tcheon Nahm Park, Ban Ejung, Young Ok Kim, Dong Hee Yoon, Sumi Kang, Cody Choi, Manu Park, Myung Ji Bae, Suk Tae Park, Jin Sang Yoo, Ji Hyun Lee, Nam Soo Kim, Jung Kang Yoon, Jae Bok Lee, Il Woo Joo and Suk Tae Park. *2011 Plateform Artis*. Korea: Incheon Art Platform, 2012.

Park, Kyung-Mee, Mike Kelley, Cody Choi, Jeremy Gilbert-Rolfe, David Pagel, Saul Ostrow, John C. Welchman, Jeffrey Deitch, Jerry Saltz, Laurence A. Rickels, Michael Cohen, and Peter Halley. *Cultural Shift Hatter: Cody Choi 1986–2003*. Korea: Paradise Media Art, 2003.

Choi, Byung Hoon, Charles Swanson, Fujie Kazuko, and Cody Choi. *Furniture as an Object*. Korea: Korea Furniture Society, 2006.

Griffin, Susan, Liao Wen, Ji-Young Shin, Young-Paik Chun, Cody Choi, and Sung-Hee Kim. *2006 Pre-International Incheon Women Artists Biennale International Symposium*. Exhibition catalogue. Korea: International Incheon Women Artists Biennale, 2006.

Welchman, John C., Nancy Barton, Laurence A. Rickels, Ken Feingold, Jean Baudrillard, Cody Choi, and Sung-Hee Kim. *International Symposium Media_City Seoul 2002*. Exhibition catalogue. Seoul: Media City Seoul, 2002.

Choi, Cody, and Jeffrey Deitch. *Cody Choi: Farewell to the 20th Century*. New York: Deitch Projects, 1998.

Contributing Editor
Being On Line, Net Subjectivity.
New York: Lusitania Press, 1997.

Provisional Utopias Sites & Stations.
New York: Lusitania Press, 1995.

SELECTED BIBLIOGRAPHY
BOOKS, EXHIBITION CATALOGUES,
AND JOURNALS

Welchman, John C., ed. *Cody Choi: Culture Cuts*. Exhibition catalogue. Cologne: Verlag der Buchhandlung Walther König, 2015.

Lee, Kenshu. *Busan Biennale: Voyage to Biennale*. Exhibition catalogue. Korea: Busan Biennale Organizing Committee, 2014.

Lee, Sun-Young. "Special Artist Cody Choi." *Monthly Art*, no. 316 (2011).

Lee, Sulbee. "Interview Cody Choi." *Monthly Art*, no. 316 (2011).

Kim, Hong-hee. *The New Epicenter: Chapter 2 Post-Human*. Exhibition catalogue. Korea: Wumin Art Center, 2011.

Welchman, John C. *Digifesta 2010: Media Art Festival*. Exhibition catalogue. Korea: Media Art Festival Digifesta, 2010.

Kim, Hong-hee. *Oh, Masterpiece*. Exhibition catalogue. Korea: Gyeonggi Museum of Modern Art, 2009.

Kim, Wonbang. *Busan Biennale 2008*. Exhibition catalogue. Korea: Busan Biennale Organizing Committee, 2008.

Kim, Sung Hee. *Meme Trackers*. Exhibition catalogue. Peking: Songzhuang Art Center, 2008.

Lunday, Elizabeth. *The Secret Lives of Great Artists: What Your Teachers Never Told You*

About Master Painters and Sculptors. Philadelphia: Quirk Books, 2008.

Jeong, Dong-Am. *Media Art: The Temptation of Digital*. Korea: Communication Books, 2007.

Choi, Cody. "Interview with Myself." *Monthly Art*, no. 268 (2007).

Huang, Du, ed. *Shanghai Biennale 2006: Hyper-Design*. Exhibition catalogue. China: Shu Hua Publishing House, 2006.

Welchman, John C. "Images of Thought and Deleuze's Pictures: Diagram, Line, Film and Face," *On Verbal/Visual Representation: Word and Image Interactions IV*. [Textxet 50] [Studies in Comparative Literature]. Edited by Martine Heusser, Michele Hannoosh, Eric Haskell, Leo Hoek, David Scott, and Peter de Voogd. Amsterdam and New York: Editions Rodopi BV, 2005.

Joo, Yeon-Hwa Henna. *Standing on a Bridge*. Exhibition catalogue. Korea: Arario Gallery, 2004.

Rhee, Wonil, Iris Haung, and Lin Chi-ming. *Digital Sublime: New Masters of Universe*. Exhibition catalogue. Taipei: Museum of Contemporary Art, Taipei, 2004.

Rimanelli, David. "Reviews: Cody Choi." *Art Forum* (February 2004).

Kelley, Mike. *Foul Perfection: Essays and Criticism*. Edited by John C. Welchman. Cambridge, MA: MIT Press, 2003.

Kim, Young Ho. "Review: Cody Choi." *wolganmisool* (October, 2003).

Yoo, Kyung-Hee. "Focus: Cody Choi."
Art in Culture (October, 2003).

Vine, Richard. "Report from Seoul, Cyber City." *Art in America* (February, 2003).

Rhee, Wonil, ed. *Media_City Seoul 2002*. Exhibition catalogue. Seoul: Seoul Museum of Art, 2002.

Diamond, Sara. "Media_City Seoul 2002." *Flash Art* (November–December 2002).

Park, Nam Hee. "Media Art Biennale Special Feature." *Korea Art* (November–December 2002).

Lee, Yong Woo. "Media_City Seoul." *wolganmisool* (November 2002).

Rhee, Wonil. "Interview." *wolganmisool* (November 2002).

Baudrillard, Jean. "Violence de L'image." *wolganmisool* (September 2002).

Welchman, John C. "Culture/Cuts: Post-appropriation in the Work of Cody Hyun Choi." *Art After Appropriation: Essays on Art in the 1990s*. Amsterdam: G+B Arts International, 2001.

Cohen, Michael. *Ghost World*. Exhibition catalogue. Korea: CAIS Gallery, 2001.

Roe, Jae-Ryung. "Reviews: Cody Choi." *Art Forum* (September 2000).

Ostrow, Saul. *Mug Shots: Performing Personae*. Exhibition catalogue. Diane R. Karp, 2000.

Becker, Wolfgang. *Continental Shift: A Voyage between Cultures*. Exhibition catalogue.

Aachen: Ludwig Forum Aachen, 2000.
Welchman, John C. "Culture/Cuts: The Work of Cody Hyun Choi." *Third Text*, no. 48 (1999).

Choi, Cody and Jeffrey Deitch. *Cody Choi: Farewell to the 20th Century*. Exhibition catalogue. New York: Deitch Projects, 1998.

Oh, Saeng-Keun, and Sou-Kyoun Lee. *Body in Painting*. Exhibition catalogue. Daejeon: Hanlim Museum, 1998.

Heartney, Eleanor. *Images of Self: The Search for Identity Through Art*. Exhibition catalogue. Saratoga Springs: Schick Art Gallery and Skidmore College, 1996.

Vergne, Philippe. *L'art au corps: le corps exposé de Man Ray à nos jours*. Paris: Réunion des musées nationaux, 1996.

Deitch, Jeffrey, and Kyung Mee Park. *Border Crawl*. Exhibition catalogue. Korea: Kukje Gallery, 1995.

Ostrow, Saul, and Sung-Hee Kim. *Blow My Top*. Exhibition catalogue. Korea: Mee Gun Gallery, 1993.

Kelley, Mike. *Cody Choi*. Exhibition catalogue. Korea: Mee Gun Gallery, 1992.

Pagel, David, and Jeremy Gibert-Rolf. *Deep the Pink*. Exhibition catalogue. Korea: Total Museum, 1992.

Contributors

MARIE DE BRUGEROLLE is an independent curator and writer. She's organized retrospectives of Allen Ruppersberg (CNAC Magasin, Grenoble, 1995), John Baldessari (Carré d'art, Nîmes, 2005), and Larry Bell (Carré d'art, Nîmes, 2010). In 2004 she curated the first international exhibition of work by Guy de Cointet, entitled *Who's That Guy?*, authored *Guy de Cointet* (JRP | Ringier, 2011), and directed the documentary film *Who's That Guy: Tell Me More About Guy de Cointet* (2011). In 2006 she organized *Faire des choses avec des mots/ Making Words With Things* (Cointet, Paul McCarthy, Mike Kelley, Catherine Sullivan) at CRAC, Sète, France. Her most recent projects include, *LA Existancial* (LACE, Los Angeles, 2013), *All That Falls* (Palais de Tokyo, 2014), and *RIDEAUX/Blinds* (IAC, Villeurbanne, France, 2015).

. . .

GREGOR JANSEN is the director of Kunsthalle Düsseldorf since 2010. From 2005 to the end of 2009, Jansen headed the ZKM | Museum of Contemporary Art in Karlsruhe. He wrote his doctorate on the Berlin-based painter Eugen Schönebeck. From 1991 onwards he worked variously as an exhibition manager, curator, lecturer, art critic, and publicist. Until 2013 he lectured in media theory and cultural and visual art history at several universities and fine arts academies. In 2000 he curated the Japan/Korea section of the transnational exhibition *Continental Shift* in Belgium, Germany, and the Netherlands. In 2002 he was appointed curator for the 2nd SeMA Biennale Mediacity Seoul and in 2005 curated *Beijing Case*, a scholarship program organized jointly by the Federal Cultural Foundation and the Goethe-Institut Beijing, which furthered artistic research into international urban developments in megacities.

. . .

SUMI KANG is a Korean art critic and aesthetician and professor of art theory at Dongduk Women's University in Seoul whose areas of research include the writings of Walter Benjamin, contemporary art, and the philosophical history of art. She is the author of *The Art of Criticism* (2013), *Aisthesis: Thinking with Walter Benjamin's Aesthetics* (2011), *The Wonderful Reality of Korean Contemporary Art* (2009), and *Rediscovering of Seoul Life and Discovering of Seoul Life* (2003). Her essays include "The Order of Heterotopia: Walter Benjamin and Archive-based Contemporary Art" (2014), "Against Mortality: Reconsidering the Relationship between Image and Death in Contemporary Art" (2014), "Prosthetic Beauty: 'Technostress' or 'Technopleasure' in Contemporary Art" (2013), and "Reconfigurations of the Visual Arts: Images for Sustainable Community" (2010/2012).

. . .

MIKE KELLEY's work (1954–2012) embraced performance, installation, drawing, painting, video, sound works, and sculpture. Beginning in the late nineteen-seventies with solo performances, image/text works, and gallery and site-specific installations, Kelley came to prominence in the nineteen-eighties with a series of sculptures composed of common craft materials. His more recent work addressed architecture and filmic narrative using the theory of repressed memory syndrome, and a sustained biographic and pseudobiographic inquiry into his own aesthetic and social history. Kelley's work has been seen in numerous solo exhibitions including *Mike Kelley* (Stedelijk, Amsterdam, 2012; Centre Pompidou, Paris, 2013; Museum of Modern Art/PS1, New York, 2013; MOCA, Los Angeles, 2014), *Mobile Homestead* (MOCAD, Detroit, 2013), *Mike Kelley: Educational Complex Onwards: 1995–2008* (Wiels, Brussels, 2008), *The Uncanny* (Tate Liverpool; Museum Moderner Kunst Stiftung Ludwig, Vienna, 2004), and a traveling retrospective of his work that opened in 1993 at the Whitney Museum of American Art in New York.

· · ·

JOHN C. WELCHMAN is professor of art history at the University of California, San Diego, chair of the Mike Kelley Foundation for the Arts, and advisor, Rijksakademie van Beeldende Kunsten, Amsterdam. His books include *Modernism Relocated: Towards a Cultural Studies of Visual Modernity* (1995), *Invisible Colors: A Visual History of Titles* (1997), *Art After Appropriation: Essays on Art in the 1990s* (2001), *Vasco Araújo* (2007), and *Paul and Damon McCarthy: Caribbean Pirates* (2015). He is coauthor of *The Dada & Surrealist Word-Image* (1989), *Mike Kelley* (1999), *On the Beyond* (with Mike Kelley and Jim Shaw, 2011), *Kwang Young Chun* (2014), and *Joseph Kosuth: Re-Defining the Context of Art: 1968–2014* (2015). *Past Realization: Essays on Contemporary European Art* [*XX to XXI* vol. I] (Sternberg, 2015) is the first of a series of six volumes of his collected writings.

Credits

Photo

pp. 8–9, 17, 23, 33, 41, 50, 51, 53, 54–59, 60, 64–69, 108–109, 128, 134–135: © Achim Kukulies, Düsseldorf

pp. 14, 15, 24–25: © Seung Yong Yoo

pp. 26, 27 (upper image), 29, 112, 113: © Nikki S. Lee

pp. 37, 78: © S.M. Jeon

pp. 49, 75, 88, 98, 123: © Gigi Sue

p. 72: © Digital Image, The Museum of Modern Art, New York/Scala, Florence, 2015; Succession Marcel Duchamp/VG Bild-Kunst, Bonn 2015

pp. 81, 125: © Seo Woo Kim

p. 82: © Katja Illner

p. 99: © Gregor Jansen

p. 110: © Kwang-min Noh

It has not been possible to establish copyright unequivocally in certain cases, despite intensive research. The editors and publisher hereby request details where applicable.

Colophon

The publishing of this catalogue coincides with the following exhibitions:

Cody Choi · *Culture Cuts*

Coordinating Curator · John C. Welchman

May 9–August 2, 2015, Kunsthalle Düsseldorf
Curator · Gregor Jansen

April 8–August 28, 2016, Musée d'Art Contemporain, Marseille
Curators · Marie de Brugerolle; Thierry Ollat

CATALOGUE

Editors · John C. Welchman; Gregor Jansen, Kunsthalle Düsseldorf; Thierry Ollat, Musée d'Art Contemporain, Marseille

Authors · Marie de Brugerolle; Gregor Jansen; Sumi Kang; Mike Kelley; Thierry Ollat; John C. Welchman

Graphic design · Büro Boris Dworschak

Editorial assistant · Irina Raskin

Copyediting · Leina González

Translation · Klaus Roth, Anthony DePasquale (Gregor Jansen essay)

Printing and binding · Druckerei zu Altenburg

Lithogaphy · Joseph Sappler

Published by · Verlag der Buchhandlung Walther König, Köln

Printed in Germany; First edition
ISBN: 978-3-86335-779-5

Bibliographic information published by the Deutsche Nationalbibliothek The Deutsche Nationalbibliothek lists this publication in the Deutsche Nationalbibliografie; detailed bibliographic data are available in the Internet at http://dnb.d-nb.de.

© 2015 the artist; the authors; Kunsthalle Düsseldorf gGmbH; Musée d'Art Contemporain, Marseille; Verlag der Buchhandlung Walther König. © for all reproduced works by Cody Choi: the artist and PKM Gallery.

Distribution
Buchhandlung Walther König, Cologne
Ehrenstraße 4, 50672 Cologne
Fon +49 (0) 221/20 59 6 53, Fax +49 (0) 221/20 59 6 60
verlag@buchhandlung-walther-koenig.de

UK & Ireland
Cornerhouse Publications, HOME
2 Tony Wilson Place, UK - Manchester, M15 4FN
Fon +44 (0) 161 2123466
publications@cornerhouse.org

Outside Europe
D.A.P./Distributed Art Publishers, Inc.
155 6th Avenue, 2nd Floor, USA - New York, NY 10013
Fon +1 (0) 212 627 1999, Fax +1 (0) 212 627 9484
eleshowitz@dapinc.com

The exhibitions are supported by

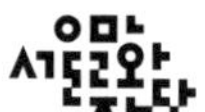

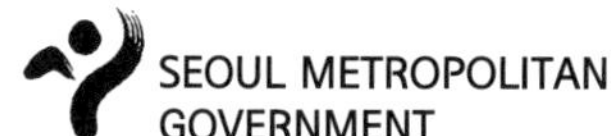

PKM GALLERY

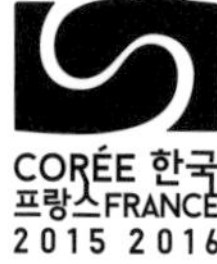

The exhibition in Marseille is part of the Korea-France Year 2015–2016 program. It has received the support of the Korea Arts Management Service, and the Secretariat of the Organizing Committee of the Korea-France Year 2015–2016, Seoul, Korea.

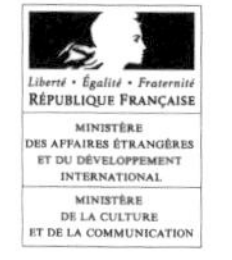

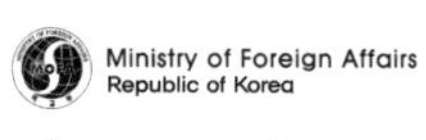

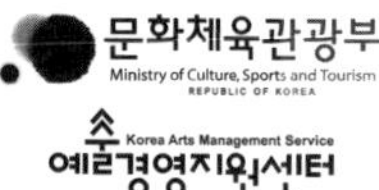

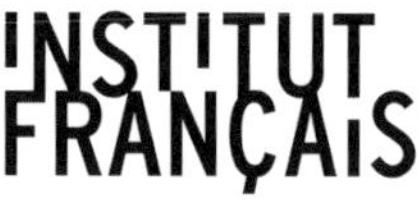

Ressources humaines/Human resources manager ·
Christine Gozzi

Accueil des publics/Department of the public ·
Fanny Leroy

Chef d'équipe/Head of technical team ·
Jean-Claude Rosa

Équipe technique/Technical team ·
Jean-Pierre Bocognano; Pascal Cahuac;
Michel Lalanne; Patrick Menicucci; Roland
Milani-Aluno; Frédéric Ribaud; Paul et
Antoine Toscano

MUSÉE D'ART CONTEMPORAIN
Directeur · Thierry Ollat

Assistante expositions et collections ·
Ségolène Périneau

Régisseur · Jasmine Grisanti

Chargée de conservation préventive ·
Nancy Racine-Vie

Iconographie et relation presse · Olivia Mistrih

Centre de documentation Ernst Goldschmidt ·
Guy Peralo

Accueil des publics · Pascale Stauth;
Nicolas Féodoroff; Francis de Hita;
Frédérique Darbas

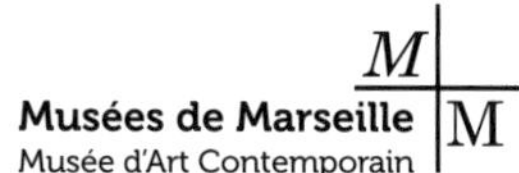
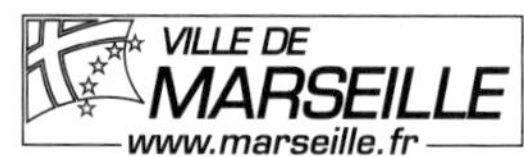
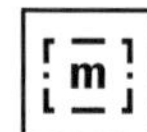